PRISONS IN THE LATE OTTOMAN EMPIRE

Edinburgh Studies on the Ottoman Empire
Series Editor: Kent F. Schull

Published and forthcoming titles

Migrating Texts: Circulating Translations around the Eastern Mediterranean
Marilyn Booth

The Kizilbash-Alevis in Ottoman Anatolia: Sufism, Politics and Community
Ayfer Karakaya-Stump

*Çemberlitas̩ Hamami in Istanbul: The Biographical Memoir
of a Turkish Bath*
Nina Macaraig

*Nineteenth-Century Local Governance in Ottoman Bulgaria:
Politics in Provincial Councils*
M. Safa Saraçoğlu

Prisons in the Late Ottoman Empire: Microcosms of Modernity
Kent F. Schull

Ruler Visibility and Popular Belonging in the Ottoman Empire
Darin Stephanov

edinburghuniversitypress.com/series/esoe

PRISONS IN THE
LATE OTTOMAN EMPIRE

MICROCOSMS OF MODERNITY

⁂

Kent F. Schull

EDINBURGH
University Press

Edinburgh University Press is one of the leading university presses in the UK. We publish academic books and journals in our selected subject areas across the humanities and social sciences, combining cutting-edge scholarship with high editorial and production values to produce academic works of lasting importance. For more information visit our website: www.edinburghuniversitypress.com

Edinburgh University Press Ltd
The Tun – Holyrood Road
12 (2f) Jackson's Entry
Edinburgh EH8 8PJ
www.euppublishing.com

First published in hardback by Edinburgh University Press 2014

Typeset in 11/13 JaghbUni Regular by
Servis Filmsetting Ltd, Stockport, Cheshire
and printed and bound by
CPI Group (UK) Ltd, Croydon CRO 4YY

A CIP record for this book is available from the British Library

ISBN 978 0 7486 4173 4 (hardback)
ISBN 978 1 4744 3572 7 (paperback)
ISBN 978 0 7486 7769 6 (webready PDF)

Contents

Illustrations

Abbreviations

AHR	*The American Historical Review*
ARIT	American Research Institute in Turkey
BNA	The British National Archives
BOA	Başbakanlık Osmanlı Arşivi (The Prime Ministry's Ottoman Archives)
c.	circa
CUP	Committee of Union and Progress
DHEUMTK	*Dahiliye Nezareti, Emniyet-i Umumiye Müdiriyeti, Tahrirat Kalemi* (The Secretariat of the Directorate of Public Security, Ministry of the Interior)
DHMBHPS	*Dahiliye Nezareti, Mebani-i Emiriyye ve Hapishaneler Müdiriyeti* (The Directorate of Prisons and Building Construction, Ministry of the Interior)
DHMBHPSM	*Dahiliye Nezareti, Mebani-i Emiriyye ve Hapishaneler Müdiriyeti Belgeleri Müteferrik* (Various Documents of the Directorate of Prisons and Building Construction, Ministry of the Interior)
DHMUİ	*Dahiliye Nezareti, Muhaberat-ı Umumiye İdaresi* (The General Communications Office of the Ministry of the Interior)
DHTMIK	*Dahiliye Nezareti, Tesri-i Muamelat ve Islahat Komisyonu* (The Commission for Expediting Initiatives and Reforms, Ministry of the Interior)
FO	The British Foreign Office
IIE	Fulbright Institute of International Education
IJMES	*International Journal of Middle East Studies*
IOPC	Imperial Ottoman Penal Code
ITS	The Institute of Turkish Studies
MMZC	*Meclis-i Mebusan Zabıt Ceridesi*
r.	reigned
UCLA	University of California, Los Angeles
WWI	World War I
YEE	*Yıldız Esas Evrakı*
ZB	*Zaptiye Belgeleri*

Note on Transliteration and Pronunciation

I have utilised a modified system of transliterating Ottoman Turkish and Arabic proper names and terms as suggested by the *International Journal of Middle Eastern Studies* (*IJMES*). I have chosen not to use diacritical markings except for the occasional apostrophe to signify both the 'ayn' and the *hamza*. Most Ottoman Turkish proper names and places are spelled according to modern Turkish conventions, except for the fact that I have maintained the final voiced consonant that corresponds to the Ottoman spelling: 'Mehmed' instead of 'Mehmet' and 'İzmid' rather than 'İzmit'. Place names and words that are more familiar to English-language speakers, such as 'Istanbul', 'Beirut', 'qadi', and 'pasha' are spelled according to common English usage.

The following is a guide to pronouncing certain letters in modern Turkish and transliterated Ottoman Turkish:

- c = j, as in 'jet'
- ç = ch, as in 'church'
- ğ = gh, as in 'though'
- ı = short 'e', as in 'often' or 'i' as in 'girl'
- j = zh, as in 'gendarme'
- ö = German oe, as in 'Goethe'
- ş = sh, as in 'short'
- ü = ew, as in 'ewe'.

Preface

When I tell people that I research Ottoman prisons, or better yet, 'Turkish prisons', their horrified response is normally along the lines of, 'Have you seen the movie *Midnight Express*?' and often, 'Have you ever spent time in a Turkish prison?' The truthful answer to both queries is, 'Yes.' It was my first-hand experience in an Ottoman prison that led me to this book. In 2002, I spent a few days in Istanbul in the company of a Turkish friend. He suggested that we sit and drink tea in one of the poshest hotels in the world, the Four Seasons. As we sat, drank, and chatted in the hotel's courtyard, my friend informed me that the hotel was nothing other than a former Ottoman imperial prison. I was flabbergasted. As I looked around the courtyard, I noticed the still discernible prison architecture, such as its high walls, turrets, and enclosed courtyard. I wondered what the reaction of the guests would be if they found out the history of this edifice. Incidentally, the Four Seasons Hotel stands on *Tevkifhane Sokak* or 'Jail Road' in the former imperial centre of Ottoman Istanbul, right between the Blue Mosque, Aya Sofya (Hagia Sophia), and the Topkapı Sarayı.

Upon learning the former life of this hotel my interest was immediately peaked. I had recently finished Michel Foucault's *Discipline and Punish* and I knew that the historiography for prisons in North America and Europe was robust, but I had no idea what the current state of the scholarship was for the Ottoman Empire. I quickly found out that it was sorely underdeveloped and included only a few short articles on related topics and a couple of MA theses, all in Turkish.

While researching in the Imperial Ottoman Archives in Istanbul I found a treasure trove of untapped documents related to penal institutions and prison reform in the late Ottoman Empire. I quickly realised how integral criminal justice reforms, including prisons, were to Ottoman plans to restructure the empire comprehensively. I also recognised that prisons were intrinsic to many facets of Ottoman modernity and nation-state construction during the nineteenth and the early twentieth centuries.

Similar to Foucault's assessment of French prisons, I argue that various late Ottoman administrations utilised prisons as important instruments of social control and discipline. The primary purpose of penal institutions is to control and discipline the population, specifically those portions of the population deemed threats to regime security. My argument, however, goes far beyond Foucault's. Not only were they important instruments of social control and discipline, but prisons became microcosms of Ottoman modernity. It was within the walls of Ottoman prisons that many of the pressing questions of Ottoman modernity played out, such as administrative reform and centralisation, the role of punishment in the rehabilitation of prisoners, economic reform and industrialisation, issues of gender and childhood, the implementation of modern concepts of time and space, identity, social engineering, the rationalisation and standardisation of Islamic criminal law, and the role of the state in caring for its population. These are all in addition to social control and discipline. Prisons, therefore, possess the unique ability to act as windows into the process of Ottoman modernity and provide clear insights into broader socio-economic, political, cultural, and ideological issues and developments occurring in late Ottoman history throughout its entire empire. In the end, this is not a book about 'Turkish' prisons, but a book concerned with a prison system that encompassed all the territories of the former Ottoman Empire during the late nineteenth and the early twentieth centuries: from Yemen to the Balkans and from Van to Beirut.

While this work utilises prisons as a window into Ottoman modernity, it also juxtaposes reform and intention with the reality of incarceration from the points of view of inmates and local prison personnel. Too much of Ottoman history is written and conceptualised from the perspective of the central state. This history tempers the grand transformational designs of Tanzimat, Hamidian, and Second Constitutional Period reformers with the realities of prison life. In other words, it discusses the intended reforms, investigates their implementation, and discusses the acceptance, success, failure, resistance, and augmentation they faced through the stories and experiences of prison guards and prisoners.

As I delved deeper into my research on Ottoman prisons I realised just how intertwined prisons were with larger issues of crime, policing, courts, legal reform, and criminal justice in the empire. Unfortunately, this study is neither comprehensive, nor exhaustive. In the end, I have only scratched the surface of the rich sources available for the study of Ottoman criminal justice. Excellent work is being done on other facets of this subject that need to be integrated into a more comprehensive picture. My work is simply an initial interpretive foray into this vast and understudied topic in Ottoman and Middle East history. My hope is that this work spurs fruitful discussion, constructive criticism, and further enquiry.

An earlier version of portions of Chapter 3 was presented as a paper, entitled 'Conceptualizing Difference during the Second Constitutional Period: New Sources, Old Challenges', at the Swedish Research Institute in Istanbul and published in *Religion, Ethnicity and Contested Nationhood in the Former Ottoman Space*, edited by Jorgen Nielsen (2012). Another small portion of Chapter 3 was published as an article, entitled 'Identity in the Ottoman Prison Surveys of 1912 and 1914', in *IJMES*, volume 41 (2009). A third portion of Chapter 3 was presented as a paper, entitled 'Counting the Incarcerated: Young Turk Attempts to Systematically Collect Prison Statistics and their Effects of Prison Reform, 1911–1918' at Boğazici University in Istanbul and was published in Turkish as 'Tutuklu Sayımı: Jön Türklerin Sistematik Bir şekilde Hapishane İstatistikleri Toplama Çalışmaları ve Bunların 1911–1918 Hapishane Reformu Üzerine Etkileri' in *Osmanlı'da Asayiş, Suç ve Ceza: 18.–20. Yüzyıllar*, edited by Noémi Lévy and Alexandre Toumarkine (2007). Portions of the discussion on theoretical approaches to the study of penal institutions found in the Introduction to this book were also published in Turkish, entitled 'Hapishaneler ve Cezalandırmaya İlişkin Yaklaşımlara Eleştirel Bir Bakış', in the same volume edited by Noémi Lévy and Alexandre Toumarkine (2007).

The generous permission policy of the Office of the Prime Minister's Ottoman Archives (Başbakanlık Osmanlı Arşivleri) has allowed me to use the images found on the book cover and in Figures 3.1, 3.2, 4.1, 4.2, 4.3, and 4.4.

I owe an enormous debt of gratitude to many people and institutions for their assistance in the development and completion of this book. I am overwhelmed by the generosity of so many. They have truly had an effect on my life and I only wish this effort could better reflect their attention, care, assistance, support, and friendship.

Many institutions generously provided me with financial and residential support for this project. They include the Foreign Language and Area Studies (Title VI) grants administered through the University of California, Los Angeles (UCLA) Center for Near Eastern Studies, the Fulbright Institute of International Education (IIE), the Fulbright-Hays Doctoral Dissertation Research Fellowships, the Institute of Turkish Studies (ITS), Brigham Young University's David M. Kennedy Center for International Studies, and the Istanbul Branch of the American Research Institute in Turkey (ARIT). I am extremely grateful for their help and assistance.

To my wonderful friends and former colleagues at Brigham Young University and the University of Memphis I owe an enormous debt of gratitude for their collegiality, guidance, support, and critique of various chapters of this work. I am also very grateful to my new colleagues and friends at Binghamton University who have provided me with a supportive and intellectually stimulating environment in which to write, revise, and finish this book. The staff at the Office of the Prime Minister's Ottoman Archives in Istanbul, Turkey deserves special thanks for their wonderful help, warmth, kindness, patience, and hospitality as they steered me through the intricacies and complexities of the Ottoman archives.

I continue to hold a debt of gratitude to those scholars and mentors who guided my own academic development and nurtured within me a curiosity and love for all things Middle East. In particular, I wish to express my gratitude to James Gelvin, Arnold Green, Güliz Kuruoğlu, David Montgomery, and Gabriel Piterberg. I can only hope that I am able to offer my own students the kind of personal and intellectual training and inspiration that they have provided me.

I also wish to thank the thoughtful, careful, and very patient editors at Edinburgh University Press (EUP) who have guided me through the publication process. The anonymous reviewers whose encouragement and constructive criticism helped to make this a much better finished project also have my sincere gratitude. I also wish to thank Michael Lejman for his editing skills. Special and heartfelt thanks must be extended to Jonathan Lohnes and Darin Stephanov who both read this manuscript and provided incredibly useful and substantive suggestions. Obviously all mistakes are my own, but if this work has any merit it is because of their help.

No acknowledgement would be complete without paying tribute to the contributions, love, and support of so many friends along the way. They have given generously of their friendship, time, thoughts, sources, insights, and critiques and they deserve my expression of sincere thanks: Iris Agmon, Ebru Aykut, Rifat Behar, Peter Brand, Michele Campos, Julia Phillips Cohen, Y. Tolga Cora, Roger Deal, Heather Dehaan, Fatmagül Demirel, Arnab Dey, Kazım Dilek, Yasemin Dilek, Eric Dursteler, Howard Eissenstat, Ferdan Ergut, Eyal Ginio, Anthony Gorman, Yasemin Gönen, Aram Goudsouzian, Melis Hafez, Will Hanley, Andy Johns, M. Erdem Kabadayı, Vangelis Kechriotis, Elektra Kostopolous, Scott Marler, Kevin Martin, Jonathan McCollum, Milena Methodieva, Hüseyin Ozkaya, Omri Paz, Catherine Phipps-Mercer, Najwa al-Qattan, Donald Quataert, Jean Quataert, Avi Rubin, Brett Rushforth, Mehmet Safa Saracoğlu, Janann Sherman, Ara Topakian, Dikran Topakian, Zeynep Türkyilmaz, Richard Wittmann, Gültekin Yıldız, Murat Yıldız, and Sara Yıldız.

Finally, and most importantly, I must thank those closest to me, without whom I would never have been able to complete this work: my family. I wish to express my love and appreciation to my dear spouse and partner,

Kimberli, and to our amazing children – Bethany, Joseph, Joshua, and Richard Kazım – who have travelled the world with me in pursuit of my education and career. It is hoped that we shall continue to have many more adventures together. You provide me with the love, stability, support, and sanity that academia can never supply. I love you more than can ever be expressed adequately in written words.

Introduction

In 1851 and again in 1918–19 British officials assigned to the Ottoman Empire conducted extensive inspections of the empire's prisons and drew up detailed reports of what they found. Notwithstanding their imperialist and orientalist undertones, these reports describe Ottoman prisons as being in a serious state of disrepair.[1] Stratford Canning, the famous British Ambassador to the Ottoman Empire, commissioned the 1851 inspections with the intent to assist the Ottomans in reforming their criminal justice system. He ordered British Foreign Office representatives stationed throughout the empire to undertake a comprehensive inspection of prisons in order to ascertain their deficiencies and to report back to him. Canning justified prison improvement and inspection according to civilisational principles:

> But in the present advanced state of human knowledge and public opinion no government which respects itself and claims a position among civilised communities can shut its eyes to the abuses which prevail. Or to the horrors which past ages may have left in that part of its administration which separate the repression of crime and the personal constraint of the guilty or the accused.[2]

The inspection questionnaire consisted of thirty questions requesting a variety of information on many aspects of the empire's prisons in every major urban centre. Questions included the number of prisoners, prison dimensions and layout, living conditions, hygiene and health concerns, rations, prison routines, prison cadre conduct, and governmental funding. The comprehensive nature of the questionnaire is quite impressive, as are the reports that were subsequently generated, which overwhelmingly demonstrate the poor state of Ottoman prison conditions.[3] After the British Embassy in Istanbul received the inspection results, officials drafted a summary report containing multiple suggestions for the general improvement of prisons throughout the empire and submitted it directly to the 'Sultan's confidential advisors'. The majority of the suggested improvements referred to health and hygiene issues, living conditions, facility repair, and prison regimens.[4]

Shortly after the unconditional surrender of the Ottomans to the *Entente* powers ending World War I (WWI), British officials conducted

1

a series of inspections of Istanbul's prisons in the period of late 1918 and early 1919 and found prisons to be in a similar state to the state detailed in the 1851 inspections.[5] There are four striking features of the second set of reports. First, inspectors paint a dreadful picture of the state of Istanbul's prisons, including note of widespread disease, malnutrition, poor sanitation, rampant prison cadre neglect, abuse of prisoners, and corruption. Second, the reports display a deep bias for incarcerated Christians vis-à-vis their Muslim counterparts; the British inspectors express a greater concern for the welfare of Christian inmates even though all prisoners suffered similarly from the poor conditions. Third, the reports exude the British inspectors' absolute contempt for 'Turks'. Fourth, two of the British military officers (Commander Heathcote-Smith and Lieutenant Palmer) tasked with conducting the initial inspections and reporting their findings clearly express an ulterior motive regarding the potential use of these reports. They suggested that the reports be added to a number of other documents in preparation for the Paris Peace Conference and utilised to achieve three of Britain's post-war goals: that is, being used to justify British calls for the abrogation of 'Turkish sovereignty in Constantinople'; being used to substantiate further the disallowance of 'Turkish independence in Anatolia'; and, finally, being used as propaganda to dampen pro-Ottoman sentiments among Muslims in India. In fact, one British official felt 'certain that if the Indian population were instructed systematically as to the real truth concerning the Turk and all his ways, we should hear little more of their sympathy for him'. In fact, he suggested that 'some judicious propaganda' should be distributed in India in order to achieve this aim.[6]

Notwithstanding the sixty-eight year gap between the two sets of inspections and their different purposes, both resulted in reports that exposed the dire state of Ottoman prisons, especially in the areas of health, hygiene, sanitation, administration, corruption and abuse, nutrition, clothing, and the general state and condition of the facilities. Anyone reading these reports and even remotely familiar with the extensive reform programmes undertaken by various Ottoman administrations over the course of the nineteenth century would conclude that prisons had been completely ignored. These two British prison reports, however, do not reveal the extensive Ottoman expenditures in time, energy, money, and human capital spent over the final eighty years of the empire's existence – all with the goal of overhauling its prisons and creating a modern criminal justice system comparable with contemporary states in Europe, Asia, and the Americas.

Instead, these reports reinforce assumptions about Ottoman prisons all too familiar to Western audiences. The topic of Ottoman or better yet 'Turkish' prisons inevitably produces particular visceral reactions and conjures up certain horrific images that usually centre on three things: brutal sexual abuse, narcotics, and torture. Oliver Stone's *Midnight Express* emblazoned this 'Anglo-American Orientalist' image of Turkish prisons upon our minds.[7] However, even *Lawrence of Arabia* and comedies such as *Airplane* and *The Simpsons* reinforce these stereotypes. Western accounts of Turkish venality and barbarity are legend, especially regarding prisons and the treatment of the incarcerated. These fables and stories are rife with salacious tales of torture and indiscriminate cruelty that say more about Western fears and fantasies regarding its medieval and early-modern past than about actual circumstances within Ottoman prisons.[8] Stereotypes aside, Ottoman prison conditions are, in fact, comparable to those found in supposedly more 'enlightened' and 'civilised' countries in Western Europe and North America during the long nineteenth century (1770s–1922).[9]

Unfortunately, such stereotypes hinder serious academic inquiry into Ottoman penal institutions, particularly concerning their role in modern state formation in the late Ottoman Empire and the actual lived experiences of the incarcerated. As a result, scholars have produced very few academic works investigating Ottoman prisons, penal institutions, the empire's criminal justice system, or the everyday lives of non-political prisoners. Apart from two monographs, an edited volume, and several master's theses (all in Turkish), and a few English-language articles on general prison reform and conditions in the broader Middle East, a large lacuna exists in the scholarly work done on Ottoman and Middle Eastern prisons. In fact, none of these works treats Ottoman prison reform during the long nineteenth century from both an imperial and a local perspective. Most are limited in scope to a particular time period and a particular region, and only a few go beyond basic descriptions of archival documents and apply important interdisciplinary theoretical and methodological approaches.[10]

This study focuses on the transformation of the Ottoman criminal justice system, particularly prisons and incarceration, during the late Ottoman Empire (c. 1840–1922) with an emphasis on the Second Constitutional Period (1908–18). First, it demonstrates the interconnected relationship between the development of modern penal institutions and state construction in the late Ottoman Empire. Second, this study attempts to link prisons and punishment more broadly with the creation of a modern criminal justice system defined by the codification of Islamic criminal law, the establishment of criminal courts, and more intrusive policing and surveillance during the long nineteenth century. Third, it argues that prisons act as effective windows into broader state and societal developments within the empire during this era of reform. This era, however, is better characterised as one of transformation centred on continuity and change rather than a rupture imposed by the West. It was within the walls of these prisons that many of the pressing questions of Ottoman modernity played out. Bureaucrats addressed issues related to administrative reform and centralisation, the rationalisation of Islamic criminal law and punishment, the role of labour in the rehabilitation of prisoners, economic development and industrialisation, gender and childhood, the implementation of modern concepts of time and space, issues of national identity based on ethnicity and religion, social engineering, and the increased role of the state in caring for its population. In other words, prisons are microcosms of imperial transformation and exemplify a distinctive Ottoman modernity created by the spread of capitalist market relations and the application of modern methods of governance within a specific Ottoman context. Fourth, this study pushes theoretical models and methodological approaches to penal institutions beyond Michel Foucault's depiction of prisons as modern instrumentalities of governance for social control and discipline. It does so by looking at the competing ideological, social, economic, and practical concerns affecting prison reform and realities on the ground. Fifth, and most importantly, this study looks at prisons on both a local and an imperial level, thus integrating top-down and bottom-up approaches to historical inquiry in order to juxtapose reform and reality. This is accomplished by looking at the centre's reform programmes, intentions, and actions in conjunction with an appraisal of the effectiveness of implementation and mitigated by recourse to the lived experiences of prisoners and local cadre in order to ascertain compliance, resistance, and augmentation to these reforms. This approach is very important in order to overcome the state-centric bias that studies of Ottoman imperial reform generally produce. Finally, this volume adds an additional voice to the bourgeoning scholarship, arguing that the development of the modern Middle East and South-eastern Europe must be situated in the late Ottoman Empire as a result of an internally devised and implemented response to internal concerns and European imperialism. More specifically, the Second Constitutional Period needs to be viewed as the culmination of transformation that left an important inheritance to the region. It is frequently portrayed as the last gasp of a dying empire waiting to expire at the hands of nationalists and imperialists.

Ottoman Modernity

'Modernity' is a highly contested theoretical concept whose academic efficacy has been debated extensively.[11] It is not the purpose of this section to provide a detailed account of the development of this concept, its relationship to modernisation theory, and its problematic nature. Other works have already effectively accomplished this task.[12] For the purposes of this study, modernity is both a 'mood' and a 'socio-cultural construct'. It is a mood insomuch as it is a powerful assumption about the supposed superior nature of the 'modern' world as compared to a 'traditional' one characterised as backward, irrational, superstitious, undemocratic, religious, and/or anti-individualistic. Modernity is a socio-cultural construct insomuch as its emphasis lies in its institutional, social, and economic particularities that have come to dominate the contemporary era, for example, capitalist market relations, an expanding and increasingly integrated world economy, new technologies, new methods of governance, the nation-state, and nationalism.[13] Several scholars have recently critiqued this concept and applied it to Ottoman and Middle Eastern contexts.[14] In this study, especially for the reformers and nation-state builders of the late Ottoman Empire, 'modernity' was both a 'mood' and a 'socio-cultural construct'. It dominated their ideological and tangible goals of centralising, standardising, and rationalising administrative, economic, military, and social power within the hands of the state in order to preserve the empire's territorial and administrative integrity.

Penal institutions, including prisons and policing, not only facilitate the development of states, but they also act as windows into the process of modernity and its effects on a specific cultural and historical context. While modernity is a global phenomenon that is comparative across the world during the recent past, it is also uniquely specific to each region. The spread of capitalist market relations and the implementation of new methods of governance were not progressively uniform throughout the world. In many cases, different regions experienced the effects of these phenomena haphazardly and often in fits and starts. Various regions 'blended' these global processes with their own administrative and economic systems, cultural traditions, and ways of life in very unique ways. Each region, therefore, created distinct modernities that are globally comparable on some levels, but also cultural and historically unique on others. Ottoman, British, Japanese, or American modernities all possess similarities, but also exhibit peculiarities specific to their historical contexts and development. None represents an authentic or original form of modernity that was then copied and exported around the world.[15] This view of modernity allows for comparison between the development and use of penal institutions among other modernising states during this era. The Ottoman experience of modern state construction and its particular use of penal institutions, therefore, should not be construed as Westernisation. Instead, the blending of global practices, such as administrative centralisation, rationalisation, and standardisation with Ottoman bureaucratic practices produced an entirely new dynamic. This blending, culminating in the creation of an Ottoman criminal justice system and modern penal institutions, is the central focus of this study.

Approaches to Prisons and Incarceration

As mentioned above, there exists a very limited scholarly literature on punishment and penal institutions for the Ottoman Empire. The vast majority of academic work on this topic consists of descriptive, close readings of state archival documents. They are very state-centric and decree-oriented studies that often do not follow the reforms through to their implementation or lack thereof. The few works that approach prisons theoretically tend also to utilise an overly state-centric approach that is closely informed by Michel Foucault's work. Foucault's approaches provide wonderful insights into penal institutions and state-society power relationships, however, if imposed heavy-handed the result is a severely limiting interpretation. These limitations shall be discussed in greater detail below. This investigation of prisons and punishment in the Ottoman Empire draws upon an eclectic and interdisciplinary array of theoretical and methodological approaches, the core of which comes from the social sciences and attempts to integrate socio-legal and Foucaldian analytical frameworks, history from below, David Garland's concept of 'overdetermination', and the debates surrounding modernity into a coherent interpretive apparatus that explicates the complexities of a specific Ottoman modernity and the role that prisons and punishment played therein. This nuanced approach to prisons and punishment traces its roots to studies of penal institutions in other world regions during the long nineteenth century, namely Western Europe and North America, as well as Latin America, Russia, and other regions in Asia.[16] This literature contains a wealth of theoretical and methodological approaches that can provide an appropriate foray into the Ottoman world through judicious selection and application.

European and North American penal historiography can be broken up into four major groups in terms of methodology and theoretical approach: Durkheimian, Marxist, neo-Marxist, and Foucauldian. Besides eighteenth-

and nineteenth-century prison reform literature and treatises by John Howard, Alexis de Tocqueville, G. Beaumont, Baron de Montesquieu, and Jeremy Bentham,[17] one of the first scholars to investigate crime, punishment, and penality was the renowned sociologist Émile Durkheim. He wrote three important works dealing with crime, punishment, and penality.[18] His theoretical and methodological approach to punishment is closely associated with his sociological theories of society, especially his concept of the 'conscience collective'. The 'conscience collective' is the sum total of the morals, values, and shared identity found within a society that governs its laws, actions, and attitudes and helps to create a bond of solidarity among its population.[19] Durkheim viewed punishment as 'an index of society's invisible moral bonds' where its values are constantly expressed and reproduced. These rituals of punishment act as windows into society itself.[20] To Durkheim, punishment also demonstrates society's emotional reaction and need to extract revenge for a violation of its norms and mores. It is this irrational emotional response to crime that helps re-establish the balance and solidarity that must exist in a society in order for it to function properly.[21]

Durkheim's methodological approach to punishment makes a tremendous contribution to penal studies, because it connects penal practices, laws, institutions, and acts of punishment with society's morals and values. He demonstrates the importance of analysing the relationship of penal institutions to public sentiment, how moral solidarity creates punishment practices, and how these practices reaffirm societal solidarity.[22] Durkheim's methodology, however, treats the 'conscience collective' as if it is an uncontested fact of social life. He never accounts for the ideological struggles that are associated with a society's morality, nor does he acknowledge that any society's moral order or legal system is a contested and constantly negotiated process. In fact, legal regulations or systems represent a compromise of various and diffuse 'conscience collectives' within a given society and do not equate in a one-to-one ratio with a society's collective morality.[23]

The Marxist approach to crime and punishment, as exemplified by George Rusche and Otto Kirchheimer's *Punishment and Social Structure*, centres on the ruling elite's relationship to the means of production and its desire to preserve and strengthen its hold on power.[24] Penal practices and institutions are held to be economically determined since the key dynamic in history and society is class struggle, which, in turn, drives social change and gives shape to concrete institutions. The ruling class creates these institutions, such as schools, the military, and the criminal justice system, to quell political opposition, promote its social and economic interests, preserve the status quo, and legitimate its domination over subordinate classes.[25] A society's particular mode of production, be it feudal, capitalist, or Asiatic, determines the amount of corporeal punishment meted out to the offender. This approach successfully highlights the relationship between economic interests and the existence, function, and purposes of penal institutions. Its myopic economic determinism, however, ignores a host of other factors that shape penal institutions and practices, many of which have nothing to do with economics. These include the importance of ideology and political forces in determining penal policy, popular support for penal practices among the lower classes, and penal reform discourse based on humanitarian arguments, judicial rhetoric, or the dynamic negotiation between penal legislation and practice. Marxist approaches to penality, however, dismiss these factors as irrelevant.[26]

The neo-Marxist approach as epitomised by David Rothman and Michael Ignatieff is much more nuanced than the traditional Marxist approach.[27] It continues to view punishment and penal institutions as a means of social control by the ruling class over lower classes, but it also investigates state power, law and legal practices, cultural influences, and ideology. The ruling class needs this 'superstructure' in order for it to maintain its economic dominance.[28] The strengths of the neo-Marxist approach are found in its historicisation of the emergence of penal institutions from specific social, cultural, political, and economic contexts. It asserts that penal policies and institutions are not a result of a monolithic process determined simply by one's relationship to the means of production, but are instead a result of multiple forces and determinants, which are both conflicting and concurring in any specific historical conjuncture. Unfortunately, neo-Marxism still makes penal institutions and policies a result of one's relationship to the mode of production and class interests in the 'last instance'. It still assumes that penal policy debates, which are often motivated by issues other than class interests or economics, such as humanitarian, religious, or scientific concerns, are still 'constrained by the structures of social power and the invisible pressures of the dominant class culture'.[29]

Michel Foucault's *Discipline and Punish* exemplifies the Foucauldian methodological approach to penality and penal institutions. The central purpose of this work is to explain the disappearance of punishment as a public spectacle of violence against the body and to account for the emergence of prisons and incarceration as the normative form of modern punishment in France. His argument centres on how power interacts with knowledge through technologies of discipline and surveillance in order to gain increased social control by one societal class over another. This relationship between power and knowledge delineates the parameters within which all societal relations and social institutions function. The prison and other institutions of social control, as well as the techniques of discipline and surveillance, are direct products of this power and knowledge relationship. Foucault's argument treats class conflict and economic determinism as superficial reasons for achieving social control. Punishment then becomes a 'political tactic' used to exercise power over the body. Similar to all institutions, penal institutions utilise systems of production, domination, and socialisation to subjugate and render the body docile, malleable, and self-disciplining.[30] Foucault's argument has made an invaluable contribution to the study of penality. It elucidates the relationship between power and knowledge, how techniques of discipline and surveillance increase power, how power is exercised through these new technologies, and the effects that these new technologies have upon individuals in terms of control.

Foucault's approach and methodology, unfortunately, remains in the realm of the ideal. *Discipline and Punish* bases much of its argument upon Jeremy Bentham's theoretical reform plans, especially the prison panopticon design. To Foucault, Bentham's panopticon represents the ultimate example of exercising knowledge and power to gain maximum control over the inmate's body and soul. Bentham's panopticon, however, remained in the conceptual realm. His grand scheme never materialised as a physical, operating penitentiary in any European country. Foucault never acknowledges this important point. As Rothman points out, 'for Foucault, motive mattered more than practice. Let public authorities formulate a programme or announce a goal, and he presumed its realisation. He mistook fantasy for reality.'[31] Granted Foucault's argument is not solely focused on the establishment of these mechanisms of power or their physical manifestation, but on what these new technologies and practices tell us about intent and ideology. However, if such an important design as Bentham's panopticon was never realised, does not this fact reveal important insights into a society's sensibilities towards punishment?

Foucault's argument also denies agency to those who are the objects of these new technologies of power. He does not afford them the ability to resist and alter the intended outcomes of these practices. In Foucault's account of penal institutions and practices, he never discusses how resistance undermines and augments the effects that these tactics were supposed to produce within a 'total institution', such as the penitentiary.[32] Patricia O'Brien demonstrates how prison subcultures in nineteenth-century French penitentiaries defied penal institutions' idealised instrumentalities of discipline, surveillance, and social control through various actions, including tattooing, covert communications, bribing guards, and prostitution. These actions undermined many of the tactics utilised by penal institutions to control and rehabilitate the criminal. As a result, resistance often leads to the development of more effective techniques of discipline and control.[33]

Foucault's argument, in many cases, is also ahistorical. He makes it perfectly clear that he is not a historian, but a philosopher. His eclectic style, incredible explanatory power, and quasi-historical approach all make him very popular with academics aspiring to be interdisciplinary in their theoretical approaches. In many cases, he attempts to universalise his claims, when in reality his studies are centred on modern France. He also claims that all systems, functions, decisions, morals, and actions within any society are fundamentally based upon control with power as its primary determinant. This is simply replacing Marx's all-encompassing economic determinant with a different one, which in turn ignores the numerous countervailing forces that attempt to protect human rights, extend freedoms, and improve living conditions and prisoner quality of life. He also ignores the political and practical decision-making processes, including budgetary restraints that act to limit the effective use of discipline and surveillance in controlling the prisoner's body and mind. Finally, Foucault's approach to prisons as examples of the modern state's dominance over society incorrectly draws an impenetrable barrier between these two reified entities. Foucault portrays power as flowing unidirectionally from the state to society when in reality the divide between the two is actually porous, convoluted, and constantly shifting through negotiation and conflict.[34]

Each of these four approaches is useful for limited inquiries into specific areas of punishment and prisons. Also each one effectively focuses upon a particular aspect of penality and provides important insights into the overall picture of the prison as a complex social institution. All of these approaches, however, treat incarceration and prisons in a vacuum. None of them integrate prisons into their broader context, namely the development of modern systems of criminal justice.

In contrast, this study attempts to place incarceration and prisons within a broader context of criminal justice by demonstrating the interconnected nature of policing, criminal codes, courts, and incarceration. It also makes use of a more comprehensive approach to the study of penality along the lines of what David Garland calls a 'multidimensional interpretative approach, which sees punishment as an overdetermined, multifaceted social institution'.[35] This approach views penal institutions as 'social artifacts' that embody and regenerate wider cultural categories and serve as a means of achieving particular penological ends. Similar to architecture, clothing, or diet, punishment cannot be explained by its instrumental purpose alone, but must also take into account its cultural style, historical tradition, and dependence upon institutional, technical, and discursive conditions. Punishment is a legal institution, administered by the state, but it is also grounded in wider patterns of knowing, feeling, and acting that depend upon these social roots and supports for its continuing legitimacy and operation. It is also grounded in history, similar to all social institutions; modern punishment is a historical outcome that is imperfectly adapted to its current situation. It is a product of tradition as much as present policy. There are many conflicting logics that go into punishment in any given society. Similar to all social institutions, punishment shapes its environment as much as it is shaped by it. Penal sanctions and institutions are not simply dependent variables at the end of some finite line of social causation. Punishment interacts with its environment, forming part of the mutually constructing configuration of elements that make up the social world.[36]

Building off Garland's notion that prisons are 'social institutions', this study investigates punishment and prisons utilising a socio-legal approach. According to Avi Rubin, the sociolegal approach is:

> an interpretive framework that explores the law as an aspect of social relations. As such, it offers a starting point for formulating a new set of questions and methodologies for understanding Ottoman legal change in the context of modernity . . . it is not the laws or codes of any given society that form the focus of sociolegal analysis but rather, the detailed, varied practices and meaning that constitute legal systems and that may not be studied in isolation from key social and cultural developments.[37]

In other words, for this study the socio-legal approach looks at normative laws, regulations, and reforms together with the actual lived experiences of both prison cadre and inmates. This approach moves far beyond Foucault's focus on the ideal of social control and discipline by incorporating the reality of Ottoman incarceration in the age of modernity.

Book Outline

This study weaves together six intersecting themes: 1. Transformation through continuity and change as opposed to rupture, 2. A focus by reformers on prisoner rehabilitation, 3. Administrative centralisation and governmentality, 4. Order and discipline, 5. The creation and expansion of the Ottoman 'nanny state'[38] in which the government increasingly assumes greater amounts of responsibility for the welfare of its population, and 6. The juxtaposition of prison reform with the reality of prison life. The first two chapters of this study provide an overview of Ottoman criminal justice practices in the early modern period and their transformation during the nineteenth century. These two chapters are primarily constructed from a state-centric administrative perspective and are meant to provide a context for understanding the developments, transformations, and experiences of the late Ottoman Empire's penal reforms and realities. Chapters 3 to 6 contrast particular reform efforts with the actual experiences of inmates and prison officials to investigate how these interactions affected reform efforts and everyday life within prisons.

Chapter 1 provides a brief overview of the early modern Ottoman legal system and its transformation during the long nineteenth century with special emphasis on the creation of a comprehensive criminal justice system including policing and surveillance, new courts, penal codes, and prisons. The purpose of this chapter is to highlight the relationship between prisons and the transformation of Ottoman criminal justice, especially the links between the Imperial Ottoman Penal Code (IOPC) and incarceration. This transformation was fully rooted in past legal practices while also appropriating and adapting new legal policies from abroad. This process of transformation does not represent an Ottoman progressive march towards Westernisation and secularisation, but one that consciously reinterpreted its Islamic legal system and transformed it through the application of modern methods of governance, such as legal codification, administrative centralisation, the rationalisation and standardisation of legal practice, and the utilisation of incarceration as the primary form of punishment for criminal behaviour.

Chapter 2 consists of a general survey of Ottoman prison reform from the 1850s until the end of the empire (c. 1919) from a state-centric perspective. It pays particular attention to the development of programmes and policies, where they originated, the foundations they built for successive reforms, and how these reforms exemplify particular regime ideologies and world views. Woven throughout the chapter are the six broad themes associated with Ottoman prison reform discussed above in order to lay out the major topics of investigation that constitute the book's remaining chapters.

The third chapter investigates Ottoman efforts to gain knowledge and power over prisons through the collection of statistical information via prison questionnaires and surveys. Not only did these efforts provide invaluable knowledge about prison conditions and the prison population, but they also yield important insights into the ideology and world view of prison reformers. This chapter also includes a discussion of the prison population itself, in terms of its socio-economic and religious composition, criminality, and how individual prisoners were identified and categorised.

Chapter 4 looks closely at prison conditions and structure, particularly in terms of organising the prison population according to crimes committed, convicted or accused, age, and gender. This chapter investigates the everyday life of prisoners, both female and male, their experiences, and the conditions of incarceration. Despite the Ottoman Prison Administration's attempts to improve living conditions through assuming responsibility for health and hygiene, nutrition, and prisoner rehabilitation, prison conditions remained poor and they remained overcrowded. Nowhere else are the limits of reform more evident. Nevertheless, Ottoman reformers still made significant improvements.

Chapter 5 investigates the Ottoman Prison Administration's attempts to professionalise its prison cadre in order to combat corruption and prisoner abuse. Ottoman administrators viewed the prison cadre as linchpins of successful prison reform and prisoner rehabilitation. This chapter looks at these attempts to reform the prison cadre and its effectiveness in light of actual prisoner experiences that reveal a culture of corruption, collusion, and exploitation. These relationships concretely demonstrate the blurred boundaries between guards and criminals, their power relationships, and consequently between state and society.

Chapter 6 delves into Ottoman conceptions of childhood, particularly regarding incarcerated minors. During the Second Constitutional Period, the Committee of Union and Progress (CUP) went to great lengths to protect children from serving prison sentences by rationalising the legal definition of childhood and by centralising power into the hands of the IOPC and the state-run criminal courts. By assuming greater responsibility for the protection of juvenile delinquents, the CUP increased the state's intervention into the private sphere and simultaneously reshaped the public sphere.

Finally, the Conclusion returns to the initial British inspections of Ottoman prisons discussed in this Introduction in order to re-evaluate their findings and place them in the context of a complete breakdown of most state functions in the immediate aftermath of WWI. It then draws larger conclusions concerning the robust penal reforms undertaken by the Ottoman Government during the long nineteenth century and the legacy of criminal justice reform and penal practice this left to its successor states in the Middle East and South-eastern Europe. Finally, the Conclusion makes some initial observations regarding the applicability of studying Ottoman penal reform in a comparative global context.

A Note on Sources

The sources for this book consist primarily of state-centric documents from The Prime Ministry's Ottoman Archives (BOA) in addition to Ottoman penal and legal codes. The archival documents are particularly rich in terms of extensively detailed statistics collected from every prison across the empire, photographs of prisons and prisoners, architectural designs, building projects, expenditure reports, and reports on prison sanitation and health conditions. Some documents also convey debates regarding prisoner nutrition, punishment, rehabilitation, and the condition of incarcerated women and children. These documents reveal elaborate prison reform programmes, new penal codes, and new prison regulations formulated and implemented by reformers that also dealt with larger imperial issues and concerns. This study also utilises interrogation documents called *istintaknameler*.[39] These documents are remarkable sources reflecting the prisoner's or official's own words about events usually involving prisoner abuse, guard–prisoner collusion, and corruption. Unfortunately, most archival documents make it very difficult to capture the voices of ordinary prisoners. Very few prisoners were literate and the vast majority did not leave behind memoirs, letters, or such describing their circumstances and experiences. This genre of document (state generated) presents certain pitfalls and limitations, but if 'read against the grain' can still offer a window into the subaltern's world, even if only a glimpse, and enable the re-creation of some aspects of their everyday lives that in turn assist in adjusting the biased perspective of the state.[40]

Finally, this book relies on evidence gathered from a variety of libraries and the national archives in the Republic of Turkey, the United States, and Great Britain. These sources consist of bureaucratic, administrative, and diplomatic documents, memoirs, travel volumes, newspapers, journals, letters, and statistical records in Arabic, English, French, German, Greek, Italian, Russian, Ottoman Turkish, and Turkish. These additional sources also help to overcome state-centric bias and provide further insights into the lives of everyday prisoners and prison cadre.

Notes

1. BNA, FO 195/364, 608/52/13, and 608/114/4.
2. BNA, FO 195/364, pp. 6–8.
3. BNA, FO 195/364, and 226/113.
4. BNA, FO 195/364, p. 8. A copy of this report was also submitted to the Foreign Office; see BNA, FO 195/364, pp. 1–32.

5. BNA, FO 608/52/13, and 608/114/4.
6. BNA, FO 608/52/13, pp. 235–7.
7. *Midnight Express* (1978) was directed and produced by Alan Parker. The screen play, written by Oliver Stone, was based on Billy Hayes' book *Midnight Express* about his experiences as a convicted drug smuggler in a Turkish prison. Recently both Billy Hayes and Oliver Stone have admitted that the movie grossly misrepresented and exaggerated Hayes' actual experience in a Turkish prison. See *The New York Times* Monday, 18 June 2007, under The Arts section, B2.
8. Said, *Orientalism*; and Wolff, *Inventing Eastern Europe*.
9. Morris, and Rothman, *Oxford History of the Prison*, Chapters 3–7.
10. For studies on Ottoman and Middle Eastern prisons written in Turkish and English see Şen, *Osmanlı'da Mahkum Olmak*; Yıldız, *Mapusane* and 'Osmanlı Devleti'nde Hapishane Islahatı'; Gürsoy, *Hapishane Kitabı*; Lévy, and Toumarkine, *Osmanlı'da Asayiş, Suç ve Ceza*; Bozkurt, 'Kütahya Hapishanesinin Genel Durumu'; Atar, 'Turgutlu Hapishanesinin Genel Durumu'; Uslu, 'Erzincan'da Suç, Suçlu ve Hapishane'; Yıldıztaş, 'Suç Unsurları ve İstanbul Hapishanleri'; Adak, 'Aydın Vilayeti'ndeki Hapishaneler'; Çiçen, 'Cesaevi Islahatı'; Hasan Şen, 'Transformation of Punishment Politics'; Peters, 'Controlled Suffering', 'Prisons and Marginalisation', and 'Egypt and the Age of the Triumphant Prison'; Gorman, 'Regulation, Reform and Resistance'; and Fahmy, 'Medical Conditions in Egyptian Prisons'.
11. For an excellent discussion about the benefits, limitations, and pitfalls of the theoretical concept of modernity see Anonymous, 'AHR Roundtable'.
12. Rubin, *Nizamiye Courts*, pp. 2–8; and Lockman, *Contending Visions*, Chapters 4–7.
13. Rengger, *Political Theory, Modernity, and Postmodernity*, pp. 39–42.
14. A few of these recent works include Rubin, *Nizamiye Courts*; Agmon, *Family and Court*; and Levine, *Overthrowing Geography*.
15. Gluck, 'The End of Elsewhere'.
16. There is a burgeoning literature on penal institutions and nation-state construction in the developing world, see Dikötter and Brown, *Cultures of Confinement*; Dikötter, *Crime, Punishment and Prisons in Modern China*; Botsman, *Punishment and Power in the Making of Modern Japan*; Bernault and Roitman, *History of Prisons and Confinement in Africa*; Salvatore, and Aguirre, *Birth of the Penitentiary in Latin America*; Adams, *Politics of Punishment*; Zinoman, *Colonial Bastille*; Arnold, 'Colonial Prison'; and Singha, *Despotism of Law*.
17. Howard, *State of Prisons in England and Wales*; Beaumont and de Tocqueville, *Penitentiary System in the United States*; de Montesquieu, *Spirit of the Laws*; and Bentham, *Introduction to the Principles of Morals and Legislation*.
18. Durkheim, *Moral Education, The Division of Labor in Society*, and 'Two Laws of Penal Evolution'.

19. Garland, *Punishment and Modern Society*, pp. 33–6.
20. Ibid., pp. 2 and 23.
21. Ibid., pp. 34–40.
22. Ibid., pp. 27–8.
23. Ibid., pp. 49–57.
24. Rusche and Kirchheimer, *Punishment and Social Structure*.
25. Garland, p. 84.
26. Ibid., pp. 108–9; and O'Brien, 'Crime and Punishment as Historical Problem'.
27. Rothman, *Discovery of the Asylum*; and Ignatieff, *Just Measure of Pain*.
28. Garland, p. 87.
29. Garland, pp. 124–5.
30. Foucault, *Discipline and Punish*.
31. Rothman, p. xix. For critiques concerning the applicability of Foucault's arguments to areas outside of Western Europe see Redfield, 'Foucault in the Tropics'; and Kaplan, 'Panopticon in Poona'.
32. According to Daniel Goffman, a 'total institution' is 'a place of residence and work where a large number of like-situated individuals, cut off from the wider society for an appreciable period of time, together lead an enclosed, formally administered round of life'. Examples of 'total institutions' include asylums, hospitals, some types of schools, the military, and prisons (Goffman, *Asylums*, p. 4).
33. O'Brien, *Promise of Punishment*. Also see Fahmy, *All the Pasha's Men*, Chapters 2–3 for a discussion on how attempts to conscript peasants for military service resulted in widespread resistance that shaped military policy and practice.
34. Mitchell, 'The Limits of the State'.
35. Garland, p. 2.
36. Ibid., pp. 19–22.
37. Rubin, 'Ottoman Judicial Change in the Age of Modernity', p. 7. Ottoman history has a growing number of works that apply a socio-legal approach to the study of law and legality transformation during the nineteenth century. The publications of Agmon and Rubin are among the most notable.
38. For a brief discussion of the Ottoman 'nanny state', see Paz, 'Crime, Criminals, and the Ottoman State', p. vi. This book uses the terms 'nanny state' and 'state patriarchy' interchangeably. For a discussion of state or 'public patriarchy', see Hatem, 'Economic and Political Liberation in Egypt'.
39. Quataert and Gutman, 'Coal Mines, the Palace, and Struggles' is an example of research that heavily utilises *istintakname* documents.
40. See Guha and Spivak, *Selected Subaltern Studies*, Introduction.

1

Ottoman Criminal Justice and the Transformation of Islamic Criminal Law and Punishment in the Age of Modernity, 1839–1922

Over the course of the long nineteenth century (c. 1770s–1922) the Ottoman Empire experienced a series of internal and external crises that included separatist movements, rebellions, fiscal problems, numerous wars, and European imperialism. In the face of these threats, sultans and administrators attempted vigorous plans of reform aimed at transforming the bureaucracy, legal and education systems, economy, population, and military. As part of this overall restructuring programme, Ottoman statesmen included efforts to create a criminal justice system. Therefore, when the Young Turks, led by members of the Committee of Union and Progress (CUP), deposed Sultan Abdülhamid II and created the first of their two major penal institutions in August 1909 (the Directorate of Public Security), the association between penal reform and concepts, such as civilisation, developmentalism, social engineering, and the centralisation and rationalisation of government power were already part of Ottoman political and intellectual *mentalité*. The close correlation between penal and broader imperial reforms makes the prison an effective window into the process of Ottoman modernity as the empire appropriated and adapted processes of modern statecraft and nation building to its particular imperial context.

This chapter highlights the change and continuity of Ottoman criminal justice policy and practice as lawmakers applied greater measures of state consolidation, standardisation, and rationalisation in order to transform the empire's Islamic legal structures over the course of the long nineteenth century. Taken in aggregate, these changes to criminal justice are astounding, however, seeing only the forest while disregarding its individual trees results in making one forest indistinguishable from another. In other words, without historical specificity, the description and analysis of the dynamism of Ottoman criminal justice and imperial transformation often obfuscates the process of adoption and adaptation, continuity and change, and innovation that took place within the empire. Instead, this dynamism is often replaced with a narrative of rupture, Westernisation, and secularisation that disregards the uniqueness of Ottoman modernity.

Although a relatively neglected field in Ottoman studies, several scholars have recently made forays into topics such as crime, punishment, policing, and criminal law in the eighteenth and nineteenth centuries.[1] A major purpose of this chapter is to synthesise this growing literature in order to provide a brief overview of Ottoman criminal justice on the eve of modernity as a backdrop to the tremendous transformations of the nineteenth and the early twentieth centuries. It is not the purpose of this chapter to go into great detail regarding all facets of Ottoman criminal justice, but to draw its broad outlines in an attempt to establish the context from whence the transformations that occurred during the late Ottoman Empire emerged, thereby elucidating the deep connections between 'modern' Ottoman criminal justice and its supposed 'medieval' predecessor. This overview includes a discussion of the philosophy of Ottoman criminal law and its practice in order to demonstrate the antecedents upon which nineteenth-century administrators built, such as the concepts of prisoner rehabilitation, the Circle of Justice, recourse to law, surveillance and public order, and punishments consisting of fines, incarceration, and hard labour.

Building upon this foundation, the second purpose of this chapter consists of another brief discussion concerning the creation of a comprehensive and integrated criminal justice system along generally recognised international standards wherein law and practice became streamlined, centralised, codified, and standardised. During this period, Ottoman administrators transformed policing and surveillance, codified Islamic law into civil and criminal codes, established modern schools of law, selectively adapted European legal codes and practices, and instituted a centralised prison system for the first time in the empire's history. Officials did not create this system *ex-nihilo*. Instead, they built upon existing structures and practices and transformed them into an entirely new Islamic criminal justice system. Finally, this chapter focuses closely on three intertwined aspects of this new criminal justice system, namely the concrete links between these new penal codes, the extensive delineation of crimes, and the adoption of incarceration as the primary form of criminal punishment. Through the promulgation and then expansion of these new penal codes together with other aspects of this new criminal justice system, the Ottoman administration gradually gained a monopoly over the adjudication of criminal matters. This effectively circumscribed the discretionary power of local administrators and Islamic court judges (*qadi* and *naib*) in adjudicating criminal cases and meting out punishments. With the exception of fines, incarceration and thus the prison became the primary site of criminal punishment within the empire.

Ottoman Criminal Justice on the Eve of Modernity

Since the reign of Sultan Süleyman I (r. 1520–66) and through the early nineteenth century Ottoman criminal justice policy and practice functioned in a relatively consistent manner in which Sultanic law (*kanun*) and Hanafi Islamic law (*shari'a*) were closely integrated and mutually legitimated. Rulers of Islamic states, including Ottoman sultans, regularly issued decrees to supplement Islamic law in areas where *shari'a* was silent, such as land law, state organisation, public order and security, and various criminal matters. Theoretically, none of the decrees was supposed to contradict Islamic law; instead, they were supposed to preserve it. For example, in the case of criminal matters, various sultans issued decrees providing punishments for theft in which the evidence or specific crime did not meet exact Islamic legal stipulations. These types of decrees were meant to supplement Islamic law and provide authorities with the discretionary means to maintain public order, safeguard sovereignty, protect personal rights including life and property, uphold Islamic law, and punish criminals, thus abiding by the Circle-of-Justice ruling philosophy.[2] Scholars, however, have generally characterised sultanic decrees prior to the 1530s as completely distinct and 'secular' in relation to Islamic law. In other words, the criminal codes issued by Ottoman sultans from the reign of Mehmet II until Süleyman I were not necessarily in 'harmony' with *shari'a*, but allowable since Islamic law made provisions for rulers to keep public order and uphold justice.[3]

Sultan Süleyman I's chief jurisconsult, Ebu's-Su'ud, is credited with 'harmonising' Ottoman sultanic decrees with Islamic law, specifically in the realms of land tenure and taxation, trusts in mortmain, marriage, and crimes and torts.[4] He is also credited with expanding the authority of the Caliphate and applying it to the Ottoman sultan. Not only was Sultan Süleyman I ruler of the Ottoman Empire and leader of all Muslims (*ummah*), but now he was also 'the interpreter and executor of God's law', thus uniting the powers of sovereign and chief jurisconsult in the hands of the Ottoman ruler.[5] This in turn completely blurred the lines between a supposedly secular (*kanun*) and the sacred (*shari'*) law. It also brought the Islamic legal offices of jurisconsult (*mufti*) and judge (*qadi*) fully under the ideological and fiscal authority of the sultan, a process that began centuries earlier.

As early as the fourteenth century, the Ottoman Sultanate founded a network of Islamic courts within the urban centres down to the village level of its expanding polity in order to exert its authority and legitimacy. This network of courts served the legal, commercial, social, and political needs of the surrounding areas and reigned supreme in legal matters for all the empire's subjects regardless of socio-economic status or communal identity. Non-Muslims also had recourse to their own religious legal institutions. Those institutions, however, existed only at the express consent of Ottoman authorities. Islamic courts dealt with all aspects of the law, including civil, familial, and criminal, and worked closely with other local authorities, such as military and administrative leaders, to maintain order and uphold the sovereignty of the sultan. In cooperation with other local authorities, court officials often engaged in many of the functions fulfilled by contemporary criminal justice systems, such as investigation, prosecution, surveillance, policing, and punishment.[6]

Islamic court judges, arguably, were the most important local royal officials. They were responsible for a host of other legal and administrative functions, such as marriage and inheritance transactions, public notary, mediation, and protecting civil justice. The judge's salary came from the state as did much of his training and each of his appointments. Notwithstanding imperial oversight, which included declarations of how certain cases should be adjudicated and the standardising of some legal interpretations, Islamic court judges possessed relative autonomy in dispensing justice and mercy, having the ability to consult various sources, including Islamic scholars, the cannon of Islamic jurisprudence, sultanic decrees, and local custom in order to decide the best resolution for a particular case. This was done while attempting to balance numerous personal, local, regional, and imperial interests and power dynamics, one of which was the preservation of Islamic law and practice.[7]

As the Ottoman sultan's most visible dispenser of justice and mercy, as well as preserver of harmony at the local level, the *qadi* worked with many local officials to mete out punishment and maintain public order. These two functions often went hand in hand, each reinforcing the other. As a minimalist or 'reactive state' the Ottoman Empire relied upon a multifaceted array of official and unofficial actors to impose order, punish criminals, and settle disputes.[8] These methods and actors included guarantors (*kefil*), character witnesses, village and neighbourhood watch programmes, local gangs (*kabadayı*), religious officials from various sects, Janissary networks, local governors, garrison troops, market inspectors, guilds, kinship and tribal groups, and – perhaps most importantly – collective responsibility.[9] While many of these groups had competing interests that could lead to unrest, they regularly cooperated out of common interest.[10]

The purpose of punishment according to Islamic criminal law and sultanic supplements was threefold: retribution for the victim, rehabilitation of the offender, and protection of state sovereignty and society by removing the offender through execution, banishment, or incarceration.[11] These three purposes are not mutually exclusive and often overlapped in terms of intent and application. Punishments meted out ranged from death sentences, to fines, financial restitution, exile, incarceration, and corporeal punishments (flogging, the bastinado, mutilation, and/or amputation). Another common form of punishment combined incarceration and hard labour wherein criminals served time as oarsmen (*kürek*) in the galleys of the imperial fleet.[12]

The vast majority of punishments meted out for criminal offences were discretionary (*ta'zir*), inflicted by a court judge when the crime or evidence did not meet the strictures of Islamic law. Islamic legal procedure, however, still governed these punishments, which could not exceed *shari'* punishments. In the Ottoman Empire, after the reforms of Ebu's-Su'ud, these punishments were deemed to be in conformity with Islamic law and were sanctioned by it.[13] Ottoman executive officials also possessed other discretionary punishment options (*siyaset*) that were not restricted by Islamic law and could be imposed directly without judicial oversight. *Siyaset* punishments often led to claims of abuse against executive power. Ottoman authorities regularly interceded to curb this type of punishment by virtue of the empire's Circle-of-Justice ruling philosophy. Eventually, *siyaset* punishments were completely circumscribed by various nineteenth-century reforms, as discussed below.[14]

Our contemporary views of the rule of law and rationalised legal systems often characterise this 'classical' system of criminal justice as capricious and despotic.[15] Ottoman court records, archival documents, and even some foreign travel accounts, however, describe a relatively well-organised and implemented system of justice wherein a majority of Ottoman subjects, regardless of religious or communal background, possessed access to legal recourse through official government institutions and procedures, such as *shari'* courts and official petitioning. Limits of communication and technology notwithstanding, the Ottoman justice system possessed relatively clear lines of authority and jurisdiction that theoretically began and ended with the sultan who simultaneously acted as sovereign and caliph, thus bridging the supposed divide between secular and sacred.[16]

Creating a Modern Criminal Justice System

By the time of its dissolution in 1922, the Ottoman Empire had significantly transformed its criminal justice system to include modern centralised criminal codes, policing organisations, criminal courts, modern law schools, and a centralised prison system wherein the vast majority of convicted criminals received incarceration as their punishment. This transformation did not happen overnight, but often in uneven and haphazard ways, as imperial and local officials attempted to deal with the challenges and crises experienced during this volatile period. This new system was not conjured out of thin air or borrowed wholesale from Western Europe. Instead, it possesses deep roots and antecedents in the Ottoman 'classical' justice system outlined above. Themes such as prisoner rehabilitation, prison labour, the Circle of Justice, links between Islamic law and imperial practice, and the rule of law, however, still functioned and took precedence in Ottoman legal circles. The assumptions and world view associated with Ottoman modernity governed this transformation. In other words, Ottoman officials implemented these reforms in order to centralise power over existing criminal justice institutions and practices through the rationalisation and standardisation of legal procedure, criminal codes, court practices and jurisdictions, and the establishment of powerful police forces.

Significant developments that altered this 'classical' system can be traced back to the reign of Sultan Selim III (r. 1789–1807) and that of Sultan Mahmud II (r. 1808–39). These developments include early legal codification attempts (Selim III's *Nizam-i Cedid Kanunları*), the transformation of surveillance and policing in the imperial capital, the destruction of the Janissary corps, and consequently the weakening of the empire's system of guilds. Both the Janissaries and the guilds played a major role in maintaining public order in urban areas. Undermining these institutions resulted in the adoption of new methods of surveillance and the creation of new organisations for the maintenance of public order while still relying on neighbourhood and village networks, guarantors, military units, and local religious leaders to fill in the gaps as these new organisations developed.[17]

Taking advantage of these opportunities to expand centralised state power, Sultan Mahmud II created a new policing force as part of his restructured military under the command of the *Serasker* (Minister of War). This force was still responsible for public order and fire fighting in urban areas. Its functions and structure, therefore, were not much different from the Janissaries. Its authority and power, however, were more centralised under the sultan through his new military force. Eventually, through trial, error, and revision, these police forces were separated from the military, assigned to the Ministry of the Interior and given clear lines of civil authority and power to police the empire's urban areas.[18]

Throughout the provinces, particularly in villages and rural areas, the Ottoman administration haphazardly established gendarme forces during the 1840s, patterned after the French original to maintain order, collect taxes, safeguard highways, and supress rebellions.[19] These paramilitary forces worked together with local governors and military garrisons. Both urban police and rural gendarme were primarily engaged in crime prevention with very little investigative authority. Criminal investigations were still the responsibility of court judges. Police forces, however, had authority to interrogate and torture suspects in order to extract evidence. Judges and these organisations, therefore, worked very closely together to arrest suspects, collect evidence, and investigate cases.[20]

From 1840 to 1880 Ottoman administrators and bureaucrats completely transformed the empire's legal codes and court systems. In so doing, Islamic civil law was codified in the form of the *Mecelle* and new city and provincial councils were given power to adjudicate in many matters alongside *qadis*.[21] Ottoman administrators also established new courts and adopted new procedures for judging criminal cases. In 1840, lawmakers simultaneously created a new criminal court system and promulgated the first Ottoman penal code. Reformers also extended powers of criminal adjudication to police and provincial councils in urban and rural areas. By 1849 these judicial proceedings became standardised throughout the empire. Then in 1854 the empire established criminal tribunals called *Meclis-i Tahkik*, which assumed responsibility for handling criminal matters from the provincial councils. These courts functioned similarly to Islamic courts, because the accused had no access to legal counsel, judges represented state interests, and proceedings were conducted in local vernaculars.[22]

In 1879, the Ottoman administration officially created the *nizamiye* court system. The foundations of this court system date back to the 1864 Provincial Regulations. The *nizamiye* courts stood alongside *shari'* courts in adjudicating both criminal and civil cases. Avi Rubin's work convincingly demonstrates the blurred boundaries in authority and jurisdiction between *nizamiye* and Islamic courts, because, in most cases, *qadis* presided over both courts. Also in 1879, the empire promulgated the Law of the *Nizamiye* Judicial Organisation (*Mehakim-i Nizamiye'nin Teşkilât Kanunu*) and the Codes of Criminal and Civil Procedure (*Usul-ı Muhakemat-ı Cezaiye Kanunu* and *Usul-ı Muhakemat-ı Hukukiye,* respectively). Coupled with the new law schools established by Sultan Abdülhamid II, these courts and new legal codes and procedures became the foundation upon which the empire built its criminal justice system.[23]

Parallel to the creation of the *nizamiye* courts, the Ottoman Ministry of Justice also adopted wholesale the 1808 French Criminal Justice Code and named its new code the 1879 Code of Criminal Procedure (*Ceza Muhakemeleri Usulü Kanunu*). Most significantly, this new procedural code established the office of public prosecutor in fulfilment of Article 91 of the 1876 Ottoman Constitution, despite the constitution's suspension by Abdülhamid II in 1878. This was the first time that such an office had ever been established in the empire. This new procedural code also regulated criminal legal proceedings, witnesses, and evidence. For example, there was now a clear separation between the roles and responsibilities of prosecutors from those of judges, which is non-existent under Islamic law. The new code strictly circumscribed the judge's role in the adjudication of the assigned cases. It also more clearly delineated the role of the police by assigning them sole responsibility for conducting criminal investigations and for writing up their findings so that public prosecutors could build their cases against the accused. The police could no longer act as judges under any circumstance. Previous to this new code, the police and market inspectors (*muhtasib*) were, under certain circumstances, empowered to arrest, investigate, try, and punish suspected criminals at the scene of the crime.[24]

Punishment also underwent a dramatic transformation in the nineteenth century. With the exception of capital punishment, which became very rare after 1839, corporal punishments, including torture, were outlawed. While technically still an allowable punishment according to the 1858 Imperial Ottoman Penal Code (IOPC), exile was severely curtailed. Beside fines, imprisonment became the most common form of punishment meted out for criminal behaviour. Incarceration in prisons, jails, citadels, dungeons, and government buildings was not an innovative punishment for nineteenth-century Ottomans. It existed from the empire's earliest days as did incarceration with hard labour. By the middle of the nineteenth century, incarceration with hard labour, however, no longer involved serving in the galleys at the Imperial Shipyards, although it maintained the name *kürek*. Tanzimat-era reformers also established several labour camps for prisoners in places such as Cyprus, Rhodes, and Mytilene.[25] By the early twentieth century, the Ottoman Prison Administration built prison factories in major urban areas. Finally, during WWI the Ottoman regime pressed many prisoners into work battalions to build roads and raise crops as part of the empire's war effort.[26]

In the age of modernity there is an inherent logic found in bureaucratic and administrative standardisation and centralisation. Ottoman sultans and administrators shared this global logic and applied it to their imperial context. Intimate relationships are to be found in the creation of the IOPC, the increased delineation of crimes and punishment, the circumscription of discretionary punishment, and the shift to the almost exclusive use of incarceration as punishment.[27] The remainder of this chapter focuses on the exposition of these interconnections over the course of the long nineteenth century culminating in the Second Constitutional Period.

Penal Codes, Incarceration and Circumscribing Discretionary Punishment

Ottoman bureaucrats created the empire's first modern penal code in 1840 shortly after the declaration of the 1839 Imperial Rescript of the Rose Garden (*Hatt-ı Hümayun-u Gülhane*).[28] This Penal Code (*Ceza Kanunnamesi*) consisted of thirteen articles in forty-two sections and an epilogue. The main criminal issues covered by this code included treason, incitement to rebellion, embezzlement of state funds, tax evasion, and resistance to authority. The code was neither comprehensive nor exhaustive regarding the many crimes punishable by *shari'* law or local administrative practice. It did stipulate that the punishment of incarceration with hard labour would be added to the traditional penalty of blood-money for homicide. This code, however, did not change traditional forms of punishment, especially exile or hard labour. It still allowed for discretionary corporal punishments and fines (*ta'zir* and *siyaset*) meted out respectively by *qadis* and local governors.[29] In other words, local Islamic court judges and state officials continued to possess great autonomy in identifying, trying, and punishing criminals according to their discretionary powers. This code, however, constituted an important combination of administrative and religious law not previously codified within the empire.[30]

Other items covered in the code include changes in legal procedure and punishments for a variety of criminal offences. For the first time, a code stipulated specific punishments for offences, such as reprimands, corporal punishments, incarceration, banishment, and hard labour. It did not, however, sever the dual system of Islamic law and administrative regulation within the empire. Some offences continued to be adjudicated by the separate systems outlined above, with others being handled jointly. Islamic legal procedures, however, still applied to all criminal proceedings.[31] Reformers intended this code to serve as a bulwark against administrative corruption and abuse of power, thus maintaining the Circle of

Justice.[32] The majority of its articles dealt with these issues as a means to centralise power and impose more effectively the rule of law in government administration.[33]

Ottoman legal reformers addressed some of the inadequacies of the 1840 Code by promulgating the 1851 New Penal Code (*Kanun-i Cedid*). This code consisted of forty-three articles organised into three chapters. It better fulfilled the demands of the 1839 *Gülhane* Decree by focusing on offences involving crimes against life, honour, and property, such as forgery, abduction of girls, and sexual advances toward minors. Additionally, it better clarified procedures adjudicating homicide; stipulated provisions for prisoner medical care; mandated assistance for poor prisoners; and regulated the punishment of slaves. In general, the purpose of the 1851 Penal Code was to assist in the maintenance of public order, prevent tyranny and corruption by government officials, and protect individual rights. It still did not, however, circumscribe the discretionary power of judges and local officials, but it did continue the process of greater delineation of crimes.[34]

Sultan Abdülmecid and Mustafa Reşid Pasha replaced this penal code in 1858 with the Imperial Ottoman Penal Code (*Ceza Kanunname-yi Hümayunu*). Over the next sixty years, lawmakers continued to expand and augment the IOPC.[35] It, therefore, became the foundation for criminal justice transformation including the transition from corporal punishments to fines and incarceration as the primary forms of criminal punishment. In addition to the penal codes of 1840 and 1851, the origins of the IOPC are also closely linked to broader imperial reforms, specifically the promulgation of the 1856 Imperial Decree of Reform (*Islahat Fermanı*).

Five years after Ambassador Canning submitted his 'Memorandum for the Improvement of Prisons in Turkey' to Sultan Abdülmecid, he assisted Reşid Pasha in drafting the *Islahat Fermanı*. It announced a wide range of legal and economic reforms including equality for all before the law, protection of property rights, citizenship, and liberty. It also contained a very important passage related to penal reform:

> Penal, correctional, and commercial laws . . . shall be drawn up as soon as possible and formed into a code . . . Proceedings shall be taken, with as little delay as possible, for the reform of the penitentiary system as applied to houses of detention, punishment, or correction, and other establishments of like nature, so as *to reconcile the rights of humanity with those of justice*. Corporal punishment shall not be administered, even in the prisons, except in conformity with the disciplinary regulations established by my Sublime Porte, and everything that resembles torture shall be entirely abolished.[36]

These portions of the *Islahat Fermanı* not only exemplify the early beginnings of Ottoman prison reform, but they also map out a robust programme to raise Ottoman punishment to the idealised standards of 'modern' civilisation.

In accordance with the *Islahat Fermanı*, the empire promulgated the IOPC on 9 August 1858.[37] Portions of the new code included adaptations of the 1810 French Criminal Code. The most striking difference between this new code and its predecessors was that it included a section devoted to the protection of individual rights. Crimes against individuals were divided into three categories: '(1) crimes committed against lives and individual security, (2) crimes against honour and dignity, and (3) crimes against the property of citizens.'[38]

The IOPC's promulgation represents a fundamental shift in Ottoman and Islamic criminal law. Personal rights were codified and rationalised within an Islamic legal framework wherein the state acted as guarantor and supervisor. Contrary to the views of contemporary scholarship, this was not the Westernisation of Ottoman criminal law. While it was the bureaucratic Ottoman state that codified these laws, Islamic court judges still rendered judgments and presided over all proceedings. Additionally, the very first article of the code claims legitimacy based upon Islamic principles and precedence.[39] The rationalisation and codification of these rights, however, abrogated some of the autonomy of Islamic courts judges and regulated outcomes in a much more standardised way than ever before.[40] Instead of characterising these reforms as the secularisation of Ottoman criminal law and proceedings, they should be viewed as the continuation of a standardising and centralising process of Islamic criminal law that built upon the 1840 and 1851 penal codes.

The IOPC was the forerunner to larger reform efforts intended to overhaul, centralise, standardise, and rationalise the entire Ottoman judicial system. This restructuring eventually included the drafting of the *Mecelle*. As mentioned above, it also laid the groundwork for the circumscription of *qadi* discretionary power. Judicial reforms, standardising legal procedures, practices, and punishments and codified legal codes limit a judge's autonomy in legal interpretation. The IOPC also facilitated the creation of *nizamiye* courts. While the *nizamiye* and *shari'* courts worked in close cooperation for several decades, by 1917 the *nizamiye* courts superseded *shari'* courts in all civil and criminal matters, except concerning inheritance and family law.[41] While transforming the empire's courts and legal codes to meet the strictures of the Modern World System, administrators still utilised the same Islamic legitimating structures employed for centuries.[42] Ottoman rulers and lawmakers built off the empire's own traditions while applying modern instrumentalities of governance to their specific imperial context.

An analysis of the transformation of the IOPC from 1858 to 1911 clearly demonstrates the shift in the conceptualisation of crime and punishment in the Ottoman Empire during this period. The code was greatly expanded by stipulating many new crimes with fixed punishments. With the exception of execution, lawmakers discontinued all forms of corporal punishment. They also outlawed torture and completely circumscribed the ability of local officials to impose discretionary punishments (*ta'zir* and *siyaset*). Administrators replaced these punishments with clearly delineated fines and prison sentences according to the type and severity of the crime committed. Some prison sentences included hard labour (*kürek*), especially in cases of serious crime (*cinayet*).[43]

By 1911 the IOPC contained 264 articles dealing with criminal legal procedures, crimes, liabilities, and punishments. The code was divided into four sections, a 'Preliminary' section and three chapters. The 'Preliminary' consisted of forty-seven articles split into four parts. These parts set forth the general grades and degrees of offences, legal procedures, and punishments for serious crimes (*cinayet*) and lesser offences (*cünha* and *kabahat*). The 'Preliminary' also stipulates the guidelines for determining criminal culpability.[44]

The first chapter of the IOPC delineates crimes against the Ottoman state and the general well-being of its populace as well as their associated punishments. It includes 121 articles divided into sixteen parts. The first two parts deal with crimes that threaten the external and internal security of the empire, such as espionage, incitement to riot and civil war, brigandage, banditry, and abrogation of the constitution. The vast majority of these crimes carry the death sentence. Other parts of this chapter deal with bribery, theft of state property, abuse of office, negligence of duty, disobedience to government officials, aiding and abetting criminals, impersonating government officials, interfering with religious privileges, disrupting imperial telecommunications, censorship, counterfeiting, forgery, and arson. The majority of these crimes are punishable by fine, loss of office and privilege, and imprisonment.[45]

The second chapter is divided into twelve parts containing eighty-six articles detailing individual crimes. The enumerated crimes include homicide, bodily injuries, threats, abortion, selling adulterated beverages and medicines, violations of honour (rape, molestation, or kidnapping), improper arrest and incarceration, perjury, slander, vituperation, theft, bankruptcy, embezzlement, breach of contract, fraud, and the destruction of private property. According to the stipulated punishments, the vast majority of these crimes are punishable by various lengths of incarceration, fines, and death.[46] The third chapter of the IOPC consists of twelve articles all detailing minor offences (*kabahat*) and their associated punishments. These offences all pertain to matters of sanitation, cleanliness, and the police. Some of the particular offences include improper maintenance of chimneys and furnaces, disturbing the peace with loud noise or raucous behaviour, public drunkenness, and the improper burial of corpses. Most punishments consist of fines and very short prison sentences (usually incarceration for a period of twenty-four hours to a week).[47]

The changes to the IOPC during the Second Constitutional Period culminated a continuous process of revision since the code's adoption in 1858. On 4 June 1911, the Ottoman Parliament repealed and reissued the IOPC in its most expansive form.[48] The major modifications of 1911 include:

1. new stipulations regarding the punishment of repeat offenders
2. outlawing the use of torture in order to extract the payment of court fees, fines, and the restitution of stolen properties
3. the seizure of articles prepared and/or used for committing an offence
4. the use of incarceration for unpaid fines or the inability to pay fines
5. the deduction of time served prior to trial and sentencing
6. regulations about determining the criminal culpability of children, the insane, and those who committed an act of self-defence
7. punishments for criminal intent
8. offences and punishments pertaining to the external and internal security of the empire
9. new bribery-related crimes and punishments
10. crimes related to the opposition or the circumvention of state regulations, particularly those concerning public health, hygiene, security, and order
11. punishments meted out for dereliction of duty by state officials
12. regulations concerning the unlawful entry into private premises
13. regulations forbidding the ill-treatment of individuals by government officials, particularly in relation to torture or bodily harm
14. regulations and punishments related to persons opposing, disobeying, or insulting government officials
15. offences and punishments pertaining to impersonating government officials
16. punishments pertaining to the destruction of telephone and telegraph communications
17. regulations and punishments related to forgery

18. regulations and punishments pertaining to arson and the manufacture, possession, and selling of illegal weapons and explosives
19. crimes and punishments related to homicide and physical assault
20. crimes and punishments pertaining to persons causing abortion, selling adulterated drinks, or selling poisons without guarantee
21. regulations and punishments regarding persons who violate honour, such as through molestation, illicit sexual relations, kidnapping, or rape
22. punishments and amendments pertaining to unlawful incarceration and the kidnapping of infants and children, especially girls
23. punishments and regulations regarding calumny, vituperation, and the divulgence of secrets
24. regulations and punishments pertaining to theft
25. regulations and punishments concerning the destruction of government and private property
26. punishments pertaining to persons guilty of misdemeanours (*kabahat*) against matters of sanitation, cleanliness, and the police.[49]

Lawmakers altered every section of the code. In fact, out of the 265 articles, a total of fifty-six were rescinded, revised, and/or expanded.[50] This constitutes the revision of more than 17 per cent of the code.

These 1911 revisions demonstrate the CUP's intent to consolidate greater amounts of power into the hands of the state and rationalise the practice of its criminal legal system by reigning in the autonomy of local judges and administrators; upholding state sovereignty, individual rights, and the protection of private property; and maintaining public order. CUP motivations to gain greater access to the lives of the population were also at work. The June 1911 IOPC transformations regarding 'Crimes against Honour', 'Theft', and 'Violent Crimes' demonstrate these changes and CUP goals in terms of criminal delineation, punishment, and discretionary authority.

Prior to the promulgation of the IOPC, local officials and Islamic court judges usually punished those guilty of violent crimes, theft, or crimes against honour according to their discretionary authority (*siyaset* or *ta'zir*), especially since Islamic law is silent on most crimes associated with these categories. As long as these punishments did not equal or exceed those stipulated in *shari'a*, the vast majority of punishments meted out for these offences consisted of a combination of fines and corporal punishments. This gave local officials enormous autonomy in dealing with these offences and often led to accusations of abuse of power.[51] With the promulgation of the IOPC and its greater delineation of crimes and punishments, more and more of local official's discretionary penal authority was abrogated.

For example, in 1911 the Ottoman Parliament significantly altered the section of the IOPC dealing with crimes against an individual's honour, including sexual offences, perjury, calumny, slander, and vituperation (Articles 197–215 inclusive).[52] Originally Article 201 only dealt with the corruption of youth. In 1860, however, this article was expanded to include adultery and its related punishments. According to Islamic law, adultery is a *hadd* offence and carries with it the penalty of death by stoning. This punishment was rarely applied, because

> to prove adultery/fornication, four male witnesses must independently testify to the fact that they have . . . seen the man's sexual organ penetrate the woman. Should any of the four testimonies contradict the other three in any fashion . . . the four witnesses will be charged with slander and whipped eighty lashes each. [Slander of this type, consequently, is a different *hadd* offence.][53]

Punishment for this crime was regularly handed over to local authorities whom exercised their discretionary power to punish the guilty with lashes, imprisonment, and so on. The punishments called for in the 1860 version of the IOPC were very one sided and harsher on the female perpetrator than on the male. This revision mirrored exactly the 1810 French Penal Code. In 1911, however, the punishments of incarceration were made exactly equal for both males and females, but in addition to jail time, males also had to pay a fine.[54] This is, no doubt, an interesting discriminatory reversal of the earlier code.

The 1911 version of Article 206 represents an example of the CUP completely rescinding the previous versions of the article and replacing it with a highly modified and more comprehensive one. All versions of the article deal with the crime of kidnapping children and girls at the age of puberty. The most significant changes consisted of, first, expanding the victims of kidnapping to include adults as well as children; second, expanding the victims of kidnapping to include males as well as females; third, even though victims now included both sexes, female victims were still the primary focus of the article; fourth, altering the criteria for determining a child's criminal culpability – originally determined by the commencement of puberty according to Islamic law, it was now set uniformly at the age of fourteen; and, finally, unlike the 1858 version of Article 206, the 1911 version removed all jurisdictions regarding 'Crimes of Honour' from *shari'* courts. Only the *nizamiye* courts could adjudicate these types of crimes, thus abrogating the *qadi*'s authority to mete out discretionary punishment by subjecting his decisions to *nizamiye* court procedural provisions.[55]

The crime of vituperation and its associated punishments was the subject of Article 214. The original 1858 version briefly outlined only the basics of the crime, such as '[falsely] ascribing some vice or otherwise' to another person, and stipulated as punishment a fine or a short period of incarceration.[56] In 1911, however, parliament rescinded the 1858 version and replaced it with a substantially larger article that extensively expanded the definition of vituperation. This expansion stipulates what constitutes vituperation, in what setting the crime must be committed (in public with witnesses or in print), the rights of the accused, and the requisite punishments (from twenty-four hours to six months of incarceration and/or a fine of five to fifteen Liras). In fact, the original article is only fifty-six words long, but the 1911 version is almost 1,000 words in length.[57]

Theft (*sirkat*), in all its related forms, including petty theft, violent theft, breaking and entering, fraud, embezzlement, and armed robbery, constituted the second most prevalent crime in the Ottoman Empire during the nineteenth century.[58] Several of the IOPC's articles relating to theft were among the most heavily revised. For example, out of the twenty-six articles dealing specifically with theft, six were almost completely restructured in 1911. These revised articles were 220, 222, 224, 225, 226, and 230. Articles 216–41 inclusive stipulate the various offences associated with theft related crimes.[59]

The specific types of revisions made in 1911 include strengthening the punishments and expanding the criteria for breaking and entering. In the 1858 version of Article 220, breaking and entering only referred to drilling through, digging under, climbing a wall, or breaking down a door or window in order to gain access to a building. In 1911, this type of crime was expanded to include the breaking and entering into any type of closed structure, be it a building, safe, cupboard, and so on.[60] This augmentation greatly expanded the definition of theft in order to strengthen protections for private property. It also expanded the Islamic definition of breaking and entering, upon which the 1858 definition was based.

Islamic criminal law was still the basis of the definition for this crime, since theft is one of the original *hudud* offences described in the Quran and Islamic jurisprudence. According to these sources, however, theft is a very circumscribed crime.[61] Out of necessity, therefore, Islamic law allotted enormous amounts of discretionary authority to court judges and local officials to punish all theft-related crimes. With the Ottoman Parliament's expansion of the IOPC's definition of theft, it severely limited the exercise of discretionary punishments.

Many revisions either delineated more crimes and/or made punishments more severe. For example, revisions to Article 222 in 1911 simply increased the punishment according to the circumstances under which people committed theft, such as whether the theft occurred at night or day, whether the thief was armed or not, and whether the crime was committed by a servant or apprentice against her/his master. The punishment was increased from six months to three years of incarceration to one to three years of incarceration.[62] Other revisions simply imposed harsher penalties for crimes already stipulated in the code. In many cases, officials doubled the stiffest penalties of incarceration as demonstrated by Articles 224, 225, and 226. An additional revision to Article 224 included an expansion of the number of items whose theft would incur a certain punishment. These items were mainly agriculturally related, such as draft animals, horses, and tools.[63]

The most extensively revised theft-related article was Article 230. The original version dealt only with petty theft and its associated punishments. The Ottoman administration, however, expanded and revised this article several times from 1858. The most significant changes included making those who purchase, receive, and/or sell stolen goods liable for the theft of the items. Revisions also included the reduction of punishment for those who voluntarily came forward regarding their crimes, confessed them, and made restitution prior to arrest or judicial hearing.[64]

The protection of private property was a key facet of CUP penal reform, as reflected by the number of revisions made to theft-related IOPC articles and by the number of prisoners arrested, convicted, and sentenced for theft-related crimes. Protecting private property had always been important to Ottoman rulers and Islamic polities in general, dating back centuries.[65] During the nineteenth century, theft-related regulations and Islamic law were brought into close synchronisation. Many scholars characterise these rationalising legal reforms as the Westernisation and secularisation of Ottoman legal norms eventually resulting in the abrogation of Islamic law.[66] This portrayal is incorrect; Ottoman bureaucrats during the nineteenth century were not abrogating Islamic criminal or civil law, but standardising and rationalising it in the hands of the state. Administrators utilised Islamic law to justify these changes and at the same time transformed *shari'a* to fit the needs of a modern imperial state. No Ottoman administration did this more than the CUP during the Second Constitutional Period. The protection of private property was particularly important to the CUP, because of its attempts to build a middle class, increase private enterprise, foster industrialisation, and promote the economic development and independence of the empire.[67]

Violent crime represents the most prevalent crime in the Ottoman Empire, according to the 1910–11 crime statistical reports and the 1912

Ottoman prison surveys.[68] IOPC articles 168–91 dealing with violent crimes, such as threats, physical assault, and homicide were among the most heavily augmented and expanded in 1911.[69] According to Islamic law, 'provisions regarding offenses against persons, i.e. homicide and wounding, [are] subdivided into (a) those regarding retaliation (*qisas*) and (b) those regarding financial compensation (*diya*) . . . and . . . are expounded in the *fiqh* books with great precisions and in painstaking detail'.[70] Islamic court judges oversaw the restitution and retribution demanded by these crimes, but Islamic law also allotted discretionary punishments associated with these crimes to *qadis* and other local officials.[71] Revisions to the IOPC continued to circumscribe these discretionary punishments and eventually subjugated all homicides to court proceedings.

Article 170 was the first article related to violent crime to be amended in 1911. The original article mandated the death penalty for premeditated homicide ('*amden katl*). In 1911, Ottoman lawmakers amended it to include the death penalty not only for those convicted of premeditated homicide, but also for those who wilfully kill (*katl-i kasdi*) their 'ancestors of either sex even . . . without premeditation'.[72] This change is significant, because when combined with the changes made to Article 179, violence against an elder relative of either sex, for the first time, falls under the jurisdiction of *nizamiye* courts, thus limiting the authority of *qadis* to adjudicate these crimes according to Islamic legal procedures. This is an important example of the CUP consolidating more power over the family within the hands of the state rather than leaving it in the hands of Islamic courts. It is also an important example of the state attempting to gain more power over all facets of Ottoman life.[73]

Regarding homicide, lawmakers significantly changed and expanded Article 174, which originally read:

> If a person has killed an individual without premeditation he [or she] is placed in kyurek [*kürek*] for a period of fifteen years; but if this matter of destruction of life has taken place while committing another Jinayet [*cinayet*] either before the commission or after the commission, or for the sake of committing a Junha [*cünha*], the person destroying life is punished with . . . death according to [the] law.[74]

The 1911 article expanded the 1858 version by providing greater protection for government officials while performing their duties and made significant clarifications regarding punishments associated with accidental homicides.[75] Other alterations to homicide-related articles include more severe punishments for accomplices.[76] Article 177, which dealt with assaults that result in the loss of use of a bodily member, was further strengthened and clarified in 1911. Punishment now consisted of a prison sentence of at least six years' hard labour and the perpetrator was responsible for the victim's medical expenses.[77]

It should not be surprising that the prosecution of violent crimes, such as assault, rape, and homicide, would comprise a major portion of IOPC reforms. Central to Ottoman administrative goals was the need to maintain public order and discipline. As the state relied less on intermediaries and increasingly sought to centralise its authority over the use of force and punishment, there was an increased confluence of what has been characterised as 'secular' and 'religious' law and legal practice. Islam was not being abrogated, but increasingly standardised to fit the demands of a rapidly changing world.

Conclusion

By 1918, the Ottoman Empire possessed a powerful police force, codified penal codes, law schools, a fully developed court system with extensive procedural regulations, and a modern prison system. This functioning criminal justice system arrested criminal perpetrators and took them to police stations for interrogation as part of a criminal investigation. A lawyer was assigned to the accused, and a criminal prosecutor was assigned to the case. Judges oversaw the proceedings of the court case and issued a decision and punishment as prescribed by the IOPC. Depending on the seriousness and circumstances of the crime, judges imposed a fine, a prison sentence for a set period of time, or both. Additionally, the convicted even had the right to appeal the judge's decision. Once convicted criminals had served their prison sentences then they could expect a return of their full citizenship rights. They were, however, placed under probationary supervision, usually equal in length to their prison sentence.[78]

In sum, this criminal justice process constitutes an enormous transformation from early modern practices. Lawmakers and administrators, however, built this new system upon existing legal structures, procedures, and legitimation. This transformation possesses deep roots in Ottoman sensibilities towards notions of justice, law, rights of subjects and rulers, and punishment. In other words, this transformation should not be interpreted as Ottoman Westernisation, but the empire's appropriation, adaptation, and implementation of the assumptions of the modern world to its own imperial context. Ottoman imperial needs for greater rationalisation of procedure, standardisation of practice, and concentration of power all influenced this transformation of legal practice and punishment.

The confluence of the need for more consolidated administrative power, a desire to impose increasing amounts of social control and public order, and a greater need for access to and control over the lives of the population led the Ottoman administration to create and then greatly expand the IOPC over the second half of the nineteenth century by standardising punishment and extensively delineating criminal offences. These actions had the cumulative effect of reining in the discretionary power of local officials (judges and governors) and making incarceration the primary type of punishment imposed for criminal offences. Violent crime, theft, and crimes against honour as stipulated in the IOPC all demonstrate this confluence and its associated outcomes.

In the end, the Ottoman drive for state centralisation, standardisation, and rationalisation of Islamic criminal law circumscribed the discretionary power of the *qadi* to such an extent that the practice of Islamic criminal law became much more rigid. Consequently, these efforts laid the foundation for Islamic criminal legal practices in many contemporary Muslim states. The harsh punitive legal actions carried out in Saudi Arabia, Iran, Nigeria, or by the Taliban are not medieval, but wholly modern. They are primarily a response to the demands of the modern state. With the application of new methods of governance, the processes built into Islamic law to maximise the restoration of communal harmony and minimise harsh punishment have been undermined in order to create a rationalised, codified, standardised, and uniform Islamic legal system for the Ottoman Empire. It was not the Ottoman reformers' intent to make Islamic criminal law more punitive. The punishments meted out for particular crimes by the IOPC parallel their Western counterparts in terms of jail sentences, fines, and even the death penalty. However, when a codified and standardised Islamic criminal code meets a centralised state apparatus and a radical ideology, the overwhelming outcome appears to be the extreme application of Islamic punishment as the norm rather than the rare exception as practised throughout Islamic history.

At the same time that lawmakers were creating comprehensive penal codes, the empire was also transforming its prisons in order to accommodate the transition to incarceration as the empire's primary punishment for criminal activity. This prison reform programme culminated in the Second Constitutional Period. As the CUP overhauled the IOPC, it also implemented the first of its extensive prison reforms in late 1911 and early 1912. This included the creation of the first centralised Ottoman Prison Administration, the conduct of a comprehensive prison survey, and the development of a comprehensive programme to refurbish and modernise the empire's prisons and jails. It is no accident that Ottoman officials enacted interrelated judicial, criminal, and penal reforms in 1911–12.

Notes

1. See, for example: Ginio, 'Administration of Criminal Justice in Ottoman Selanik'; Zarinebaf, *Crime and Punishment in Istanbul*; Başaran, 'Remaking the Gate of Felicity'; Şen, *Osmanlı'da Mahkum Olmak*; Yıldız, *Mapusane*; Gürsoy, *Hapishane Kitabı*; Lévy and Toumarkine, *Osmanlı'da Asayiş, Suç ve Ceza*; Lévy-Aksu, *Ordre et désordres*; Rubin, *Nizamiye Courts*; Peters, *Crime and Punishment*; Miller, *Legislating Authority*; Deal, *Crimes of Honor*; Lévy, Özbek *et al.*, *Jandarma ve Polis*; Türker, 'Alternative Claims on Justice and Law'; and Paz, 'Crime, Criminals, and the Ottoman State'.
2. Peters, *Crime and Punishment*, pp. 71–5; and Darling, *History of Social Justice*, pp. 2–12. Darling (p. 2) argues that the Circle of Justice possesses deep roots in the Middle East dating back to ancient Mesopotamia and was appropriated by all Islamic polities including the Ottomans. This self-referential ruling strategy linked sovereignty and prosperity to the maintenance of justice and protection of the population from administrative exploitation: 'There can be no government without men; No men without money; No money without prosperity; And no prosperity without justice and good administration.'
3. Imber, *Ebu's-Su'ud*.
4. Ibid.; and Heyd, *Studies in Old Ottoman Criminal Law*.
5. Imber, pp. 75–6.
6. Imber, *Ottoman Empire*, pp. 216–51; Peters, *Crime and Punishment*, pp. 69–102; Inalcik, *Ottoman Empire*, pp. 71–5; and Pierce, *Morality Tales*, pp. 1–125.
7. Ergene, *Local Court, Provincial Society and Justice*, pp. 43–55, 99–124; Gerber, *State, Society, and Law*, pp. 25–78; Imber, *Ebu's-Su'ud*, pp. 3–8; Pierce, pp. 86–125; and Peters, pp. 69–102.
8. A minimalist state limits its societal intervention to preserving public order and regime sovereignty. It also provides an official forum whereby subjects can settle difficult disputes and gain official legitimacy for particular actions. See Damaška, *Faces of Justice and State Authority*, p. 73; and Paz, p. 15.
9. Collective responsibility is the principle of holding accountable a community or group for a crime when an investigation produces no guilty party, such as a murder committed in a city quarter or village. It is the community or village that becomes responsible to produce the perpetrator or make restitution for the crime. See Baer, 'Transition from Traditional to Western', p. 151; and Zarinebaf, pp. 125–40.
10. Başaran, pp. 120–56; Paz, pp. 15–21; Peters, *Crime and Punishment*, pp. 8–19, 30–8, 75–9, and 96–102; and Zarinebaf, pp. 73–80, 128–40, and 164–77.
11. Peters, *Crime and Punishment*, pp. 30–1 and 96–102.
12. Başaran, pp. 120–56; Paz, pp. 15–21; Peters, *Crime and Punishment*, pp. 8–19, 30–8, 75–9, and 96–102; and Zarinebaf, pp. 73–80, 128–33, and 164–77.
13. Imber, *Ebu's-Su'ud*, pp. 210–13.

14. Peters, *Crime and Punishment*, pp. 125–33 and 195–6; and Darling, pp. 138–53.
15. Weber, *Economy and Society*, pp. 976–8. For a detailed discussion of the merits and problems of Weber's *Kadijustiz*, see Gerber, pp. 25–42; Powers, 'Kadijustiz or Qadi-Justice?'; Semerdjian, *'Off the Straight Path'*, pp. xxi–xxiv; and Zarinebaf, pp. 141–6.
16. Imber, *Ebu's-Su'ud*, pp. 1–62; Gerber, pp. 25–78; and Peters, *Crime and Punishment*, pp. 69–71.
17. For Sultan Selim III's reign see Başaran, pp. 106–16, 137 and 150–6; and Zarinebaff, pp. 74–5 and 126–40. For a discussion about the relationship between the guilds and Janissaries, see Quataert, *Ottoman Empire*, pp. 134–40. Regarding the *Nizam-i Cedid Kanunları* see Koç and Yeşil, *Nizâm-i Cedîd Kanunları*.
18. Ergut, *Modern Devlet ve Polis*; Özbek, 'Osmanlı İmparatorluğu'nda İç Güvenlik'; Swanson, 'The Ottoman Police'; and Fahmy, 'Police and the People'.
19. Özbek, 'Policing the Countryside'.
20. Peters, *Crime and Punishment*, pp. 8–11.
21. Adopted as the empire's official civil code in 1877, the *Mecelle* represents the first systematic attempt to codify and modernise Islamic civil law (*shari'a*) according to Hanafi jurisprudence. It was prepared and written from 1869–76 by a commission directed by Ahmet Cevdet Pasha and consists of sixteen volumes containing 1,851 articles. For a detailed discussion of the creation of the *Mecelle* and its affect on the practice of Islamic law, see Messick, *Calligraphic State*. For an English translation of the *Mecelle*, see Tyser and Demetriades, *Mejelle*.
22. Paz, p. 18.
23. Rubin, *Nizamiye Courts*, pp. 1–54.
24. Rubin, 'Legal Borrowing and its Impact' and 'Ottoman Judicial Change'; Peters, *Crime and Punishment*, p. 80, 90, and 129; and Young, 'Code of procédure pénale', 26 June 1876, *Corps de Droit Ottoman*, vol. VII, pp. 226–300.
25. See Yıldız, *Mapusane*, pp. 225–61 for a thorough discussion of the transformation of *kürek* punishment during the nineteenth century. Also see Zarinebaf, Chapter 9 for a discussion of the transformation of punishment in Istanbul during the eighteenth century.
26. Chapter 4 discusses the topic of prison labour.
27. A comprehensive study of the transformation and practice of Ottoman criminal law for the long nineteenth century has yet to be written, but the following section was culled from a number of secondary and primary sources that treat this topic in a cursory manner. The texts of the various Ottoman Penal Codes can be found in Akgündüz, *Mukayeseli İslam*, pp. 811–19 and 821–3; *Düstur, İkinci Tertip*, vol. I, pp. 400–68; and Bucknill and Utidjian, *Imperial Ottoman Penal Code*. Scholars who work on the legal history of the Middle East, par-

ticularly the penal codes of the Ottoman Empire and Egypt, include Ahmet Akgündüz, Gabriel Baer, Serpil Bilbaşar, Ahmet Gökçen, Ruth Miller, and Rudolph Peters. Of particular importance is Miller's *Legislating Authority*. Her argument centres on 'looking at the discourse of law in and of itself – law as it was understood apart from its social context'. She claims that 'Ottoman and Turkish law was in fact detached from its social context'. This is what defines the transformation of criminal law in the late Ottoman Empire: its 'increasing abstraction' (pp. 1–2). Her argument goes through the promulgations of the various Ottoman penal codes and their transformation, but does not link them to the ways in which the law was implemented or practised.

28. This 1839 Imperial Decree called for 'guarantees to all Ottoman subjects of perfect security for life, honour, and property; a regular system of assessing taxation; and an equally regular system for the conscription of requisite troops and the duration of their service'. See Hurewitz, *Middle East and North Africa*, pp. 268–70. This decree, along with the *Islahat Fermanı* (discussed below), was the basis of Ottoman reform programmes during the Tanzimat. They declared that all Ottoman subjects, regardless of religious affiliation, communal identity, or socio-economic status, were equal before the law.

29. Peters defines *siyaset* punishments as 'discretionary justice exercised by the head of state and executive officials, not restricted by the rules of the *shari'a*, whereas *ta'zir* are 'discretionary punishments' meted out by Islamic court judges and authorised by Islamic law in cases where the accused could not be convicted according to the stipulations of Islamic law, but who were obviously guilty. Thus, *ta'zir* punishments could not exceed *shari'* punishments. Both *siyaset* and *ta'zir* consisted of corporal punishments, such as flogging or amputation, and could also include fines. See Peters, *Crime and Punishment*, pp. 196 and 127–33; and Baer, pp. 147–8.

30. Baer, pp. 139–58.

31. Bucknill and Utidjian, pp. xii–xiii; and Peters, *Crime and Punishment*, pp. 127–33.

32. Miller, pp. 25–40; and Darling, pp. 157–67.

33. Miller, pp. 26–31.

34. Peters, *Crime and Punishment*, pp. 127–33; and Baer, 'Transition from Traditional to Western', pp. 143–4.

35. Peters, *Crime and Punishment*, pp. 127–33; and Bucknill and Utidjian, pp. xiii–xvi.

36. Hurewitz, pp. 315–18; italics added.

37. For a brief, but useful, discussion of the source and significance of the initial 1858 IOPC, see Baer, pp. 139–58; and Bucknill and Utidjian, pp. ix–xvi.

38. Bozkurt, 'Reception of Western European Law', p. 287.

39. Bucknill and Utidjian, p. 1.

40. Baer, 'Transition from Traditional to Western', pp. 144–5.

41. Rubin, *Nizamiye Courts*, pp. 1–54; and Peters, *Crime and Punishment*, p. 131.

42. Rubin, *Nizamiye Courts*, pp. 1–54.
43. Bucknill and Utidjian reproduce the original 1858 IOPC and its subsequent changes in chronological order, thus enabling side-by-side comparison of all of the code's articles.
44. Bucknill and Utidjian, pp. 1–36.
45. Ibid., pp. 37–123.
46. Ibid., pp. 124–98.
47. Ibid., pp. 199–208.
48. Ibid., p. xiv.
49. Ibid., pp. 10–13, 24–31, 33–5, 37–69, 76–7, 79–83, 86–92, 99–100, 102–4, 109–62, 164–83, and 192–208.
50. The fifty-six articles modified on 4 June 1911 include Articles 8, 11, 12, 37, 39, 40, 42, 45, 46, 47, 55, 67, 68, 69, 76, 99, 102, 105, 106, 113, 114, 115, 116, 130, 134, 135, 136, 155, 166, 170, 174, 175, 177, 178, 179, 180, 188, 189, 190, 191, 192, 197, 201, 202, 206, 213, 214, 220, 222, 224, 225, 226, 230, 252, 253, and 255.
51. According to Wael Hallaq and Rudolph Peters, Islamic law only has six *hudud* offences considered 'violations of the claims of God'. These offences consist of theft, banditry, unlawful sexual intercourse, unfounded accusation of unlawful sexual intercourse (slander), drinking alcohol, and apostasy. The Quran and books of Islamic jurisprudence (*fiqh*) delineate these offences and their prescribed punishments in great detail. They also make the procedural laws concerning these crimes so strict that their punishments were rarely applied. Islamic jurisprudence, however, stipulates wide-ranging provisions giving discretionary authority to various state actors (magistrates, rulers, and *qadis*) to mete out punishments (*ta'zir* and *siyaset*) 'for sinful or forbidden behaviour or . . . acts endangering public order or state security'. See Peters, *Crime and Punishment*, pp. 6–7 and 53–68; and Hallaq, *Introduction to Islamic Law*, pp. 72–82, 173.
52. Bucknill and Utidjian, pp. 149–70.
53. Hallaq, *Introduction to Islamic Law*, p. 173.
54. Bucknill and Utidjian, pp. 152–6.
55. Ibid., pp. 159–62. Regarding *nizamiye* court procedural law and its differences from *shari'* procedural law, see Rubin, *Nizamiye Courts*, Chapter 1.
56. Bucknill and Utidjian, p. 166.
57. Ibid., pp. 167–70.
58. For imperial crime statistics for 1910–11 see BOA, DHEUMTK 8/23, 8/28, and 32/3. For crimes committed by convicted criminals, see DHMBHPS 145/31, DHMBHPSM 3/36, 4/4, 4/21, 5/1, and 5/9.
59. Bucknill and Utidjian, pp. 171–90.
60. Ibid., p. 174.
61. 'The jurists define the *ḥadd* crime of theft very narrowly. It contains the following elements: surreptitiously taking away of (movable) property with a certain minimum value (*niṣāb*) which is not partially owned by the perpetra-

tor nor entrusted to him from a place which is locked or under guard (*ḥirz*)' (Peters, *Crime and Punishment*, pp. 55–7).

62. Bucknill and Utidjian, pp. 175–6.
63. Ibid., pp. 177–9.
64. Ibid., pp. 180–3.
65. Concerning property rights in Islamic law, see Hallaq, *Shari'a*, pp. 296–307.
66. Berkes, *Development of Secularism*, pp. 161–72, 417, and 467–73; Karpat, *Politicization of Islam*, pp. 421–2; and Peters, *Crime and Punishment*, pp. 127–33.
67. Regarding CUP economic policies during the Second Constitutional Period, see Toprak, *'Milli İktisat' 1908–1918, İttihad-Terraki ve Cihan Harb*, and *Milli İktisat, milli burjuvazi*.
68. BOA, DHEUMTK 8/23, 8/28, and 32/3, DHMBHPS 145/31, DHMBHPSM 3/36, 4/4, 4/21, 5/1, and 5/9.
69. Bucknill and Utidjian, pp. 124–45.
70. Peters, *Crime and Punishment*, p. 7.
71. Ibid., pp. 38–53.
72. Bucknill and Utidjian, p. 125.
73. Ibid., pp. 133–5.
74. Ibid., pp. 127–8.
75. Ibid., pp. 128–9.
76. Ibid., p. 129.
77. Ibid., p. 131.
78. Paz, pp. 20–1.

2

Prison Reform in the Late Ottoman Empire: The State's Perspectives

The 1850s constitute a very important transitional period for prison reform in the Ottoman Empire. As discussed in the Introduction and in Chapter 1, the convergence of British inspections of Ottoman prisons, the *Islahat Fermanı*, and the promulgation of the Imperial Ottoman Penal Code (IOPC) drew attention to many criminal justice related issues and prepared the ground for extensive prison reform efforts. First, the inspections revealed the dire state of the incarcerated and the need for state intervention to improve conditions. Second, the *Islahat Fermanı* announced an aggressive agenda to create, expand, and overhaul the Ottoman criminal justice system, including prisons. Finally, the promulgation of the 1858 IOPC transformed the empire's criminal justice practices by extensively delineating criminal behaviour and their associated punishments and outlawing corporal punishments including torture. This effectively circumscribed the discretionary punitive powers of local Islamic court judges and administrative officials. In so doing, the IOPC mandated incarceration as the primary punishment for criminal behaviour, thus making prisons the principal site for this newly standardised penalty.

Practical reasons for prison reform aside, Ottoman rulers and administrators also engaged in it for ideological purposes. Over the course of the nineteenth century the notion that prisons and punishment demonstrate a particular society's level of civilisation was adopted worldwide.[1] In fact, this association between civilisation and punishment dates back to the second half of the eighteenth century with Jeremy Bentham, Cesare Beccaria, and others.[2] By the mid-nineteenth century, Ottoman bureaucrats firmly linked nation-building and civilisation with criminal justice and prisons. The mutual association of these concepts entered the Ottoman intelligentsia's *mentalité* from both internal and Western European sources. One of the most influential was the long-serving British Ambassador to the Ottoman Empire, Sir Stratford Canning.[3] Canning devoted a great deal of time and energy to promoting reform within the empire and viewed its advancement in 'European civilisation' and 'Christian civilisation' as the only hope for solving the Near Eastern Question.[4] According to Ambassador Canning, it was Britain's 'duty . . . [and] vocation . . . not [to] enslave but to set free'. Britain's task was 'to lead the way and to direct the march of other nations', thus encapsulating British Orientalist and 'White Man's Burden' views towards the Ottoman Empire.[5]

In Canning's 1851 'Memorandum on the Improvement of Prisons in Turkey', he clearly associates modern penal practices such as the moral rehabilitation of prisoners, proper health and hygiene, and crime prevention, with progress, reason, scientific advancement, and European 'civilisation'.[6] Reşit Pasha and Sultan Abdülaziz expressed similar views in the 1856 *Islahat Fermanı*: 'Proceedings shall be taken . . . for the reform of the penitentiary system as applied to houses of detention, punishment, or correction . . . so as to reconcile the rights of humanity with those of justice.'[7] The connection between prison reform and 'the civilisation of a country' was part of Ottoman imperial discourse and it continued to grow throughout the rest of the empire's existence.[8]

In addition to civilisational uplift, Ottoman administrators also shared the world view that a centralised, standardised, and rationalised administrative state founded on the principles of what Foucault terms 'governmentality' was essential to the empire's survival.[9] Ottoman bureaucrats and rulers attempted to implement this administrative approach on all governmental levels. Imperial prison reforms were, therefore, carried out for both practical and ideological purposes.

The purpose of this chapter is to provide an overview of the central administration's prison programmes, philosophy, and ideology in order to establish the groundwork for understanding the developments, transformations, and realities of late Ottoman criminal justice and incarceration. It also discusses the broad themes associated with Ottoman prison reform: civilisational transformation, prisoner rehabilitation, increased administrative centralisation, standardisation, and rationalisation, order and discipline, and the creation and expansion of state patriarchy. In so doing, it argues that prisons act as effective windows into broader imperial transformation and the intricacies of Ottoman modernity. It was within the walls of prisons that many of the pressing questions of Ottoman modernity played out. Bureaucrats addressed issues related to administrative reform and centralisation, the rationalisation of Islamic criminal law and punishment, the role of labour in the rehabilitation of prisoners, economic development and industrialisation, gender and childhood, the implementation of modern concepts of time and space, issues of national identity based on ethnicity and religion, social engineering, and the increased role of the state in caring for its population. In other words, prisons are microcosms of imperial transformation and exemplify a distinctive Ottoman modernity created by the spread of capitalist market relations and the application of modern methods of governance to a specific Ottoman context.

It also argues that prison reform and the transformation of Ottoman penal practice did not occur overnight or in a systematically progressive way, but the groundwork was laid in the 1850s for extensive Ottoman criminal justice reformation that included the empire's sprawling and dilapidated network of prisons, jails, fortresses, and other governmental structures used for incarceration. Each Ottoman administration (Tanzimat, Hamidian, and CUP) built on the previous regime's efforts, emphasising certain aspects so that by the time the CUP came to power, it was able to take full advantage of past reforms and implement them more fully according to its Positivist world view.

This chapter's discussion of prison reform is broken into two main parts. The first discusses prison reform during the Tanzimat and Hamidian eras (c. 1850–1908). The second section focuses on prison reform during the Second Constitutional Period until the empire's dissolution (c. 1908–22). This discussion further develops themes in Chapter 1 by beginning in the 1850s and includes the empire's participation in international prison conferences, drafting and adoption of detailed prison regulations, engaging in regular prison inspection routines, collecting extensive prison statistics, creating unified prison regimens that attempted to standardise practice and behaviour, professionalising the prison cadre, and constructing new prisons. Reforms culminated in the Second Constitutional Period as the CUP created the empire's first centralised Prison Administration and overhauled its prisons on an unprecedented level. The CUP continued these efforts throughout WWI by expending large sums of money, time, and effort. Prisons constituted an important facet of its programme to transform the empire into a powerful, centralised, and industrialised nation-state.

By providing this state-centric overview of prison reform, this chapter contextualises subsequent chapters that offer detailed studies of many of these reforms, how they were implemented, and how they affected local prison officials and inmates. These chapters, therefore, bring state- and people-centric histories together in order to complicate the picture of the late Ottoman Empire, particularly concerning crime, punishment, and incarceration.

Prison Reform in the Tanzimat and Hamidian Eras (c. 1850–1908)

According to Canning's 1851 Ottoman prison report, health and living conditions were dreadful. Most prisoners had little access to fresh air, exercise, adequate food, or medical treatment. Prisons were makeshift structures usually located in local military compounds, fortresses, or in government building annexes. Inmates primarily depended on family, friends, or religious endowments for their meagre subsistence. All kinds of prisoners were incarcerated together: the accused with the convicted, the petty criminal with the felon, adults with children, and sometimes even men with women. According to Canning, immediate and extensive reforms were required for both Ottoman prisons and the imperial criminal code.[10] As stated above, this report in combination with the promulgation of a series of penal codes and the *Islahat Fermanı* securely entrenched criminal justice and consequently prisons on the imperial reform agenda.

Just prior to the promulgation of the 1858 IOPC, the Ottoman administration hired Major Gordon, a British military officer, to direct prison reform in the empire. The Ottoman Government paid him a handsome sum and allocated a budget of more than 1,250,000 *kuruş* to administer and reform the empire's dilapidated network of prisons, jails, dungeons, and fortresses. Gordon complained profusely about how 'hellish' Ottoman prisons and dungeons were, and held up the Tersane Dungeon (*zindan*) as the epitome of brutality and neglect. He attempted, without much success, to introduce prisoner work discipline into the empire by adopting the British and American concepts of labour prisons. Idleness, however, continued to typify Ottoman prison life.[11]

Gordon did have some influence on the delineation of crimes found in the 1858 IOPC. In a report he presented to the Ottoman Meclis-i Tanzimat (Tazimat Council), Meclis-i Vükela (Ottoman State Cabinet), and Sultan Abdülmecid, Gordon successfully lobbied that the penal code adopt a four-part classification of criminal behaviour: accused (*zanlı*), misdemeanour (*kabahat sahiplerine*), less serious offence (*erbab-ı cünhaya*), and serious offence/felony (*mürtekib-i cinayet*).[12]

Notwithstanding Gordon's efforts, Ottoman bureaucrats were slow to invest a great deal of time and money in reforming prisons during the Tanzimat era, although they did commission, fund, and undertake some projects.[13] For example, Ottoman administrators constructed a model penitentiary (*Dersaadet hapishane-yi umumisi*) in the Sultanahmet district of Istanbul in 1871.[14] This prison was supposed to be replicated in each provincial centre of the empire, but it never came to fruition. It was located next to the *At Meydanı* (Hippodrome) and near Sultanahmet Jail in the centre of the imperial capital. This penitentiary represents the fulfilment of a prison reform recommendation by Ambassador Canning in 1851.

> Those [the prison reforms] which relate more directly to the building, to the construction of new or the improvement of old ones, require more time and a larger expenditure. Much, however, would be gained by adopting the whole as a system, and carrying it into practice gradually – If a single prison, by way of model, were established on sound principles in the Capital, for instance, where one of a better kind has already been formed under the Zaptie [police], the improvement confirmed by experience might be extended with ease throughout the empire according to local circumstances and the command of means.[15]

Perhaps it is difficult to substantiate the connection between a model prison constructed in 1871 and Canning's recommendation in 1851, but the construction did take place and the prison was designated a penitentiary (*hapishane-yi umumi*).[16]

Besides the obvious need for prison reform, another reason for building such an edifice was to procure greater political, judicial, and financial autonomy from European powers. Many late nineteenth century Ottoman officials hoped that such reforms would convince the Great Powers that the empire deserved equal status in the Concert of Europe and lead to the abolishment of exploitative capitulations.[17] Despite the adoption of the 1858 IOPC and the creation of a model prison in the imperial capital, it was not until the Hamidian era that administrators began replicating this type of prison around the empire and penal reforms gained greater significance. As a result of these legal and judicial reforms, punishment and prisons became an issue of 'civilisation' among the rising Ottoman intelligentsia with a growing focus on rehabilitating prisoners ('*ıslah-ı nefs*').[18]

Although these changes and activities mark very important steps in the direction of concrete penal reform, further developments did not take place until the Hamidian era (1876–1908). Sultan Abdülhamid II legislated and implemented penal reforms on several fronts – judicial proceedings in criminal matters, participation in international prison conferences, the construction of new prisons, new prison administrative regulations, and regular prison inspections. His successes, however, were founded on the efforts of his predecessor (Sultan Abdülaziz) who promulgated the 'Instructions for the Administration of the Provinces' on 21 February 1876. These instructions stipulated that district officials were required to supervise prisons, maintain prison population registers, and submit regular written reports to the Ministry of Justice. Not only did it delineate administrative responsibilities for prisons, but it also affected their internal organisation by mandating the separation of convicted and accused inmates. Additionally, it contained provisions designed to combat arbitrary detentions.[19]

Building from Adbülaziz's efforts, Sultan Abdülhamid II issued the 1879 Code of Criminal Procedure and officially instituted the *nizamiye* court system (both of which were discussed in Chapter 1). Contemporaneous with these developments, Abdülhamid II ordered Müfettiş Pasha to conduct a comprehensive inspection of Ottoman prisons and submit his recommendations for improvement as part of a new prison reform campaign (*hapishane ıslahatı*). He was also given specific orders to find ways to rescue 'prisoners from their miserable conditions' (*mahbusların hâl-i sefâletten*). Müfettiş Pasha completed his inspections and submitted his report in December 1879. It contained scathing descriptions of the woeful prison conditions, complaints regarding the length of sentences, and recommendations for improvement. His most intriguing recommendation concerned the newly constructed (1871) *Dersaadet* penitentiary. He found it inadequate and in need of replacement after just eight years of use. He proposed that penitentiaries be separated from populated areas and, therefore, recommended that the *Dersaadet* penitentiary be relocated to a small island in the Marmara Sea just off the coast of Istanbul. This prison would house only criminals sentenced to fifteen or more years of hard labour.[20]

Shortly after Müfettiş Pasha filed his report, the Ministry of Justice in May 1880 issued 'The Regulation for Prisons and Houses of Detention' (*Hapishane ve Tevkifhane Nizamnamesi*). The 1880 Prison Regulation contains six sections consisting of ninety-seven articles meticulously detailing the proper administration of Ottoman prisons in both the imperial centre and provinces. The regulation includes such items as standards for health and hygiene, living conditions, and the spatial separation of different types of prisoners based on gender, age, type of crime, and status as convicted or accused. It also stipulates the types of prison officials to be employed, such as wardens, clerks, doctors, and male and female guards, and their associated responsibilities. Regulations regarding the conduct of prison personnel and internal prison order and discipline are also clearly delineated. Additionally, it specifies the types and manner of prison labour and who should perform them.[21]

This regulation was the first of its kind in the empire. It was never, however, officially adopted by sultanic decree (*irade*). Regardless of its unofficial status, it represents a significant step in Ottoman penal reform for at least two reasons. First, it signifies the Ottoman process of appropriation and adaptation of European prison regulations. Ottoman prison reformers sifted numerous sources, including French and Prussian prison administrative regulations, and adapted the measures best suited to the empire's specific needs and circumstances.[22] Second, the 1880 Prison Regulation served as the template for prison reform and administration throughout the rest of the empire's existence.

Abdülhamid II attempted to implement the first article of the 1880 Prison Regulation, which states, 'Every district (*kaza*), sub-division (*liva*) and provincial centre shall possess a prison and house of detention [jail].'[23] In almost every provincial centre and in many administrative sub-districts, officials constructed either a prison (*hapishane*) or a jail (*tevkifhane*). Abdülhamid II also constructed a number of 'model' prisons, had pictures taken of them, and showed them off to the rest of the world. These 'model' prisons were built according to new architectural designs and furnished with the latest equipment. Unfortunately, the administration of the vast majority of Ottoman prisons did not follow the 1880 Prison Regulation.[24] This represents, however, a higher degree of penal reform implementation than during the Tanzimat era.

Beginning in the 1870s, Ottoman representatives first attended and then fully participated in international prison conferences. This participation brought prestige and provided a forum for discussing important reform policies. Ottoman representatives attended the first International Penal Congress in 1872 as observers, but it was not until 1890 that they participated as full members in the international prison conference held at St Petersburg, Russia. Prior to 1890, only 'civilised' European and North American countries could be full participants. The topic of Ottoman involvement produced a great deal of consternation among the Great Powers, but, in 1890, a formal invitation to participate was finally extended. This invitation marked an important step for Ottoman self-perceptions of the empire's own civilisational progress.[25]

Ottoman representatives translated the proceedings of the conference and submitted them to the Council of State (*Şura-yı Devlet*) to be debated and ratified. Most issues discussed at the conference, however, had already been addressed in the 1880 Prison Regulation. The empire continued to participate in international prison conferences until 1910, which was the last conference held prior to the outbreak of WWI.

Eighteen ninety-six was an important year for prison reform in the empire. Under the direction of Abdülhamid II, administrators reaffirmed legislation that was passed in 1879 that authorised provincial governors to appoint committees for preliminary inquiries into corruption, abuse of official power, health and hygiene concerns, and prisoner mistreatment. The membership of these appointed committees consisted of a president, a Muslim, and a non-Muslim. Each member possessed the authority to request information from the police and to release prisoners who were unjustly detained. This legislation also authorised governors to appoint both prison directors and guards.[26]

In close association with this legislative reaffirmation, Abdülhamid II established 'The Commission for Expediting Initiatives and Reforms' (*Tesri-i Muamelat ve Islahat Komisyonu*) and placed it under the direction of the Ministry of the Interior. He charged it to conduct regular inspections in order to monitor the progress and hasten the implementation of imperial reforms. This commission spent a major portion of its time investigating health- and hygiene-related issues, particularly in prisons, hospitals, and major urban areas. The commission's efforts clearly align with Hamidan goals for the state to take greater responsibility for public health and hygiene, especially in the prevention and spread of communicable diseases such as cholera and syphilis.[27] During the time in which the commission operated (1896–1908), numerous reports detailed specific prison health concerns and described the general state of Ottoman prison disrepair. These reports provide a general picture of prison conditions in the empire, demonstrating that most prisons were not abiding by the hygiene directives issued by the Sublime Porte or to be found in the 1880 Prison Regulation.[28]

Notwithstanding these efforts, prison reform was still hampered by administrative inefficiency. No single ministry or department possessed full responsibility for administering or financing the empire's sprawling prison network. The centralisation of bureaucratic responsibilities between the palace (Sultan Abdülhamid II) and the Sublime Porte (the Ministries of Justice, Finance, and Interior) were still in the process of being rationalised. The Ottomans had yet to create a central Prison Administration with the comprehensive powers to implement the 1880 Prison Regulation. Abdülhamid II's reign, however, did result in a greater level of bureaucratic streamlining than his predecessors had brought about. He also strengthened the connections between the concepts of civilisation, the centralisation of administrative power, and prison reform. Abdülhamid II's reforms also demonstrate the state's growing intervention into the daily lives of its subjects, especially in terms of health care and preventing the spread of infectious disease. His world view focused on centralising his power and the transformation of his empire. This left an important legacy and foundation for the CUP on which to base its own reform agenda. During the Second Constitutional Period, as imperial crises worsened and the authoritarian nature of the government increased, the CUP fully integrated prisons into its nation-state construction, economic development, and social-engineering programmes.

Prisons Reform in the Second Constitutional Period

The Ottoman Empire of the early twentieth century was anything but peaceful, prosperous, and stable. In the few years leading up to the 1908 Constitutional Revolution there were waves of strikes, popular protests, and riots throughout the empire as a result of dire economic hardships, crop failures, and new taxes. CUP revolutionaries planned, instigated, and fanned many of these protest actions.[29] During 1908 and 1909, the Ottoman administration and society experienced tremendous upheaval as a result of a *coup d'état* and countercoup, the reinstatement of the 1876 Constitution, the reintroduction of parliamentary rule, extensive territorial losses in the Balkans, an initial relaxation of press censorship, a general liberalisation of politics, and extensive bureaucratic and administrative reforms.[30]

With the CUP's ascendance, there was an explosion in political activism, demonstrations, and the proliferation of printed materials throughout the empire. Various nationalist identities and ideologies competed for the hearts and minds of portions of the Ottoman population. From 1908 to 1913, vast stretches of Ottoman territory were lost, including Crete, the territories of present-day Libya, the Dodecanese Islands, and all of the Balkans, except for the eastern portion of Rumeli, resulting in a massive influx of Muslim refugees into the empire. The Ottoman world was literally 'turned upside down.'[31]

This context of social, territorial, demographic, and political crises helps illuminate the role that penal policy and reform played in CUP pragmatism and modern state construction. Police and prisons constitute key institutions for maintaining power and imposing order and discipline upon a population, especially during times of crisis. As early as 1909, the CUP clearly linked penal reform and prisons, in concrete terms, to social control and modern state formation. Penal reform also began playing a role in CUP ideology to bring civilisation, science, reason, progress, economic development, and administrative centralisation to the empire.

Shortly after coming to power, the CUP took drastic action to curb strikes and political protests, even though its members had originally promoted these activities, leading up to the 1908 Revolution. It brutally crushed these actions and passed legislation outlawing them.[32] The CUP's inner circle possessed a healthy distrust of the masses according to Gustav Le Bon's (1841–1931) elitist and racist philosophy concerning crowd psychology. CUP members read Le Bon's *The Psychology of the Crowd*, first published in 1895, and adopted its principles as a foundation of their political ideology. They viewed themselves as an elite group leading the nation to reason, science, progress, and civilisation. Le Bon was a Comtian Postivist and his views originated from the French Third Republic, whose elites believed that the French Revolution had gone terribly wrong during the Jacobin Reign of Terror.[33]

The Young Turks, and especially the leaders of the CUP, attempted to promote themselves as inheritors of the ideals of the French Revolution. They continuously portrayed Sultan Abdülhamid II as a corrupt despot similar to Louis XVI of France and labelled the sultan's administration the *'ancien régime'*. The inner circle of the CUP mainly consisted of low-level bureaucrats and junior military officers who received European-style educations in the schools established by Abdülhamid II. Their frustration grew to revolutionary levels at what they viewed as the sultan's nepotistic and sycophantic style of rule. They claimed to possess the training and expertise to save the empire from dismemberment and collapse by raising the Ottoman populace to the level of a scientific society. To Le Bon, the Third Republic, and the CUP, the masses constituted a powerful yet fickle force that needed to be controlled, dominated, and directed for the good of the nation. As a result of the 1909 countercoup the CUP viewed the masses as a real threat to its rule, and thus it established a powerful penal institution to subdue, monitor, and control the masses.

In August 1909, just four months after the failed countercoup, the CUP-led government established the Directorate of Public Security (*Emniyet-i Umumiye Müdiriyeti*). It functioned as a CUP harbinger to consolidate power and control the population. For example, one of the directorate's functions was to monitor and control vagrants, vagabonds, and the unemployed.[34] This new directorate replaced the Ministry of Police (*Zabtiye Nezareti*), was attached to the Ministry of the Interior, and was allocated a considerable budget.[35] As early as 1910, the Directorate of Public Security collected and reported to the Ministry of the Interior detailed statistics regarding crime, riots, strikes, and general political issues from across the empire.[36]

Prison reform during the Second Constitutional Period began almost immediately with the intent to exploit penal institutions for the purpose of social engineering. From 1909 to 1911, the CUP-led government, focused on developing a central prison policy. In order to develop its pro-grammes, prison officials conducted detailed inspections from Yemen to the Balkans. It suspended all major prison construction and repair projects until a general prison architectural design could be developed. In formu-lating its policy, the CUP drew heavily from the 1880 Prison Regulation and further implemented Article 1, which mandated a central prison and jail in every administrative district throughout the empire. The CUP utilised Hamidian prison regulations as the template for its own prison reforms and implemented the 1880 Prison Regulation at an unprecedented level, especially in areas associated with order, discipline, administration, and health and hygiene.[37]

Simultaneous to these initial inspections, the Ottoman administration raised the funds necessary to implement its penal reform programme. After deposing Abdülhamid II, the new government wrested administrative power from the Hamidian bureaucracy, confiscated the sultan's property, auctioned it off, reformed the Ministry of Finance, and attempted to create a more accurate, transparent, and balanced budget.[38] Administrators devised various schemes to raise funds for prison reform. These included establishing a number of labour prisons in major population centres of the empire, such as Istanbul, Damascus, Ankara, Beirut, and Baghdad. These labour prisons engaged in manufacturing and their profits went to the directorate.[39] Officials also sold dilapidated prison facilities in order to finance new prison building projects based upon a unified architectural design.[40]

In May 1911, just prior to the IOPC revisions, Ottoman legislators promulgated a regulation to reorganise the empire's prisons. This regulation called for investigations into particular prison practices aimed at disciplining and rehabilitating prisoners. It also led to the creation of the empire's second major penal institution, the Prison Administration (*Hapishane İdaresi*).[41] Except for military and consular prisons, this office streamlined and consolidated the decentralised Ottoman system of more than a thousand different prisons and houses of detention into one bureaucratic administration and placed it under the jurisdiction of the Ministry of the Interior.

The CUP-led Ottoman Parliament then passed extensive legislation related to penal policy and practice. As discussed in Chapter 1, on 4 June 1911, the Ottoman Parliament heavily revised the 1858 IOPC aimed at centralising and expanding the bureaucracy's authority over the adjudication of crime and punishment. The reformed IOPC delineated new crimes, codified and standardised punishments, expanded state authority over the use of force, further circumscribed the autonomy of court judges and local administrators, increased the state's ability to intervene in familial matters, and augmented definitions regarding criminal culpability, particularly in relation to minors. These changes solidified the central administration's control over criminal legal matters and punishment. It also entrenched incarceration as the primary punishment for criminal activity. There are deep and important connections between these IOPC revisions and the prison reforms initiated and implemented from 1911–12, especially the 1912 prison survey.

Having collected enough preliminary information, created a centralised Prison Administration, substantially augmented the IOPC, and secured the necessary funding the Prison Administration launched its first comprehensive prison census in January 1912. It distributed the survey to every province and administrative district throughout the empire and requested enormous amounts of information about the prison population and prison management. The 1912 prison survey requested details regarding crimes committed, sentences served, marital and familial status, occupation, education level, age, and the ethno-religious and national identity of each prisoner. It also collected information on prison expenditures, health care, deaths in prisons, rates of recidivism, and prison factories. Chapter 3 contains a detailed discussion of this survey and the information it yields regarding the empire's prison population.[42]

The knowledge and power gained by this questionnaire and others like it not only shaped CUP penal reform, but it also fashioned the prison into a premier institution for social control, social engineering, and Ottoman nation-state construction, surpassed only by the police and military. Prisons became microcosms of the CUP's larger plans to meld the empire's population and administration into a modern nation-state. The programmes implemented in Ottoman prisons, such as education, administrative and organisational centralisation, social engineering, health and hygiene, labour, and economic development parallel those implemented empire-wide. Additionally, the Prison Administration also initiated another statistical campaign in 1912 concerning prison employees. This survey collected the names, titles, numbers, responsibilities, salaries, and dates of service of all prison employees. Combined, these two surveys provide the most detailed picture of the Ottoman prison population and administration ever compiled.[43]

After completing these surveys and processing their results, the CUP initiated its first comprehensive prison reform programme in early 1912 aimed at bringing 'Ottoman prison standards and health and hygiene conditions in line with the Laws of Civilisation'.[44] Mandated reforms required every prison to have an outdoor courtyard for inmates and called for the hiring of qualified prison employees who were literate in penal laws and practices. Another reform made provisions for prisoner rehabilitation through education and labour. Additionally, every prison was either to be renovated or rebuilt according to modern architectural standards. After completing all of the research and initiating such an extensive programme in early 1912, the Ottoman Government suddenly suspended all of these reforms in the autumn of 1912. It has been argued that the Balkan Wars caused this discontinuance, but this is only partially correct.[45]

In the summer of 1912, the CUP won an outright majority in the Ottoman Parliament and gained sole control of the government for the first time. Notwithstanding this major victory, the CUP quickly found itself expelled from power after being accused of using its Special Organisation (*Teşkilat-i Mahsusa*) to intimidate, spy upon, and assassinate political rivals in order to manipulate election results. The *Entente Liberal*, the CUP's main opposition party, was instrumental in bringing down the CUP Government. Its political platform advocated administrative decentralisation for the Arab provinces, economic liberalisation, free trade, and Great Power intervention in the empire's economic, administrative, and social problems.[46] It is important to note that until 1912 the CUP had never held direct political power, but had remained a clandestine society influencing Ottoman politics from behind the scenes through elected representatives. Intense political pressure caused by the 1912 electoral scandal, resulted in the CUP Government resigning and being replaced by the 'Great Cabinet'-led National Unity Coalition.[47]

The 'Great Cabinet' quickly purged the government of CUP members, arresting many, executing some, and chasing others into exile. This new coalition government emasculated CUP military support in the Balkans by about 70,000 troops and demoted the military leadership loyal to the CUP.[48] Another apparent victim of the new government was the CUP's prison reform programme.

The First Balkan War did not start until 8 October 1912. As a result of the military purges of CUP officers and troops, especially in the Balkans, the Ottoman military was woefully unprepared and, therefore, soundly defeated. Edirne was on the verge of collapse, which would expose Istanbul to foreign invasion and conquest. On 28 January 1913 some members of the CUP stormed the cabinet office of the Sublime Porte, shot the Minister of War, overthrew the 'Great Cabinet' and for the first time consolidated political power firmly within their own hands. The new cabinet reconvened parliament, reinstating all the loyal CUP members who were elected in 1912.[49]

In response to the general upheaval caused by the Balkan Wars and its temporary loss of power, the CUP attempted to consolidate its political control even further by restructuring the Ministry of the Interior. On 22 December 1913, Talat Pasha (Minister of the Interior) issued the 'Regulation for the Restructuring of the Ministry of the Interior' (*Dahiliye Nezareti Teşkilati Hakkında Nizamname*). It completely overhauled, streamlined, and increased the power of the ministry. Out of all the reforms enacted by the CUP during the Second Constitutional Period, none were more extensive than what took place in the Ministry of the Interior.[50]

The new 'central organisational core' of the ministry consisted of eleven directorates, including the Directorate of Public Security (*Emniyet-i Umumiye Müdiriyeti*) and the Directorate of Prisons (*Hapishaneler Müdiriyeti*). Although similar organisations had been created shortly after the failed countercoup of 1909 and in 1911, the 1913 regulation raised the profile of both directorates within the Sublime Porte and greatly expanded their responsibilities and powers. The Directorate of Public Security was charged with 'executing and pursuing all matters, issues, and affairs that concern the maintenance of public order, security, discipline, and the rule of law within all territories under [Ottoman] dominion'. The regulation also charged it to 'gather and analyse all intelligence dealing with its assigned duties' and to be 'responsible for maintaining and administering law enforcement'. For its part, the Directorate of Prisons (*Hapishaneler Müdiriyeti*) replaced the Prison Administration (*Hapishane İdaresi*). This constitutes an upgrade in status from being an 'administration' to that of a 'directorate' in the bureaucracy, thus making it on par with the other directorates within the Ministry of the Interior. Furthermore, this directorate was given extensive new powers including 'maintaining, repairing, operating, constructing, and administering all prisons and gathering all necessary intelligence and information pertaining to any of the aforementioned responsibilities'.[51] The powers and responsibilities given to these two directorates are indicative of modern penal institutions.

From December 1913, the prison increasingly became a focus of CUP administrative and societal reform. The CUP revived, resumed, and expanded the suspended 1911–12 prison reform programme. The conduct of prison surveys and reports shifted from annual to tri-annual reporting on prison officials and the incarcerated.[52]

In 1914, the Directorate of Prisons initiated another comprehensive prison survey. Similar to the 1912 prison survey, it sent this questionnaire (*sual varakaları*) to every prison in the empire. The questionnaire requested information on the state and condition of each prison facility asking for detailed input from local prison administrators in the form of extensive written comments about the specific needs for their respective prisons.[53] To make their cases some wardens included photographs of their facilities that revealed the woeful conditions that prisoners were forced to endure.[54] Other prison directors included blueprints of the prisons that they wanted built.[55]

The findings of this survey resulted in a massive prison renovation and construction programme similar to the one initiated in 1912. Administrators designed, funded, and initiated new prison construction projects around the empire, particularly in provincial centres. In its continued adherence to the 1880 Prison Regulation, it appears that the Directorate of Prisons intended to build a prison in every administrative district in the empire.[56] Similar to the 1911–12 plans to raise the money for such a project, on 25 January 1914 the Directorate of Prisons issued a directive calling for the selling of 'ruined existing prisons and vacant lands' in order to finance the prison overhaul.[57]

This revitalised building and renovation programme launched scores of new prison construction projects. Prison officials from around the empire submitted land surveys, building estimates, and expenditure reports to the Directorate of Prisons, which in turn approved and funded them with the assistance of the Ministry of Finance. There are literally thousands of prison architectural designs, building estimates, and expenditure reports held in the Ottoman archives that illustrate the massive scale of this operation.[58] Unlike in the Balkan Wars, the CUP did not suspend prison reform during WWI. In fact, prison reform continued to expand throughout the war. The effort, time, and resources expended on prison reform during this period clearly demonstrate the importance of penal institutions to the CUP's imperial vision.

These penal reform efforts should not be attributed to pressure from Germany, its wartime ally. CUP interest and efforts regarding penal codes, practices, and institutions pre-dates its alliance with Germany and did not continue in order to curry German support. The Ottoman Empire was very successful in securing the loans and financial assistance it wanted from Berlin during the war. For the first time, a Great Power (Germany) needed Ottoman assistance more than the other way round. Germany was desperate to keep the Ottomans in the war. This gave the CUP and the Ottoman Minister of Finance (Cavid Pasha) enormous leverage over its German ally when it came to financial matters – even securing German financial assistance for the empire's prison reforms.[59]

On 6 May 1915 the Directorate of Prisons completed another statistical collection campaign. This survey did not deal with prison conditions, but focused on budgets and expenditures in relation to the number of inmates. Each province provided expenditures for the current year as well as previous ones and proposed its future budget.[60]

The importance of prisons to CUP ideology and state formation is demonstrated no clearer than during WWI. Faced again with crisis, the Ottoman administration continued to place heavy importance on penal reform. During the summer of 1916 Ottoman foreign officials in Germany began interviewing potential candidates for the newly created position of 'Inspector General of Prisons and Penitentiary Establishments for the Ottoman Empire' (*Inspecteur Général des Prisons et Etablissements*

Pénitenciers de l'Empire Ottoman). Ottoman officials narrowed the candidates to Dr Paul Pollitz and M. Alexander Klein. Both Pollitz and Klein had extensive experience of directing German prisons. The successful candidate's main responsibility would be to continue to overhaul, manage, and reconfigure the empire's prisons.[61] On 15 October 1916, the Directorate of Prisons had the Ottoman Ambassador to Berlin, Ibrahim Hakki Pasha, hire Dr Paul Pollitz as the empire's Inspector General of Prisons and Penitentiary Establishments. This hiring was approved by the highest echelons of the Ottoman Government including Grand Vizer, Mehmed Said Halim Pasha, and Interior Minister Talat Pasha.[62]

Dr Pollitz was a private German citizen, a professional prison administrator, a reformer, and a criminal psychiatrist. According to his contract, Dr Pollitz received a substantial annual salary of 1,200 Turkish Lira and also received payments of 1,500 Francs upon his arrival to Istanbul and at his departure in order to offset travel expenditures. He was hired for a five-year term beginning on 1 November 1916.[63] Upon his arrival to Istanbul, Dr Pollitz expanded and intensified the already robust penal reform programmes initiated by the Directorate of Prisons and focused his efforts on greater administrative efficiency and oversight. Additionally, he expanded the construction of new prisons, improved health and hygiene conditions, and championed the plight of incarcerated minors.

Shortly after his arrival, Dr Pollitz began reviewing Ottoman penal regulations. On 28 December 1916, Pollitz submitted a draft proposal to the Ministry of the Interior for a new comprehensive prison regulation. This massive document more than doubled the size of the 1880 Prison Regulation. Some additions included standardising salaries for all prison employees based on position and experience, clearer guidelines regarding prison health and hygiene practices, daily prison routines and organisation, and, most significantly, placing greater importance on prison labour.[64] Debate regarding this proposal continued for several months, but it was never adopted due to budgetary concerns. On 24 April 1917, however, the CUP and Directorate of Prisons officially ratified the 1880 Prison Regulation and distributed it to every prison in the empire.[65] This was the first time in the Ottoman Empire's long history that any comprehensive prison regulation was officially adopted and made binding for every prison. Prison practice, at least on paper, was finally standardised for the empire.

Shortly after submitting his revised Ottoman Prison Regulatory Code, Dr Pollitz issued a statement outlining his comprehensive plans for penal reform, which included the reorganisation of the prison population according to the gravity of the crimes committed. For example, prisoners sentenced to one to three months should all be incarcerated at the lowest administrative level (*kaza*) while perpetrators of more serious crimes should be incarcerated together at the provincial or sub-provincial level. Dr Pollitz, throughout his tenure as inspector general, championed the separation of the convicted and accused through the construction of many new jails (*tevkifhaneler*) for the better maintenance of prison order and prisoner protection. He also proposed restructuring the powers of provincial, sub-division and district governors regarding the administration of prisons on the local level.[66]

Dovetailed with these programmes, Dr Pollitz also proposed and implemented new regulations governing prison finance. In January 1917, he ordered the compilation of prison budgets and expenditures for 1916. According to the data, the 1916 budget for the Directorate of Prisons totalled 314,474 Turkish Lira (TL).[67] The 1917 proposed budget replicated the amounts spent in 1916 for supplies, medicines, and salaries, but did not estimate future building costs.[68]

The 1916 expenditures are quite remarkable considering that the empire was at war, even though the amount only represents 2 per cent of the total budget for the Ministry of the Interior in 1912. The Ministry of the Interior, however, was responsible for the maintenance and operation of all internal services, transport, infrastructure, and government administrations throughout the empire. The fact that the Ottoman prison population constituted less than 0.16 per cent of the total Ottoman population makes the amount of resources spent on prisons surprising.[69]

As a result of these budgetary inquiries, Dr Pollitz proposed a set of new regulations for Ottoman prison budgets and expenditures (*Hapishaneler Nizamnamesi'nin hapishanelerin hesap muameleleri*). It consisted of ten articles focused on greater transparency, control, and accountability of the Directorate of Prison's expenses on all levels. His assistants wrote up the new proposal and submitted it to the Ministry of the Interior on 7 October 1917.[70]

Dr Pollitz's agenda also included ascertaining prison conditions and managing the numerous building projects that were already under way. By 26 November 1916, he received a report detailing the current building projects for new jails (*tevkifhaneler*) within the empire. These projects included İzmir, Adana, Mersin, Beirut, Eskişehir, Samsun, İzmid, Kayseri, Yozgad, and Kala-i Sultaniye, in addition to projects already begun in Istanbul and Üsküdar. Each *tevkifhane* was to hold 400 prisoners separated into different quarters for men, women, and children. These houses of detention would also contain an infirmary, toilets, washrooms, a mosque, a morgue, and a kitchen. The estimated cost of each jail ranged from 10,000 to 15,000 Turkish Liras. Just to reiterate, all of these projects pre-date Dr Pollitz's arrival.

As part of his broader inquiries into the condition of the empire's prisons, Dr Pollitz requested information on several additional items, divided into four categories: 1. the physical structure of the building – its size, capacity, and age; 2. general prison conditions – ventilation, light, and dampness; 3. health and hygiene – cleanliness, disease, the existence of a clinic, mentally ill prisoners, clothing, parasites, potable water, and toilets; and 4. food – type, quality, and quantity.[71] These inquiries led directly to another massive statistical collection campaign (*izahat*) initiated on 28 December 1916 by Dr Pollitz. This campaign's design and implementation rivalled that of the 1912 prison survey in terms of size and scope.[72] It possessed, however, very specific areas of statistical collection that came to define Dr Pollitz's tenure as the inspector general. It recorded the number of inmates eighteen years of age and under, each prison's food source, the names, locations, and types of every prison throughout the empire, the number of male prisoners and the number of female prisoners, the types of crimes committed (*cinayet*, *cünha*, and *kabahat*), number of working prisoners, the number and types of employees in each prison, and the number of prisoners who possessed expertise that would benefit the war effort, such as agricultural or road construction.[73] Many of these categories match the follow-up questions Dr Pollitz had asked just a month earlier about jails (*tevkifhaneler*) under construction in 1916 and 1917.[74] In fact, there is also a close correlation between the added emphasis he placed on prison labour in his proposed prison regulation (*nizamname*) and the new prison survey.[75]

Dr Pollitz sent the questionnaires to every provincial governor and prison in the empire. The directive was issued jointly by the Directorate of Prisons and the Ministry of the Interior and signed (in Ottoman Turkish, no less) by Dr Pollitz. It stipulated that each of the provincial governors (*valiler*) was personally responsible for the completion of the survey in addition to supplying the requested information 'to the greatest degree (*en ziyade*) about the prison guards (*gardiyanlar*), prison officials (*memurler*), the prison board of directors (*heyet idaresi*), the prison directors (*müdirler*), and the general conditions of the prisons (*hapishanelerin ahval umumiyesi*)'. The provincial governors were also responsible for providing information regarding the number of prisoners being compelled to do agricultural work.[76] In the end, Dr Pollitz justified the survey by claiming that it would be the 'basis for the reorganisation (*teşkilat*)' of the empire's prisons.[77]

By March 1917, the vast majority of local prison officials had completed and returned the questionnaires.[78] The Directorate of Prisons compiled the results into a meticulously organised master copy.[79] These statistical tabulations became the basis of Dr Politz's reform campaigns for the rest of his tenure. His campaigns focused on improving prison health and hygiene conditions, relieving prison overcrowding, constructing new prisons, prison repairs, the plight of juvenile delinquents, developing programmes to rehabilitate prisoners, especially through labour, and bringing greater order and discipline to prison regimes.[80]

Dr Pollitz spent a great deal of his time inspecting prisons and verifying that reforms were being implemented. His peregrinations took him throughout the empire from Rumeli to the Aegean and throughout Anatolia and the Arab provinces.[81] This continued until he was relieved from duty in 1919 and prison reform in the empire came to a screeching halt. The post-CUP Ottoman Government slashed prison budgets as a result of losing WWI and the *Entente* occupation of Istanbul. Without the CUP in power, prison conditions quickly deteriorated as demonstrated by the British prison inspections conducted in late 1918 and in early 1919. The inspection reports described horrifying conditions including widespread corruption, abuse, and death due to poor hygiene, disease, and malnutrition. It appears that the only reforms carried out in the empire's prisons during the Armistice Period (*Mütakere Dönemi*) and the allied occupation of Istanbul occurred as a result of *Entente* pressure.[82] A comparison of acheivements during the tenures of Major Gordon and Dr Pollitz as the directors of Ottoman prison reform seventy years apart, demonstrates the empire's increased commitment to prisons and penal institutions over the course of the nineteenth century.

Conclusion

As this brief state-centric overview of Ottoman penal reform demonstrates, prisons were important sites of imperial transformation in the late Ottoman Empire. These modifications represent a coherent and internally developed system of reforms by Ottoman bureaucrats to centralise power within the hands of the state and enter more fully into the lives of the empire's citizens. These transformations do not represent a rupture from the past or a discarding of long-held beliefs and practices in some sort of secularising and Westernising mission. This transformation represents a clear example of the development and execution of a unique Ottoman modernity that consciously adapted new methods of governance to existing structures in the empire, thus creating a new dynamic distinctive to the empire's historical, ideological, and cultural development. Notwithstanding CUP claims that the *ancien régime* was gone, it clearly built on existing programmes and furthered them in an attempt to create a modern state.

This chapter also demonstrates the central government's clear intention to increase its intervention into the lives of its population at all levels of state and society, particularly the prison. Similar programmes and processes being implemented throughout the empire were simultaneously happening within prison walls, thus making the prison a microcosm of Ottoman modernity and transformation. These programmes and policies included administrative centralisation, the streamlining and standardisation of regulation and procedure, information gathering, employee professionalisation, improving public health and hygiene, economic development, and the rehabilitation of prisoners through productive work.

Subsequent chapters juxtapose particular reform efforts with the actual experiences of inmates and prison officials to investigate how these interactions affected prison reform efforts and everyday life. These include prison surveys and the prison population, prison organisation and everyday life, the professionalisation of the prison cadre and the realities of corruption and prisoner abuse, and juvenile delinquency and incarceration. These chapters further several themes discussed in this overview and go into greater detail about state intentions, ideology, implementation, and their effects on prison life as local administrators and prisoners appropriated, resisted, and/or ignored these attempts. They also continue the other intersecting themes woven throughout the book that include transformation through continuity and change, a focus by reformers on prisoner rehabilitation, administrative centralisation and governmentality, order and discipline, and the creation and expansion of Ottoman state patriarchy in which the government increasingly assumed greater amounts of responsibility for the welfare of its population.

Notes

1. There are numerous nineteenth-century examples of links being drawn between prisons and civilisation in literature, political writings, and governmental treatises. The most famous example may be Fyodor Dostoevsky's assertion that the, 'degree of civilisation in a society can be judged by entering its prisons' (Dostoevsky, *House of the Dead*). For a careful study of nineteenth-century intellectual associations between civilisation and punishment, see Pratt, *Punishment and Civilization*.
2. Bentham, *Introduction to the Principles of Morals and Legislation*; Beccaria, *Crimes and Punishments*; and Howard, *State of Prisons in England and Wales*, and *Account of the Principle Lazarettos*.

3. For biographies of Ambassador Canning, see Lane-Poole, *Life of Lord Stratford de Redcliffe*; and Byrne, *Great Ambassador*.
4. For more on the Ottoman Empire and the Near Eastern Question, see Brown, *International Politics and the Middle East*, pp. 21–81.
5. Quoted from Cunningham, 'Stratford Canning and the Tanzimat', p. 245. For a detailed discussion concerning Canning's influence on nineteenth-century Ottoman prison reform, see Yıldız, *Mapusane*, pp. 110–61.
6. BNA, FO 195/364, pp. 1–32.
7. Hurewitz, pp. 315–18.
8. In 1910, as British Home Secretary, Sir Winston S. Churchill stated that 'the mood and temper of the public with regard to the treatment of crime and criminals is one of the unfailing tests of the civilisation of a country'. As quoted by Jenkins, *Churchill*, p. 180.
9. According to Foucault, 'governmentality' is the administrative and ruling philosophy that typifies the modern era. A country's population becomes the state's object of rule. The state views it as its primary resource to be managed and harnessed for the common good through the implementation of new methods of governance, such as comprehensive censuses, military conscription, public education, promulgating new laws, and creating powerful penal institutions, resulting in the 'totalisation' and 'individuation' of the population. This process enables the state to know each citizen individually and to simultaneously organise and mobilise the population for the benefit of the nation-state (Foucault, 'Essays on Governmentality').
10. BNA, FO 195/364.
11. Şen, *Osmanlı'da Mahkum Olmak*, pp. 18–26; and Yıldız, *Mapusane*, pp. 172–225.
12. Yıldız, *Mapusane*, p. 179.
13. Ibid., pp. 172–261. This section of *Mapusane* contains a comprehensive discussion of prison reform activity and its successes and failures during the Tanzimat era.
14. Ibid., pp. 267–93.
15. BNA, FO 195/364, pp. 1–32.
16. A *hapishane-yi umumi* or penitentiary was a new designation in the Ottoman Empire and represented a prison dedicated to housing serious offenders (*cinayet*) with a sentence of at least five years. These prisons were to be located in provincial and imperial city centres. This prison, built in 1871 and located in the Sultanahmet district of Istanbul's old city, represents the first of its kind within the Ottoman Empire. BOA, DHMBHPSM 1/2, doc. 10; and Yıldız, 'Osmanlı Devleti'nde Hapishane Islahatı', pp. 190–3.
17. Yıldız, *Mapusane*, pp. 182–8.
18. Ibid., pp. 184–5.
19. Young, 'Instructions sur l'administration des vilayets', 21 Feb 1876, *Corps de Droit Ottoman*, vol. I, pp. 88–91; and Gorman, 'Regulation, Reform, and Resistance', p. 100.

20. For Müfettiş Pasha's report, see BOA, YEE 72/37.
21. BOA, DHMBHPSM 1/2, doc. 10; and Yıldız, *Mapusane*, pp. 188–204.
22. Yıldız, 'Osmanlı Devleti'nde Hapishane Islahatı', pp. 192–4.
23. BOA, DHMBHPSM 1/2, doc. 10, Article 1.
24. See Hamidian era prison photographs from the Istanbul University Library Photograph Album Collection under the following headings: *Hapishane* (Aydın) 90601/12; *Hapishane* (Dedeağaç) 90418/17; *Hapishane* (Edirne) 779–40/7; *Hapishane* (Edirne) 90455/17; *Hapishane* (Gümülcine) 90418/51; *Hapishane* (Halep) 90754/79; *Hapishane* (Kırşehir) 779-58/11; *Hapishane* (Rodos) 90807/4,13–90808/2,18; *Hapishane* (Sakız Adası) 90802/5; *Hapishane* (Sultanyeri) 90412/8; *Hapishane* (Trabzon) 90441/21; *Hapishane* (Urfa) 90430/13; *Hapishane* (Yanya) 91104/2; and *Hapishane-Koğuşu* (Dimetoka) 779-40/10.
25. Demirel, '1890 Petersburg Hapishaneler Kongresi', pp. 11–14.
26. Young, 'Code of procédure pénale', 26 June 1879, *Corps de Droit Ottoman*, vol. VII, pp. 226–8 and 295–300, and Young, 'Iradé sur les Réformes', *Corps de Droit Ottoman*, vol. I, pp. 99–103; and Gorman, p. 100.
27. For a discussion on health and hygiene reform programmes during the Hamidian era, see Yıldırım, 'Tanzimat'tan Cumhuriyet'e Koruyucu Sağlık Uygulamaları'; Kalkan, 'Medicine and Politics'; and Kranzler, 'Health Services'.
28. Findely, *Bureaucratic Reform*, p. 253 and the introduction to the BOA, DHTMIK catalogues, which have hundreds of inspections, reports, and recommendations conducted and produced by this commission. It operated from June 1896 to July 1908 and provides rich background information on the prison conditions inherited by the CUP.
29. For more details on the unrest across the empire, see Quataert, *Social Disintegration and Popular Resistance*; and Kansu, *Revolution of 1908*, pp. 29–72.
30. Turfan, *Rise of the Young Turks*; Kansu, *Revolution of 1908*, and *Politics in Post-revolutionary Turkey*; Quartaert, *Social Disintegration and Popular Resistance*, 'Economic Climate', and '1908 Young Turk Revolution'; Ahmad, *Young Turks*; Kayalı, *Arabs and Young Turks*; Brummett, *Image and Imperialism*, and 'Dogs, Women, Cholera, and Other Menaces'; Arai, *Turkish Nationalism*; Ramsaur, *Young Turks*; and Hanioğlu, *Young Turks in Opposition* and *Preparation for a Revolution*.
31. This phrase is taken from Hill, *World Turned Upside Down*.
32. Kansu, *Revolution of 1908*, pp. 24–71.
33. Hanioğlu, *Young Turks in Opposition*, pp. 16–26; and Le Bon, *Psychology of the Crowd*.
34. Ergut, 'Policing the Poor' and 'State and Civil Rights'.
35. Findely, pp. 291–337.
36. These reports and statistics are found in the Directorate of Public Security's catalogue BOA, DHEUMTK.

37. BOA, DHMBHPS 142/38, 142/54, and 143/3. The guidelines contained in the 1880 Prison Regulation and its implementation is discussed extensively in Chapters 4 and 5.
38. Findely, p. 333.
39. Chapter 4 discusses prison labour.
40. BOA, DHMBHPSM 2/117, and DHMBHPS 35/4.
41. Düstur, *İkinci Tertip*, vol. 3, p. 467, no. 156. 7/6/1329.
42. BOA, DHMBHPSM 8/3, doc. 10/b.
43. Examples of these records are BOA, DHMBHPSM 2/49, 2/75, 2/78, 2/108, 2/112, 2/113, and 2/114. Chapter 5 contains a detailed analysis of Ottoman prison employees.
44. BOA, DHMBHPS 145/31.
45. Gönen, 'Osmanlı İmparatorluğunda Hapishaneleri', p. 175.
46. See Kayalı, 'Elections and the Electoral Process' concerning Ottoman elections in the Second Constitutional Period. For more on the *Entente Liberal*, see Hanioğlu, *Preparation for a Revolution*, pp. 289–311.
47. Ahmad, *Young Turks*, pp. 92–120; and Zürcher, *Turkey*, pp. 112–14.
48. Yakut, 'Exertions for the Depoliticisation'; and Turfan, pp. 155–65 and endnote 115.
49. Ahmad, *Young Turks*, Chapters 5 and 6.
50. Findely, pp. 309 and 313–14.
51. *Düstur*, 2nd series *İkinci Tertip*, vol. VI, p. 131–2.
52. BOA, DHMBHPS 149/45 and 73/58, docs 5 and 7.
53. The general directives for this survey are contained in BOA, DHEUMTK 13/11 and 54/4; DHMBHPSM 9/59; and DHMBHPS 72/46. Each province and independent administrative sub-division returned these completed questionnaires. Some examples include DHMBHPSM 11/84 (Adana); DHMBHPSM 10/19 (Beirut); DHMBHPSM 9/94 (Çatalca); DHMBHPS 149/6 and 149/9 (Edirne); DHMBHPSM 10/40 (Halep); DHMBHPSM 9/96 (Istanbul); DHMBHPSM 10/14 (Karesi); DHMBHPSM 10/52 (Sivas); DHMBHPSM 11/25 and 18/62 (Trabzon); DHMBHPS 149/36 (Van); and DHMBHPSM 11/24 (Zor).
54. BOA, DHMBHPSM 10/14, docs 12–15.
55. BOA, DHMBHPSM 9/103 and 11/84.
56. BOA, DHMBHPS 72/30 and 73/11; and DHMBHPSM 31/82. Article 1 of the 1880 Prison Regulation refers to the building of prisons in every administrative district of the empire.
57. BOA, DHMBHPS 72/30.
58. The catalogues of the Prison Administration and the Directorate of Prisons (BOA, DHMBHPS and BOA, DHMBHPSM) contain thousands of documents related to prison repair, construction, and maintenance. Many of these construction projects were initiated in 1912, suspended after the CUP lost power, and revived in 1914. For one list of several construction projects in 1914, see BOA, DHMBHPSM 15/42.

59. For Germany and the Ottoman Empire's financial relationship during WWI, see BOA, DHMBHPS 119/23; Trumpener, *Germany and the Ottoman Empire*, pp. 271–351 and 'Germany and the End of the Ottoman Empire', pp. 111–39.
60. BOA, DHMBHPS 58/48.
61. BOA, DHMBHPS 92/18 contains the curriculum vitae of each candidate as well as deliberations about each candidate.
62. BOA, DHMBHPS 92/57, doc. 4.
63. BOA, DHMBHPS 92/18, 92/44, 92/46, and 92/57, doc. 5 concern Dr Pollitz's hire and include his employment contract.
64. BOA, DHMBHPS 158/27.
65. Ibid.; DHMBHPS 160/78; and DHMBHPSM 31/82. There are several drafts of a new and expanded version of the 1880 Prison Regulation dating to 1917. See DHMBHPS 74/66, 158/8, 158/27, 159/41, and 160/78; and DHMBHPSM 31/82.
66. BOA, DHMBHPS 76/31 contains Dr Pollitz's comments on existing prison regulations.
67. The budget included 113,500 TL for supplies (food and materials), 4,000 TL for medicines, 40,213 TL for employee salaries, 20,350 TL for repairs, 3,311 TL for prison rentals, 4,100 TL for the transport of prisoners, 110,000 TL for the construction of new prisons, and an additional 13,000 TL and 6,000 TL for the construction of two new prisons in Istanbul and Üsküdar (BOA, DHMBHPS 158/29, docs 2–4).
68. BOA, DHMBHPS 76/31.
69. Shaw, 'Ottoman Expenditures', pp. 373–8.
70. BOA, DHMBHPS 159/41.
71. BOA, DHMBHPS 158/8, doc. 1.
72. '*İzahat*' literally means 'explanations' (Redhouse, *Redhouse Sözlüğü*, p. 568).
73. BOA, DHMBHPS 76/20, doc. 3.
74. Compare BOA, DHMBHPS 158/8, doc. 1 with DHMBHPS 76/20.
75. Compare BOA, DHMBHPS 158/27 with 76/20.
76. BOA, DHMBHPS 76/20, doc. 2.
77. Ibid.
78. Examples of the returned questionnaires include: DHMBHPSM 27/24, 27/31, 29/65, and DHMBHPS 158/38 (Ankara); DHMBHPSM 23/29, 26/68, 26/70, 27/5, 27/14, 27/20, 28/4, 28/29, 31/31, and 53/11 (Beirut); DHMBHPSM 29/66 (Diyarbekir); DHMBHPSM 26/59, 27/3, 27/28, 29/69, and DHMBHPS 12/49 (Hüdavendigar); DHMBHPSM 26/47, 26/49, 27/15, and 27/25 (Istanbul); DHMBHPSM 26/63 (İzmid); and DHMBHPSM 27/39 (Jerusalem).
79. BOA, DHMBHPS 143/93.
80. Documents related to Dr Pollitz's Ottoman prison reform agenda include BOA, DHMBHPS 76/27, 76/31, 76/36, 76/60, 78/26, 78/47, 79/38, 80/2, 92/57, 123/26, 158/8, 158/27, 158/29, 158/42, 159/8, 159/41, 160/2, 160/78, 161/46, and DHMBHPSM 31/82.

81. BOA, DHMBHPS 76/36, 159/8, 160/2, 78/26, 78/47, 78/59, 161/46, 79/30, 123/26, 79/38, and DHMBHPSM 33/60. Also see DHMBHPS 79/38, docs 95–7.
82. BNA, FO 608/52/13, pp. 235–43; BNA, FO 608/114/4, pp. 118–88; and BNA, FO 608/103/3, pp. 269–72. For a description of crime and prisons in Istanbul during the *Entente* Powers' occupation (1918–21), see Yıldıztaş, 'Suç Unsurları ve İstanbul Hapishanleri'.

3

Counting the Incarcerated: Knowledge, Power and the Prison Population

As mentioned in Chapter 2, soon after its creation in May 1911, the Prison Administration began to organise a detailed prison survey. This survey commenced on 18 January 1912 by eliciting information regarding every aspect of prisons, including budgets, health care, employees, prison labour, and inmates. Categories of inquiry associated with prisoners included crimes committed, gender, date of incarceration, marital and familial status, recidivism, punishment, social class and occupation, ethno-religious/national identity, age, and literacy. The survey broke down each of these categories further into lists of specific items related to the prisoner's identity. For example, familial status differentiated its various categories according to gender. Under each gender, categories included – single, married with children, married without children, widowed with children, and widowed without children. Another example concerns the prisoner's social class and occupation. This group divided the population into twelve categories not differentiated by gender: state employees, teachers, physicians, merchants, money changers, land owners, artisans, farmers, workers, sailors, servants, and unemployed.[1]

The level of information collected and tabulated by means of this survey fits the description of what Michel Foucault called a '*tableaux vivants*'. According to Foucault, this table is 'the first of the great operations of discipline . . . which transforms the confused, useless or dangerous multitudes into ordered multiplicities'. The organising of seemingly disparate bits of information about inmates from more than a thousand prisons across a vast empire into a rational system made this questionnaire 'both a technique of power and a procedure of knowledge'.[2] The Prison Administration arranged the questionnaire to link the singular and the multiple together within one document. Foucault claimed that this combination simultaneously provided knowledge of the individual and the group. This process divided the prison population into comprehensible parts while simultaneously totalising it into an intelligible whole that Ottoman authorities could understand, control, and discipline. The knowledge and power gained by this and subsequent prison surveys conducted in the Second Constitutional Period not only shaped CUP penal reform, but also helped fashion the prison into one of the premier institutions for social control, social engineering, and modern state construction within the empire, surpassed only by the military and perhaps the police.

Building off the overview of prison reform provided in Chapter 2, this chapter explores the various ways that the Prison Administration and later the Directorate of Prisons gathered information about its prisons and inmates during the Second Constitutional Period. The chief focus of this chapter is the description and analysis of the creation, conduct, content, and results of the 1912 prison survey. Its various categories of identity provide insights into the composition of the prison population; Ottoman administrative and societal sensibilities towards crime, criminality, and punishment; and its conceptualisation of difference according to ethno-religious, communal, and national identities assigned to the incarcerated.[3] This survey provides the most detailed picture of the prison population during the empire's entire existence and its results are woven throughout this chapter in order to provide a clearer picture of the incarcerated.

The 1912 Ottoman Prison Survey and Prison Population

Population surveys provide valuable insights into the dynamics and composition of a particular institution, region, or society. The 1912 prison survey provides these kinds of insights not only for the prison population but for society as a whole. This section first discusses the development, use, and importance of statistics and censuses for the Ottoman bureaucracy during the long nineteenth century, thus providing the historical context of the 1912 prison survey. The next part analyses the development, structure, conduct, and limitations of the 1912 prison survey in order to facilitate the subsequent analysis of specific categories of the survey and the constitution of the prison population found in sections two and three.

Over the course of the nineteenth century the collection, analysis, and use of statistics in Europe developed into the standard means by which institutions studied, organised, predicted, and, ultimately, controlled large, variable, complex phenomena such as 'societies'. For social scientists and bureaucrats, statistics provided scientific authenticity to their conclusions. Society was not a passive entity to be shaped and moulded with ease by bureaucratic directives and legislation, but a dynamic force of conflicting interests and actions. In fact, statisticians were among the first to fully personify and reify the concept of 'society'. Statistics became the rational method of scientific analysis that facilitated the consolidation of power in the hands of another reified and personified entity: the 'state'. The state viewed statistics as the chief means of gaining knowledge and power to shape, control, and reform society. This, in turn, facilitated the creation of a modern nation-state. Understanding complex phenomena, such as a nation-state's population, economy, agriculture, and trade, provides the means to shape and control them for the common good.[4] Foucault even points out that 'statistics' has 'state' as its root.[5]

Throughout its existence, the Ottoman Empire conducted extensive cadastral surveys and collected population statistics for taxation, military, and security purposes. In the 1830s, the framework, scope, regularity, and efficiency of statistical collection changed as modernising reforms began in earnest. The entire population increasingly became the object of these campaigns as the bureaucracy needed to further harness social power. The administration utilised statistics for practical purposes, such as tax levies, military conscription, infrastructural improvements, land surveys, administrative organisation, and social engineering projects. It stressed efficiency and accuracy as essential elements of governance, thus laying an important foundation for the centralising reforms of the Tanzimat, Hamidian, and CUP eras. The military became the driving force behind the administration's efforts to keep accurate statistics of the numbers and ages of Muslim males eligible for conscription.[6]

Administrators increasingly recognised the importance of statistics as guides for imperial transformation. Nevertheless, no centralised statistics bureau existed before 1891. Prior to the 1870s, the Sublime Porte attempted only one major census in 1828/29–31. It was, however, not systematic, continuous, or comprehensive. In some areas officials counted individuals, but in many cases they obtained their information from population registries published by provincial bureaucracies in previous annual reports. Many of these figures were out of date and did not reflect population fluctuations resulting from migrations, war, territorial loss, and pastoral-nomadism.

One result of this census, however, was the establishment of the Office of Population Registers (*Ceride-i Nüfus Nezareti*). In 1839, census responsibilities were divided among various ministries. This system appointed population officials on the district level who were 'required to register all births, deaths, and migrations and to report several times a year to the central office in Istanbul'.[7] During its time in operation (1839–53), this system produced nearly 21,000 population registers from across the empire.[8]

Despite the existence of extensive raw population statistics, the data was not systematic or comprehensive. Population surveys were, however, conducted with chronological regularity. Provincial administrators reported these statistics to Istanbul in annual 'yearbooks' (*salnameler*). It was from these records that Ottoman and foreign officials compiled imperial population figures, although they varied in detail, accuracy, and reliability depending on where and when they were collected, for example, in pastoral-nomadic areas or before, during, or after wars and treaties.[9] Also, provincial officials rarely counted individual women and children, or the elderly. Their chief concern was military age Muslim males and the total number of individuals in a particular region or religious (*millet*) community.[10]

In 1874 the Council of State (*Şura-yı Devlet*) ordered the establishment of a new system for collecting population statistics and called for a new census. It was never conducted, however, because of political instability (1876 was the year of three sultans), the Russo-Ottoman War, and the promulgation and suspension of the 1876 Ottoman Constitution. These new orders and regulations pertaining to censuses, however, established the basis for developing a more advanced system during the Hamidian era.[11] In 1879 Grand Vizier Küçük Said Pasha recommended the creation of a 'statistical system' to monitor bureaucratic activities and provide the government with accurate information for making policy decisions.[12] As soon as the political situation stabilised, Abdülhamid II ordered a new census to be conducted jointly by the Ministries of War and the Interior for military and taxation purposes.[13]

In addition to basing the new census on the 1874 regulations, Sultan Abdülhamid II and the Council of State actively appropriated census policies and procedures from foreign governments. They shared the same world view concerning the benefits that accurate and comprehensive population statistics brought to good governance, economic development, state stability, and imperial power.[14] In 1886 Abdülhamid II approached American Ambassador Samuel Cox for assistance with the Ottoman census. Ambassador Cox had chaired the US congressional census committee and played an instrumental role in successfully completing the 1880 US Census.[15]

Conducted from 1881–93, the new Ottoman census called for every imperial subject to be counted, described, and issued an identity card (*nüfus tezkeresi*), which was required to conduct any official state business including land transactions, tax payments, and obtaining travel visas. Collected personal data included given name, nickname, surname name, address, age, religion, profession, civic, tax, voting status, and any disabilities. This level of information was unprecedented for Ottoman population surveys.[16] To expedite its completion and continue the work of recording population changes, Abdülhamid II established the Statistical Council of the Sublime Porte in 1891 and ordered it to 'collect ... information on everything that happened in the provinces ... down to the smallest detail'.[17]

The census of 1881–3/1893 resulted in a clear picture of the empire's diverse population. The government utilised this data to facilitate reform programmes throughout the empire, including prisons, and to shape society for the empire's common good. These efforts laid the foundation for CUP policies and programmes concerning the collection and exploitation of population statistics.

CUP members recognised the potential power of statistics. Many of its members possessed the same affinity for statistical information as their Western counterparts, having been educated in modern schools with European curriculums. As a result of their Comtian Positivist world view, CUP members saw themselves as the elite class of technocrats, responsible for reshaping the empire according to the scientific principles upon which all modern, civilised, and rational societies should be based.[18] For Positivists, statistics represented the pre-eminent scientific tool for 'totalising and individuating' the empire's population, including its inmates.[19] The breadth and depth of the Prison Administration's 1912 prison survey represents a culmination of the inheritance of these long-term administrative practices and CUP innovations.

As stated above, the 1912 prison survey collected information from every house of detention in the empire. The survey requested precise information on inmates, including their numbers, whether they were convicted or accused, age, gender, marital and familial status, ethno-religious and national identity, literacy, recidivism, social class and occupation, crime committed, date of incarceration, and prison sentence. The survey also requested information concerning deaths, sickness, disease, injuries, which prisons had hospitals or clinics, the types of diseases treated, and surgical procedures performed. Details concerning prison budgets were collected, including details such as projected and actual expenditures, employee salaries, repair and construction costs, and medical expenses. It also asked for data on prison factories, production, expenditures, and profits. Additional factory data on the quantity and type of goods manufactured and how many inmates it employed was also collected. The survey directive provided clear instructions on how the survey was to be conducted and how the results should be returned, and it threatened those who failed to comply with 'serious consequences'. All prisons were required to confirm with the Prison Administration that they had received their copy of the survey, and the Prison Administration went so far as to send out periodic reminders concerning the survey's due date.[20] In the end, the majority of prisons returned their completed surveys on time, but some of the completed surveys have been subsequently lost, destroyed, or withheld.[21]

The questionnaire possessed a particular organisational logic that both facilitated and hindered the usefulness of its data. It was not organised according to individual prisoners, but according to the crime committed and the prisoner's gender. The thirty-three specific crimes for which data was collected drove the rest of the tabulation process. All subsequent categories followed a particular crime in this order: gender, year of incarceration, marital status, recidivism, prison sentence (lesser crimes), socio-economic status and occupation, prison sentence (felonies), ethno-religious and national identity, age, and literacy. All categories, except for socio-economic status and occupation, differentiated according to gender (see Figure 3.1).[22]

For example, in the district prison of Cebele, located in the Trabluşşam administrative sub-division of the Beirut province, the total prison population consisted of 159 individuals in 1912. Of those 159, eighty-three were awaiting trial and seventy-six were convicted and serving their prison sentences. Among the seventy-six sentenced criminals, fifty-one

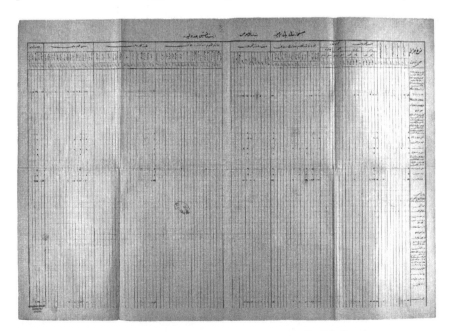

Figure 3.1 1912 prison survey questionnaire, Beirut province's Cebele prison.
Source *BOA, DHMBHPS 5/9, doc. 4*

(forty-four males and seven females) were incarcerated for assault and battery (*darb ve cerh*) with sentences ranging from one week to one month. Twenty males were single, fifteen males were married with children, and nine males were married without children. Of the seven females convicted of assault, four were married with children and the other three were married without children. The assault convicts consisted of twenty-one farmers (*zürra*), thirteen labourers (*amele*), nine artisans (*esnaf*), five merchants (*tüccar*), and three land owners (*ashab-ı akar*). All fifty-one inmates were Muslim. The ages of the male prisoners breakdown accordingly: Eighteen were aged from 14 to 20, ten were aged from 21 to 30, twelve were aged from 31 to 40, three were aged from 41 to 50, and one was aged from 61 to 70 years of age. The seven female prisoners were all aged from 21 to 30 years. Finally, twenty-five males were literate while the other twenty-six convicted of assault and battery were illiterate.[23]

The various limitations of this data result from the questionnaire's organisation and content. Since no names were recorded, it is impossible to match a specific prisoner incarcerated for a particular crime with her or his age, occupation, literacy level, or ethno-religious and national identity unless he or she was the only person incarcerated for a particular crime. Recording errors as well as omissions of pieces of information are additional limitations to the usefulness of these surveys. On many occasions prison officials regularly and purposely omitted certain information; for example, some forms do not include details on prisoners' ages or ethno-religious and national identities. On others, officials incorrectly recorded a prisoner's ethno-religious and national identity by assigning multiple conflicting identities. Confusion is to be expected, however, since the empire was so geographically, linguistically, ethnically, and religiously diverse.

Outside of raw numbers, it is impossible to reconstruct the entire Ottoman prison population at any time during the empire's existence. The surviving prison surveys, however, allow the reconstruction of more than two-thirds of the 1911–12 prison population in great detail. In fact, these surveys make it possible to reconstruct the prison population for the provinces and independent administrative sub-divisions of Istanbul, Baghdad, Beirut, Canik, Edirne, the Hijaz, Kastamonu, Mamüretülaziz, Manastır, Mosul, and Yanya.[24] Gerneral prison population statistics broken down by province are also available for 1914, 1916–17, 1918–19, and 1919–20, but they do not have nearly the level of detail as can be found in the 1912 survey (see Charts 3.1, 3.2, 3.3, 3.4, and 3.5).[25]

Conceptualising Crime and Socio-economic Status

This section investigates the categories found in the 1912 prison survery regarding crime and socio-economic status. It also utilises the prisoner data collected from these two categories to partially reconstruct the Ottoman prison population. In so doing, this section reveals important insights into CUP and broader Ottoman sensibilities towards class, crime, and social control by sheding light on which crimes were most commonly prosecuted by the state and the socio-economic status of these criminals.

As part of CUP attempts to impose social order and discipline, the prison survey collected information on each prisoner's socio-economic status and occupation. This category provides clear data on which crimes particular segments of society committed and what percentage of the prison population came from a specific social class. Not surprisingly, the vast majority of the Ottoman prison population was from the lower class. The 1912 prison survey, however, was not very specific or exhaustive in its socio-economic classifications.[26] It did, however, attempt to organise the entire prison population into twelve different categories representing both broad and specific types of employment and class status:

1. State Officials (*memurin*).
2. Teachers (*muallimin*).
3. Physicians (*atıbba*).
4. Merchants (*tüccar*).
5. Money Changers & Bankers (*sarraf*).
6. Land Owners (*ashab-ı akar*).
7. Artisans (*esnaf*).
8. Farmers (*zürra*).
9. Labourers (*amele*).
10. Ship Captains & Sailors (*kapudan ve taife*).
11. Servants (*hademe*).
12. Unemployed (*işsiz*).[27]

The survey makes interesting distinctions regarding socio-economic status and occupation, such as differentiating between skilled and unskilled workers (*esnaf* and *amele*) and between rural and urban workers (*zürra* and *esnaf/amele*). It also collected information on very specific types of occupations, such as sailors, money changers and bankers, teachers, and medical doctors, thus constituting an interesting mixture of professionals and unskilled workers filling quite specific occupations. Government employees (*memurin*), however, were grouped all together in a generic category. It seems strange that the CUP would not collect

Province and independent sub-division	Male	Female	Total
Baghdad	1,660	80	1,740
Beirut	3,930	90	4,020
Bitlis	578	43	621
Canik	1,722	45	1,767
Edirne	6,787	362	7,149
The Hijaz	414	45	459
Istanbul	5,670	272	5,942
Kastamonu	1,051	143	1,194
Mamuretülaziz	2,099	106	2,205
Manastır	3,998	168	4,173
Mosul	2,808	26	2,834
Yanya	1,867	114	1,981
Totals	32,584	1,494	34,085

Chart 3.1 1911–12 prison statistics.

Note Several provinces and independent administrative sub-divisions are not represented here because their results are not available to researchers.

Source *BOA, DHMBHPSM 3/36, 4/4, 4/20, 4/21, 5/1, 5/9, 6/27, and 12/70; BOA, DHMBHPS 145/2, 145/56, 145/78, 146/69, and 146/70*

more specific information on incarcerated government employees, since its ideological and pragmatic approaches to politics and state administration favoured centralisation, rule of law, professionalisation, and accountability. Concerning the organisation of this category, there appears to be a definite separation and gradation in socio-economic status with professionals and the higher-skilled occupations preceding the less skilled. The final two categories (servants and the unemployed) represent the lowest rungs of the Ottoman socio-economic ladder.

Despite the broad nature of these occupational divisions, these categories do provide significant insights into the composition of the Ottoman prison population. It also sheds light on the socio-economic groups about which the CUP was most concerned, such as bankers and money changers, merchants, skilled and unskilled labourers, artisans, farmers, and ship captains and their crew members, all of whom occupied vital positions in the Ottoman economy. It also provides insights into the groups that the CUP was least concerned with, such as religious scholars and clerics (*ulema*,

Province (Vilayet)	Less serious crimes (Cünha ve Kabahat)			Serious crimes (Cinayet)			Awaiting trial (Mevkufin)			Totals
	Male	Female	Total	Male	Female	Total	Male	Female	Total	
Istanbul	871	47	918	47	1	48	127	4	131	1,097
Edirne	264	14	278	90	0	90	274	9	283	651
Erzurum	113	21	134	229	6	235	229	11	240	609
Adana	367	14	381	272	1	273	478	18	496	1,150
Ankara	762	38	800	1,375	21	1,396	1,626	51	1,677	3,873
Aydın	558	65	623	454	12	466	875	27	902	1,991
Bitlis	66	0	66	155	3	158	447	6	453	677
Basra (limited data)	2	0	2	3	0	3	1	0	1	6
Baghdad	58	1	59	302	2	304	304	4	308	671
Hijaz	32	0	32	10	0	10	21	0	21	63
Haleb	449	10	459	871	7	878	1,190	9	1,199	2,536
Hüdavendigar	491	50	541	807	6	813	803	24	827	2,181
Diyarbekir	173	2	175	349	1	350	431	24	455	980
Suriye	241	14	255	69	3	72	364	6	370	697
Sivas (limited data)							1	0	1	1
Trabzon	129	14	143	141	8	149	628	13	641	933
Kastamonu	648	59	707	731	12	743	388	24	412	1,862
Konya	618	51	669	531	14	545	1,151	25	1,176	2,390
Mamuretülaziz	327	44	371	117	4	121	339	8	347	839

Province (*Vilayet*)	Less serious crimes (*Cünha ve Kabahat*)			Serious crimes (*Cinayet*)			Awaiting trial (*Mevkufin*)			Totals
	Male	Female	Total	Male	Female	Total	Male	Female	Total	
Van (limited data)	53	2	55	50	1	51	186	2	188	294
Independent sub-division (*Sancak*)										
Urfa	49	0	49	72	0	72	173	1	174	295
İzmid	164	10	174	114	0	114	213	1	214	502
Bolu (limited data)	225	35	260	23	0	23	171	2	173	456
Canik	121	20	141	51	0	51	234	10	244	436
Çatalca (limited data)	9	0	9	9	0	9	15	0	15	33
Zor	51	0	51	12	2	14	42	0	42	107
Asir	52	0	52	2	0	2	54	0	54	108
Kala-i Sultaniye	109	2	111	396	0	396	249	3	252	759
Medina (limited data)	37	2	39	9	0	9	10	0	10	58
Tekke	42	1	43	40	7	47	180	8	188	278
Karahisar-ı Sahib	305	20	325	475	5	480	406	10	416	1,221
Menteşe	215	17	232	467	4	471	233	3	236	939
Totals	7,601	553	8,154	8,273	120	8,393	11,843	303	12,146	28,693

Chart 3.2 1914 prison statistics.

Note The provinces and independent administrative sub-divisions of Beirut, Karesi, Kayseri, Küds-i Şerif (Jerusalem), Kütahya, Maraş, Mosul, and Yemen did not report any statistics.

Source *BOA, DHMBHPSM 12/38 and 17/24; and DHMBHPS 17/32*

Province (*Vilayet*)	Male prisoners	Female prisoners	Provincial totals
Istanbul	919	48	967
Edirne	558	49	607
Adana	996	53	1,049
Ankara	1,242	143	1,385
Aydın	2,618	225	2,843
Beirut	1,221	30	1,251
Hüdavendigar	799	50	849
Suriye	1,116	33	1,149
Sivas	1,141	73	1,214
Kastamonu	1,137	118	1,255
Konya	901	84	985
Bitlis	85	11	96
Haleb	646	18	664
Trabzon	180	3	183
Mosul	499	4	503
Diyarbekir	1,097	31	1,128
Mamuretülaziz	218	16	234
Independent sub-division (*Sancak*)			
Urfa	281	4	285
İzmid	266	13	279
İçil	81	4	85
Eskişehir	164	0	164
Bolu	455	47	502
Canik	280	9	289
Çatalca	13	6	19
Zor	100	2	102
Kudüs-i Şerif	628	15	643
Karesi	712	45	757
Kala-i Sultaniye	133	18	151

Chart 3.3 1916–17 prison statistics.

Note Several provinces and independent sub-divisions did not report their prison statistics in full. These include Trabzon, Bitlis, Mamuretülaziz, Edirne, Mosul, Çatalca, and Kütahya.

Source *BOA, DHMBHPS 143/93, doc. 2*

Province (*Vilayet*) Independent sub-division (*Sancak*)	Male prisoners	Female prisoners	Provincial totals
Kayseri	242	13	255
Karahisar-ı Sahib	289	13	302
Menteşe	224	23	247
Maraş	350	16	366
Niğde	360	8	368
Kütahya	0	0	0
Cebel-i Lübnan	269	6	275
Tekke	197	18	215
Grand totals	20,417	1,249	21,666

Chart 3.3 (continued)

Province (*Vilayet*)	Sentenced (*Mahkumin*)	Awaiting trial (*Mevkufin*)	Total
Istanbul	450	500	950
Edirne	600	425	1,025
Adana	750	755	1,505
Ankara	925	810	1,735
Aydın	1,955	1,325	3,280
Bitlis	645	475	1,120
Beirut	1,125	930	2,055
Haleb	1,050	580	1,630
Hüdavendigar	1,045	625	1,670
Diyarbekir	750	725	1,475
Suriye	1,450	650	2,100
Sivas	880	1,055	1,935
Trabzon	500	350	850
Kastamonu	1,250	640	1,890
Konya	1,140	755	1,895
Mamuretülaziz	650	250	900
Mosul	550	350	900

Chart 3.4 1918–19 prison statistics.
Source *BOA, DHMBHPS 163/85*

Province (*Vilayet*)	Sentenced (*Mahkumin*)	Awaiting trial (*Mevkufin*)	Total
Independent sub-division (Sancak)			
Urfa	200	150	350
İzmid	255	155	410
İçil	100	95	195
Eskişehir	240	105	345
Bolu	550	255	805
Tekke	240	210	450
Canik	50	150	200
Çatalca	55	45	100
Zor	90	85	175
Kudüs-i Şerif	240	255	495
Karesi	640	225	865
Kala-i Sultaniye	125	235	360
Kayseri	250	135	385
Karahisar-ı Sahib	220	145	365
Kütahya	325	275	600
Menteşe	325	145	470
Maraş	220	235	455
Niğde	250	345	595
Cebel-i Lübnan	155	145	300
Totals	20,245	14,590	34,835

Chart 3.4 (continued)

Province (*Vilayet*)	Sentenced (*Mahkumin*)	Awaiting trial (*Mevkufin*)	Total
Istanbul	178	241	419
Edirne	600	425	1,025
Adana	750	755	1,505
Ankara	925	810	1,735
Aydın	1,955	1,325	3,280

Chart 3.5 1919–20 prison statistics.

Note The provinces of Erzurum and Van did not report their prison statistics.

Source *BOA, DHMBHPS 165/97*

80

Counting the Incarcerated

Province (*Vilayet*)	Sentenced (*Mahkumin*)	Awaiting trial (*Mevkufin*)	Total
Bitlis	645	475	1,120
Hüdavendigar	1,045	625	1,670
Diyarbekir	750	725	1,475
Sivas	880	1,055	1,935
Trabzon	500	350	850
Kastamonu	1,250	640	1,890
Konya	1,140	755	1,895
Mamuretülaziz	650	250	900
Mosul	550	350	900
Independent sub-division (*Sancak*)			
Urfa	200	150	350
İzmid	255	155	410
İçil	100	95	195
Eskişehir	240	105	345
Bolu	550	255	805
Tekke	240	210	450
Canik	50	150	200
Çatalca	55	45	100
Karesi	640	225	865
Kala-i Sultaniye	125	235	360
Kayseri	250	135	385
Karahisar-ı Sahib	220	145	365
Kütahya	325	275	600
Menteşe	325	145	470
Maraş	220	235	455
Niğde	250	345	595
Erzincan	60	150	210
Totals	15,923	11,836	27,759

Chart 3.5 (continued)

Province and independent sub-district	State officials	Teachers	Physi-cians	Mer-chants	Money changers/ Bankers	Land owners	Artisans	Farmers	Labourers	Ship captains and crew	Servants	Unemployed
Baghdad	14	3	0	5	12	86	813	631	127	3	50	154
Beirut	18	4	0	13	0	287	1,281	1,526	237	50	39	332
Bitlis	3	1	0	0	0	61	83	319	103	0	14	33
Canik	0	0	0	0	0	1	42	893	89	5	67	194
Edirne	47	7	3	55	12	219	742	4,073	1,540	178	272	609
The Hijaz	1	0	0	15	0	0	232	20	48	13	34	87
Istanbul	199	81	7	11	0	8	3,053	397	948	127	201	617
Kastamonu	0	0	0	3	0	6	151	609	148	0	7	187
Manastır	7	6	1	20	0	31	269	1,692	553	56	164	302
Mamuretülaziz	3	0	0	0	0	10	172	1,060	188	3	87	166
Mosul	21	0	0	31	0	119	300	721	684	4	29	546
Yanya	8	2	2	6	0	44	53	1,025	191	12	86	326
Totals	321	104	13	159	24	872	7,191	12,966	4,856	451	1,050	3,553

Chart 3.6 1911–12 prisoner socio-economic and occupation statistics.

Note Several provinces and independent administrative sub-divisions are not represented here because their results are not available to researchers. Not all available surveys provided socio-economic data. These numbers, therefore, do not match total prison population numbers.

Source BOA, DHMBHPSM 3/36, 4/4, 4/20, 4/21, 5/1, 5/9, 6/27, and 12/70; DHMBHPS 145/2, 145/56, 145/78, 146/69, and 146/70

talebeler, imams, muezzins, and *hafizler).* This group, which according to the 1894–5 Ottoman census consisted of more than 583,000 practitioners, was the single largest profession in the empire.[28] Despite its prevalence, the Prison Administration did not collect data on this occupation, even though the CUP was very suspicious of religious professionals and purged many for their anti-constitutional views.[29]

The vast majority of the 1911–12 prison population came from the lowest socio-economic classes. In fact, this group made up more than 90 per cent of the entire prison population. These prisoners were of low status and when employed filled the lowest paying and least prestigious occupations in Ottoman society, such as artisans, labourers, farmers, and servants. Additionally, they represent the largest segments of Ottoman society, and they constitute the local and imperial governments' main base for tax revenues and military conscription. In other words, they are the masses that the CUP feared so intensely. The CUP, therefore, was very keen to monitor and control these segments of society (see Chart 3.6).

The prison statistics for 1912 for the provinces and administrative subdivisions that are listed in Chart 3.6 show that out of a prison population of 34,085 in 1912 there were 321 government officials, 104 teachers, 13 physicians, 159 merchants, 24 bankers and money changers, and 872 land owners. The total number of prisoners from the middle and upper classes was only 1,493. This represents less than 4.4 per cent of the total prison population. Prisoners from lower classes, however, number at least 30,067 individuals (the occupations of 2,525 inmates were not reported) and constitute at least 88 per cent of the Ottoman inmate population. The breakdown of this total number is 7,191 artisans, 12,966 farmers, 4,856 labourers, 451 ship captains and crew members, 1,050 servants, and 3,553 unemployed.[30]

In 1914, the Prison Administration updated the prison survey's questionnaire to reflect the findings of the 1912 survey by reorganising the survey's socio-economic status and occupation section. This change demonstrates a need to devote more space to the most prevalent occupations found among prisoners. In the 1914 version many of the categories for professionals were combined while others were more clearly defined. For example, the categories for physicians *(atıbba)* and teachers *(muallimin)* were combined and then expanded to include all learned professions: 'physicians, teachers, and other learned professionals' *(atıbba ve muallimin ve sair ehl-i fünun).*[31]

The 1914 questionnaire also augmented and circumscribed the 1912 'servants' category. It changed the title to 'servants of merchants, money changers, bankers, and others' *(tüccar ve sarraf ve saire hademesi).* This

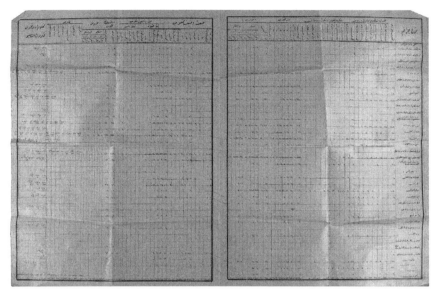

Figure 3.2 1914 prison survey questionnaire, Istanbul province.
Source *BOA, DHMBHPS 150/3, doc. 2*

alteration reflects CUP interests in protecting major actors in its economic plan. Merchants, money changers, and bankers were important financiers of Ottoman industrialisation and economic expansion, not to mention its war effort. Protecting their property and their physical safety was important, especially since theft and assault were the most common crimes committed by servants.[32] Connecting socio-economic status with crimes committed reveals additional insights into CUP and broader Ottoman conceptualisations of criminality, class, and social control.

The 'crimes committed' category is the most important section of the questionnaire since it drove the rest of the survey. The survey divides the category 'Types of Crimes' (*Nev'i-i Ceraim*) into two sections 'Misdemeanours and Less Serious Crimes Section' (*Cünha ve Kabahat Kısmı*) and 'Serious Crimes Section' (*Cinayet Kısmı*). The first section contains twenty-one categories dealing with lesser offences. Nineteen of the categories contain specific 'less serious crimes' and the two remaining categories are 'other lesser crimes' and prisoners awaiting trial for lesser crimes (*mevkufin*).[33] The 'Serious Crimes Section' contains seventeen categories. Fourteen contain specific serious offences. One category concerns those prisoners awaiting trial for serious crimes. The last two categories are for prisoners awaiting trial in martial law courts and a category for totalling all prisoner statistics.[34]

According to the IOPC, there are literally hundreds of *cinayet, cünha,* and *kabahat* crimes that are punishable by incarceration. The Prison Administration, however, only requested data for thirty-three crimes. The survey listed some crimes as a general category, such as theft, but most listed crimes were specific. A close analysis of these crimes, their relation to the IOPC, and the number of criminals convicted offers revealing insights into Ottoman society and CUP ideology regarding crime and its threat to public order and safety.

The first section of the 'Types of Crimes' category (*Cünha ve Kabahat Kısmı*) consists of the following twenty-one categories:

1. Disrespecting civil servants, gendarme, and soldiers (*me'murin, zaptiye ve askere şetm ve hakaret*).
2. Aiding and abetting the escape of a convict and concealing habitual serious offenders (*mahbus kaçırmak ve ihfayı erbab-ı cinayet*).
3. Lacking good character, such as vagrants without skills or profession (*bila salahiyet sanat-ı resmide bulunmak*).
4. Forgery of travel permits and passports (*mürur tezkeresi ve pasaport sahtekarlığı*).
5. Assault and battery (*darb ve cerh*).
6. Offering abortions and harmful medications (*iskat-ı cenin ve eczayı muzırra i'tası*).
7. Seducing and dishonouring a virgin (*hetk-i ırz ve iğfal-i bakire*).
8. Indecent sexual behaviour (*fi'il-i şeni*).
9. Verbally and physically molesting youth (*gençlere harf endazlık ve elile sarkıntılık*).
10. Unlawful arrest and incarceration (*usul ve nizam haricinde habs ve tevkif*).
11. Switching, concealing, and stealing a child and kidnapping a girl (*çocuk tebdili, sirkati ve gaybi ve kız kaçırmak*).
12. Providing false witness, oath, or evidence during a judicial proceeding (*umur-ı hukukiyede yalan şehadet ve yemin ve tehdidamiz mektup*).
13. Vituperation, insulting, and slander (*şetm ve hakaret ve iftira*).
14. Fraud (*dolandırıcılık*).
15. Theft (*sirkat*).
16. Corruption/Embezzlement (*emniyet-i suiistimal*).
17. Wasting or destroying a person's goods, property, and documents/papers (*nasın malını ve emlakini ve evrakını iza'a ve telef etmek*).
18. Opposing police directives, announcements, and warnings (*nizamat, bildiri ve tenbihat-ı zaptiyeye muhalefet*).

19. Miscellaneous lesser crimes and misdemeanours (*ceniha ve kabahat-i mütenevvi'a*).
20. Debtors (*medyun*).
21. Those arrested for lesser crimes and misdemeanours awaiting trial (*mevkufin*).[35]

Less serious offenders constituted roughly two-thirds of the 1911–12 prison population.[36]

Under the second section (*Cinayet Kısmı*) fourteen crimes were listed in the following order, together with three other categories:

1. Aiding and abetting bandits and embezzling state goods (*kat-i tarik yataklığı, zimmete emval-i miri geçirmek*).
2. Premeditated homicide (*'amden katl*).
3. Homicide without premeditation (*min gayri ta'ammüdden katl*).
4. Wilful homicide without premeditation (*katl-i kasdi*).
5. Severe assault and battery and severing a body part (*cerh ve darb-i şedid ve kat'-i uzuv*).
6. The intentional aborting of a foetus (*cebren veya kasden iskat-i cenin*).
7. Violent indecent sexual behaviour (*cebren fi'il-i şeni*).
8. Kidnapping a sexually mature female (*cebren baliğa kaçırmak*).
9. The forgery of seals and official items (*mühür ve enva'-ı resmiye sahtekarlığı*).
10. Arson (*kundakçılık*).
11. Armed theft causing injury (*mu'amele-i şedid icra ve cerh ile hırsızlık*).
12. Theft through breaking and entering (*meskun mahalden duvar delerek veyahut kapı kırarak hırsızlık*).
13. Armed theft without injury (*mu'amele-i şedid icrasıyla bila cerh hırsızlık*).
14. Possession of weapons forbidden by the Ministry of War (*esliha-i memnu'a-i divan-i harbi*).
15. Prisoners awaiting trial in martial law courts (*misafirhaneye vurud iden Divan-i Harb-i Örfiden*).
16. Those arrested for serious offences awaiting trial (*mevkufin*).
17. Total (*yakut*).[37]

Serious offenders made up nearly one-third of the prison population of 1911–12.[38]

The vast majority of the crimes listed on the questionnaire concern property, life, honour, and social order. Eighteen crimes deal with violent behaviour against an individual, fourteen deal with types of theft, nine crimes are honour related (character and sexual purity), and nine crimes deal with issues related to state responsibilities, authority, and power. Finally, all of the offences, in one way or another, deal with crimes against social order, discipline, and control. None of these crimes, however, are associated with espionage, bribery, the selling of government secrets, dereliction of duty, or state corruption. The *Cinayet* section does not even have a catch-all category similar to the one possessed by the *Cünha ve Kabahat* section in which serious offenders of other crimes not included in the questionnaire could be listed. The CUP collected information on very specific types of crimes that closely correspond with the 1911 changes to the 1858 IOPC.

As discussed in Chapter 1, the CUP furthered the process of consolidating judicial power into the hands of the state and rationalising the practice of Islamic criminal law already begun in previous regimes. Its goal was to reign in the autonomy of Islamic court judges, particularly regarding crime, individual rights, and the protection of property. In so doing, the CUP expanded state consolidation of power and its encroachment into the lives of the population. An analysis of the convergence between the 1911 penal code revisions, the crimes listed on the prison survey, and the statistical results explicates CUP ideology and pragmatism towards crime, preserving and expanding its own power, and a better understanding of criminal behaviour in the empire, particularly concerning crimes against state officials and those associated with honour, theft, and violence.

Throughout history states have placed a high priority on protecting their officials involved in tax collection, law enforcement, regime preservation, and maintaining public order. The Ottoman Empire and the CUP were no different. In fact, the amount of attention given to protecting state officials during the Second Constitutional Period reveals the importance that the CUP placed on it, even though few were incarcerated for these crimes.

The Prison Administration listed two crimes on the prison survey dealing with offences against state officials: 'Disrespecting civil servants, gendarme, and soldiers' and 'Opposing police directives, announcements, and warnings'. IOPC Articles 112–16 address these types of crimes and their respective punishments. The 1911 IOPC reforms significantly modified these articles in order to delineate crimes and punishments more clearly. In fact, only Article 112 was not altered.[39]

The number of prisoners arrested, convicted, and incarcerated for crimes against state officials was very low in comparison to other crimes listed on the prison survey. In 1911–12 the administrative areas of Canik, Istanbul, Beirut, Baghdad, Bitlis, and the Hijaz incarcerated a total of

14,549 prisoners.[40] Out of those prisoners, only 322 were convicted for crimes against state officials.[41]

The vast majority of those incarcerated for crimes against state officials served very light sentences. A total of 281 prisoners were either pardoned or spent from twenty-four hours to one month in prison. The other forty-one prisoners received varying sentences ranging from one month to one year, with just a handful of prisoners being incarcerated for a maximum of two years.[42] Generally these light punishments indicate that violations were not of a serious nature.

Only the independent administrative sub-division of Canik appears to be an exception to the generalities listed above. Out of its 1911–12 prison population of 1,767 inmates, a total of 100 were convicted of 'Disrespecting civil officials, gendarme, and soldiers'. It is not clear why there were so many arrests and convictions for such an uncommon crime, but in the end it actually did conform to the aforementioned norms. Only eight of these inmates served any jail time (three months to a year). The other ninety-two prisoners convicted of this crime were pardoned.[43] The overall results (few convictions and light sentences) appear staggeringly low for a crime that the CUP heavily modified in 1911 and then closely monitored.

Of those prisoners who served time for crimes against state officials, the vast majority were artisans (ninety-two).[44] The numbers for the rest of the occupations and professions were twenty-one farmers, twenty labourers, eighteen unemployed, nine government officials, five servants, a land owner, a merchant, and a sailor. The high number of artisans indicates the existence of tensions between this segment of society and urban state authorities as manifest by the numerous strikes and protests that happened from 1881 to 1910. As mentioned in Chapter 2, shortly after coming to power in 1908, the CUP-led government enacted a series of laws severely curtailing the right to protest and strike, thus limiting the power of artisans and guild members.[45] Tracking the number of prisoners arrested, convicted, and serving time for disturbing the peace and attempting to abrogate state authority was vitally important to the CUP, especially in the wake of the 1909 countercoup.

As discussed in Chapter 1, in 1911, the Ottoman Parliament significantly altered the section of the IOPC dealing with crimes against an individual's honour, including sexual offences, perjury, calumny, and vituperation.[46] Although these crimes also do not represent a significant statistical number of actual convictions and incarcerations, they do constitute a significant portion of the crimes for which statistics were collected. Out of the thirty-three crimes listed on the prison survey, ten crimes were related to these types of offences.

Although, the prison survey collected data on a significant number of crimes related to honour, it ignored others, such as kidnapping adults. Instead, it focused on crimes associated with kidnapping children of both sexes (considered a less serious offence) and kidnapping females at the age of puberty (nine to fourteen years old), but not yet manifesting menses (*mürahika*), which was considered a serious criminal offence.[47] With so few prisoners convicted of these crimes it is difficult to understand why the Prison Administration expended such energy tracking them.

The prison survey listed the crimes of slander and vituperation under the same heading and combined their statistics. It is, therefore, impossible to distinguish between these two closely related offences.[48] The state incarcerated only a small percentage of its prison population for these crimes. In Baghdad, the Hijaz, Istanbul, Beirut, Bitlis, and Canik inmates convicted of slander and vituperation represent less than 3 per cent of the prison population (451: 14,549) in 1911–12. More than 90 per cent of these prisoners received and served prison sentences of twenty-four hours to one month.[49]

Their crimes could not have been too serious especially since the maximum penalty for felony slander was ten years' imprisonment with hard labour. If slander or vituperation were of a less serious offence the maximum penalty was one to three years of incarceration, but the survey indicates a prevalence of short prison sentences for these two crimes.[50] This indicates that most of the perpetrators committed vituperation, which according to the IOPC is the lesser of the two offences. Regarding the socio-economic status and occupation of those convicted and incarcerated for slander and vituperation, at least 88 per cent were artisans, labourers, farmers, servants, or unemployed.[51] With so few being incarcerated for this crime it appears odd that the CUP-led Prison Administration considered it important to track. When the inmates' socio-economic backgrounds are taken into consideration, however, it makes more sense. Keeping the masses in check and protecting the reputations of the middle and upper classes, especially for a new administration, are essential to securing and maintaining power.

The second most prevalent type of crime committed in the Ottoman Empire, according to the prison survey, was theft (*sirkat*) in all of its related forms, including petty and violent theft, breaking and entering, fraud, embezzlement, and robbery. Theft-related crimes constituted nine of the thirty-three crimes listed on the questionnaire. More prisoners were convicted and incarcerated for theft-related crimes than any other except assault and battery (*darb ve cerh*). The Ottoman Parliament heavily revised theft-related portions of the IOPC in 1911 as well. The prison population of 1911–12 in Istanbul, Baghdad, Beirut, Bitlis, the Hijaz, and Canik incarcerated for misdemeanour theft consisted of 2,603 out of a total population of 14,549. Nearly 70 per cent (1,816 out of 2,603) of inmates served sentences of one week to six months incarceration. A total of 2,436 of the prisoners incarcerated for theft (more than 93 per cent) were from the lower classes (artisans, farmers, labourers, servants, and unemployed). Muslims constituted nearly 58 per cent of theft convicts at 1,501 and 449 Christians (Ecumenical, Armenian, and Bulgar Exarchate) rounded out the largest proportions of the prisoners incarcerated for misdemeanour theft.[52] Legal reform, aggressive prosecution, and incarceration for theft demonstrate CUP priorities to protect private property.

Violent crimes were the most prevalent offence in the Ottoman Empire. In fact, the 1912 prison survey collected statistics on fourteen different violent crimes. Again, the Ottoman Parliament in 1911 heavily modified all IOPC articles relating to violent crime, especially threats, physical assaults, and homicide.[53]

The actual number of prisoners convicted of violent crimes, particularly assault and homicide, constitute almost half of all inmates in 1911–12. For example, 2,926 out of the 5,942 individuals incarcerated in Istanbul prisons in 1911–12 were convicted of violent crimes. In Beirut, out of the 4,020 incarcerated persons, 2,121 were serving time for either assault or homicide, and in Bitlis 347 prisoners out of a total population of 621 were incarcerated for violent crimes. Baghdad, Canik, and the Hijaz all had a lower percentage of violent criminals in their prisons than either Istanbul or Beirut. In all three of them, however, violent crime was still the most prevalent type of offence committed. Out of a prison population of 1,740, there were 799 prisoners convicted of violent crimes in Baghdad, whereas Canik had 631 prisoners out of 1,767, and the Hijaz had the fewest, at 84 out of 460.[54]

The single-most prevalently convicted and incarcerated crime during the Second Constitutional Period was 'assault and battery' (*darb ve cerh*). In the provinces and independent administrative sub-divisions of Istanbul, Baghdad, Beirut, Bitlis, Canik, and the Hijaz 5,605 out of a total prison population of 14,549 served time for 'assault and battery'. Despite accounting for the largest percentage of convictions and incarcerations, most 'assault and battery' crimes were minor. A total of 80 per cent of those convicted for 'assault and battery' served light sentences (twenty-four hours to one month). Their crime, therefore, was most likely fisticuffs. Nearly 89 per cent of those incarcerated for 'assault and battery' were from the lower classes (artisans, farmers, labourers, servants, and the unemployed).[55] As mentioned in Chapter 2, the Second Constitutional

Period was a particularly volatile time in terms of war, uprisings, foreign interventions, separatist movements, and political instability. Maintaining public order and social control, especially among the lower classes, was a matter of top priority for the CUP.

Even the crimes for which few individuals were actually incarcerated, but still monitored by the prison surveys (vituperation, slander, and crimes against state officials) add additional insight into Ottoman administrative goals regarding its desire to consolidate power within its hands and protect government officials. Both of these goals are essential for creating and maintaining a strong, centralised, and efficient government that possesses a monopoly on the use of violence to enforce its laws. They are also key elements to imperial transformation and revitalisation. Combining statistics on criminal behaviour with socio-economic status provides even deeper insights into CUP ideology and Ottoman society.

A Marxist and neo-Marxist explanation for the predominance of the lower classes in Ottoman prisons claims that the upper and middle classes utilise prisons as a means of controlling the masses, maintaining political and economic power, protecting their personal well-being and property, and disciplining the labour force. The proletariat of all industrialised and developing countries during the Second Industrial Revolution consisted predominantly of unskilled workers and peasants. The Second Constitutional Period and the CUP fit this Marxist and neo-Marxist interpretation, except that its inner-circle rejected Great Power *laissez-faire* liberal economics and viewed it as the major cause of the empire's economic and political problems. The CUP envisioned achieving an industrialised empire via state-directed developmentalism (*étatism*), which also required a disciplined labour force to staff the factories and work the fields of a newly created Muslim bourgeoisie.[56] Monitoring and controlling the lower classes and protecting the property and well-being of this emerging bourgeoisie were high priorities for the CUP as manifested by the conceptualisation and results of the 1912 prison survey.

Conceptualising Difference: Identity and the Ottoman Prison Survey

Socio-economic status and criminality are not the only categories that offer compelling insights into the empire's prison population and CUP ideology. Likewise, the prison questionnaire's category on ethno-religious and national identity provides data on prisoner identity and understanding of CUP conceptualisations of difference, in terms of race, ethnicity, religion, and nationality.[57] As stated earlier, governments utilise censuses to identify, quantify, and categorise their population in order to harness social power and facilitate social control. The process of collecting statistics through population surveys can actually create identities. Ian Hacking coined the term 'nominalism' to signify the act of 'making people up'. According to Hacking, 'nominalism' reflects state intentionality as it assigns identity to its various populations through censuses and other population registrations.[58] This concept applies to the Ottoman prison survey, because the state is assigning identity to inmates who lack the power of self-identification.

'Nominalism' can have unintended consequences. For example, in Macedonia, European powers forced the Ottoman Empire to conduct a thorough population survey beginning in 1903 that resulted in a great deal of political and social strife.[59] In 1872, the Ottoman administration established the (Bulgarian-dominated) Exarchate and recognised it as a separate religious community (*millet*) from the (Greek-dominated) Ecumenical Patriarchate. This caused intense nationalist struggles between the different Eastern Orthodox communities in the Balkans concerning which religious and/or nationalist community the population belonged, especially among the Bulgarian, Serbian, and Greek-speaking communities. Each group struggled, especially their clergies, for potential control of the religious community and perhaps the future nation. If a certain group within the Macedonian population decided to identify with the Ecumenical Patriarchate then it was choosing to be 'Greek', even if it spoke Bulgarian or Serbian and vice versa.[60]

The 1903 census exacerbated this explosive situation of competing nationalist movements identified by religious affiliation. During the census, local religious leaders, nationalists, ideologues, and government officials intimidated and coerced local populations to identify themselves with one party or the other, either the Ecumenical Patriarchate or the Bulgarian Exarchate. The census became a site for naming and identifying elements of the population for taxation, military conscription, and their potential nationalist proclivities. Not only was the Ottoman state trying to impose its own classification upon Macedonia's population, but the people were actively identifying and naming themselves.[61]

During the first decade of the twentieth century, Macedonia was the central stronghold of the CUP and the staging ground for the 1908 Constitutional Revolution. CUP loyalists entrenched themselves in Macedonia's administrative and military hierarchy.[62] Even the Inspector General of Rumeli and director of the 1903 census Hüseyin Hilmi Pasha was an active CUP supporter.[63] He was well aware of the explosive potential of the 1903 census for the Macedonian population. For this reason, he debated whether or not to use the most benign and generic population classifications available: Muslim, Jew, and Christian. He eventually abandoned the idea because those categories went against the 1902 Mürzsteg Programme, which required the Ottomans to implement 'administrative reorganisation according to national principles' within Macedonia. According to the Mürzsteg Programme, 'national principles' meant nationalist identity based on specific religio-linguistic characteristics.[64] If utilised, perhaps the generic categories could have prevented some of the violence that resulted from the more controversial religious identities delineated in the census.

As a result of its participation in the 1903 Macedonian census and their modern educations, CUP members understood the power of statistics in nation-state construction. European meddling and Christian national-separatist activities galvanised Macedonian Muslim support for the 1908 Constitutional Revolution led by the CUP.[65] What took place in Macedonia demonstrated to CUP members the explosive power of identity appropriation and helps to explain the Prison Administration's choice of identity categories in the 1912 prison survey.

The identity categories contained in the 1912 prison survey reveal important insights into how the CUP conceptualised difference among the state's population. As a result of constant warfare and immense social upheaval characterising the Second Constitutional Period, these prison surveys represent the closest attempt to a population census ever carried out by the CUP.[66] The categories of identity found in the prison survey provide the most concrete example available for understanding how the CUP conceptualised difference in terms of ethnicity, religion, and nationality prior to the radicalisation of identity and its brutal demographic engineering programmes post-Balkan Wars and during WWI.[67]

One of the prison survey's most intriguing categories of identity concerns a prisoner's *millet* identity. The title of this category is '*Milliyet-i Mahkumin*'.[68] According to twentieth-century standards, this title should be translated as 'the prisoner's national identity'. This translation, however, actually obfuscates the multiple and contradictory meanings *millet* possessed during the late Ottoman period. Based upon the word's usage in the survey, '*Milliyet-i Mahkumin*' should be translated as 'the prisoner's ethno-religious, communal or national identity'. Under this category the possible *millet* identities of a prisoner consisted of the following ten choices:

1. *İslam.*
2. *Rum Katolik ve Protestan* (Ecumenical Patriarchate Christians who are Catholics or Protestants).[69]

3. *Ermeni Katolik ve Protestan* (Armenian Christians who are Catholics or Protestants).
4. *Musevi* (Jewish).
5. *Bulgar* (Bulgarian Exarchate).
6. *Milel-i Muhtelife-yi Osmaniye* (Other Ottoman Communities).
7. *Alman* (German), *Fransa* (French), *İngliz* (British), *ve Avustralı* (Austrian).
8. *İranlı* (Iranian/Persian).
9. *Yunanlı* (Citizens of Greece).
10. *Milel-i Muhtelife-yi Ecnebi* (Other Foreign Nationals).

This category was broken into two main divisions: Ottoman subjects and foreign nationals. The division related to Ottoman subjects consists of six groupings:

1. Muslims (*İslam*).
2. Ecumenical Patriarchate Christians who are Catholics and Protestants (*Rum Katolik ve Protestan*).
3. Armenian Christians who are Catholics and Protestants (*Ermeni Katolik ve Protestan*).
4. Jews (*Musevi*).
5. Bulgarian Exarchate Christians (*Bulgars*).
6. Other Ottoman Communities (*Milel-i Muhtelife-yi Osmaniye*).

The second division, referring to foreign nationals, consists of four groupings:

1. German, French, British, and Austrian foreign nationals (*Alman, Fransa, İngliz, ve Avustralı*).
2. Iranian foreign nationals (*İranlı*).
3. Greek foreign nationals (*Yunanlı*).
4. Other Foreign Nationals (*Milel-i Muhtelife-yi Ecnebi*).[70]

The organisation of this category, the possible *millet* options, and the use and meaning of *millet*, reveal several significant insights into CUP conceptions of difference. First, each of the *millet* categories related to the Ottoman population represents divisions and identities based on sectarian lines and not along linguistic, quasi-racial, or cultural designations. Most of these religious groups represented long-standing Ottoman administrative and bureaucratic designations based largely upon Islamic and customary law (*shari'a* and *örf-i hukuk*), thus dividing the Ottoman population along monotheistic sectarian lines: Judaism, Christianity, and Islam.[71] Previous Ottoman attempts to collect population statistics during the nineteenth century also categorised the empire's population according to these basic sectarian designations.[72]

Of these three monotheistic religions, prison officials only divided Christianity into sectarian sub-categories. These Christian *millet* subdivisions were the Armenian Patriarchate, the Ecumenical Patriarchate, and the Bulgarian Exarchate,[73] which was originally a subgroup of the Ecumenical Patriarchate, but, as mentioned above, was separated in 1872.[74] The grouping of Ottoman subjects according to religious affiliation received official recognition as the '*Millet* System' on 25 April 1861.[75] The Ottoman administration founded this system, in part, to implement the Imperial Rescripts of 1839 and 1856, which declared that all Ottoman subjects possessed equal status before the law regardless of religious affiliation. Even the final category for classifying the identity of the prisoners who were Ottoman subjects was organised along confessional lines. The category 'other Ottoman communities' or *milel-i muhtelife-yi Osmaniye*, acted as a catch-all category and would have included other religious sects (*mezhepler*) such as Alevis, Druze, Yazidis, Maronites, Assyrians, Latins, and Coptic Christians.[76]

Furthermore, these categories of identity suggest that the concept of ethnicity based upon linguistic, quasi-racial, or cultural designation was either in its infancy within the Ottoman Empire or was consciously being avoided by the CUP at this time. This is illustrated by the inclusion of Catholics and Protestants within the religious *millet* of the Ecumenical Patriarchate and Armenian populations. This inclusion implies that these two categories were not strictly based on a unified religious identity, because if Catholics and Protestants somehow fell under the category of Ecumenical Patriarchate and Armenian Christianity, then these designations were not purely religious. They also appear to represent a quasi-ethnic identity, one intertwined with religion, culture, and language. That said, within the prison survey only Christian *millets* conveyed any sense of ethnicity outside the lines of strict sectarianism.

By contrast prison officials did not request the number of Ottoman subjects considered Turks, Arabs, or Kurds among the prison population. The CUP appears to have been content to include these groups under the rubric of Islam without reference to racial, linguistic, religious, or supposed national differences among these groups. They were not viewed as separate ethno-religious communities possessing national identities of their own. Rather they were conceptualised as part of the core constituency of the Ottoman nation – Muslims. The issue of differentiating the ethno-religious national identity of Muslims that is so pervasive and perversely manipulated in the contemporary Middle East does not appear to have been an important issue to the Prison Administration.[77] Perhaps the CUP attempted to avoid similar fractious problems with its Muslim population that existed among the Balkan Christians during the 1903 Macedonian census. During the Second Constitutional Period, other CUP attempts to collect statistics on various segments of the Ottoman population regarding crime, military conscription, or taxation, either categorised the population along similar sectarian lines as the prison survey or simply identified them 'Muslim' or 'Non-Muslim'.[78]

The only place in the questionnaire where *millet* possesses the possible meaning of 'national' is in the second division of the '*Milliyet-i Mahkumin*' category. This section deals exclusively with subjects of foreign states incarcerated in Ottoman prisons and contains no sectarian differentiations. As a result, it is clear that *millet* does possess a nationalistic connotation, but only in reference to foreigners and not Ottoman subjects. Therefore, in this one category of the questionnaire ('*Milliyet-i Mahkumin*'), the term *millet* possesses several different meanings: religious, ethno-religious, and national identity. This clearly demonstrates the state of flux in which *millet* found itself during this time. The multiple meanings of *millet* caused confusion among some local prison officials who, while completing the survey, assigned multiple *millet* identities to individual prisoners.

Concepts such as nationalism, race, and ethnicity are not germane to the regions, languages, or cultures of the Middle East. There were no words in Persian, Turkish, or Arabic that adequately described what these concepts meant in the late Ottoman Empire. New words were adopted from European languages or indigenous words were imbued with new significance while still maintaining their traditional meanings. This led to great confusion as to what the terms in question actually meant. *Millet* is one such example. Its inclusion in the prison survey confused many state officials charged with assigning *millet* identity of the empire's prisoners. Sometimes these local officials even gave prisoners multiple *millet* identities within the same category of the survey.

For example, prison officials in Mecca (the provincial capital of the Hijaz) assigned multiple *millet* identities to the same prisoner. Some prisoners were identified both as Muslims and as belonging to 'other Ottoman communities'. Additionally, incarcerated German, French, British, and Austrian subjects were also given dual *millet* identities, but in this instance as simultaneously foreign nationals and Muslims.[79] Hijazi prison officials were not the only ones applying multiple *millet* identities to the incarcerated. In Baghdad province, national and religious identity was also conflated. Officials in the Baghdadi administrative district of Kazımiye felt it necessary to indicate the national, religious, and ethnic identity of its prisoners. Kazımiye prison officials indicated that prisoners who were

Iranian nationals were also Muslims and whether or not Ottoman Muslim subjects belonged to 'other Ottoman communities'.[80]

The Beirut district of Hayfa and the Yanya district of Margılıç are two other examples of this phenomenon.[81] All prisoners, not just Muslims, were given multiple *millet* identities. In fact, all Ottoman subjects who were assigned a religious *millet* identity of Muslim, Ecumenical Patriarchate, or Jewish were also listed as belonging to 'other Ottoman communities'. It appears that the Hayfa and Margılıç prison officials made a clear distinction between religious affiliation and ethnic or communal identity and that the term *millet* possessed these clear and distinct meanings in their minds. These instances are unique in comparison with the rest of the survey.

In other provinces, such as Manastır, Mamüretülaziz, Mosul, and Istanbul, local prison officials did not assign multiple *millet* identities. In fact, only a handful of administrative districts from around the empire made this mistake.[82] In other words, they did not specify the religious affiliation of foreign nationals or those labelled as 'other Ottoman communities'. However, the assigning of multiple *millet* identities to the same prisoner was not limited to one isolated province. It cannot, therefore, be explained away as a strange aberration in one obscure corner of the empire. The areas that did assign multiple *millet* identities were spread across the empire. As a result of this ambiguity and the confusion it caused, the Prison Administration adjusted this category in order to clarify *millet*'s meaning and usage in a subsequent version of the survey.

On 25 May 1914, the province of Istanbul submitted its prison statistics for 1913–14 utilising a similar version of the 1912 questionnaire. There were, however, some significant alterations, particularly regarding the ethno-religious, communal, and national identity of the inmates. The title of the 1914 version of this category was changed from '*Milliyet-i Mahkumin*' to '*Milliyet ve Tabiiyet-i Mahkumin*'. This same category was now separated into two subdivisions not previously contained in the 1912 questionnaire. The two new subdivisions were entitled '*tebaiyeten Osmaniye*' and '*tebaiyeten ecnebiye*'. Instead of ten different choices regarding the prisoner's identity, this version included twelve different designations divided equally between the two new subdivisions. The subdivision of *tebaiyeten Osmaniye* included the following:

1. *İslam*.
2. *Rum ve Rum Katolik ve Protestan* (Ecumenical Patriarchate and Ecumenical Patriarchate Catholic and Protestant).
3. *Ermeni ve Ermeni Katolik ve Protestan* (Armenian and Armenian Catholic and Protestant).

4. *Musevi* (Jewish).
5. *Bulgar* (Bulgarian Exarchate).
6. *Milel-i Muhtelife-yi Osmaniye* (Other Ottoman Communities).

The second subdivision of *tebaiyeten ecnebiye* included the following:

1. *Alman ve Avustralı* (German and Austrian).
2. *İngliz* (British).
3. *Fransa* (French).
4. *İranlı* (Iranian/Persian).
5. *Yunanlı* (Citizens of Greece).
6. *Milel-i Muhtelife-yi Ecnebi* (Other Foreign Nationals).

These new titles, subdivisions, and categories represent significant clarifications of the original 1912 questionnaire's ambiguous use of the term *millet* (see Chart 3.7).[83]

The first significant change is the addition of two related words – *tabiiyet* and *tebaiyeten* – found in the title of the entire category related to the ethno-religious, communal, and national identity of the prisoners and in the category's two new subdivisions. The words are, respectively, an adjective and adverb and possess the meanings of 'nationality or allegiance' and 'as a subject'. Both words are also closely associated with *tabi* and *tebaa*, which mean respectively 'a subject of a state or sovereign' and 'subjects; subject (of a state)'. *Tabiiyet*'s antonym *tabiiyetsizlik* means 'statelessness'.[84]

The use of *tabiiyet* and *tebaiyeten* in the 1914 prison survey represents a significant change and clarification in terminology. It indicates that the Ministry of the Interior and the Prison Administration realised the ambiguous nature of *millet* and sought to clarify its meaning regarding national and communal identity between Ottoman and foreign subjects. The 1912 questionnaire conflated the traditional diplomatic usage of the term *millet* (as religious sovereignty) with the more recently developed meaning of 'ethno-religious community' in reference to Ottoman subjects.[85] The confusion caused by this conflation was clearly demonstrated by the prison officials who incorrectly assigned multiple *millet* identities to individual prisoners.

In the 1914 version, the meaning and use of the terms *millet* and *milliyet* are much more circumspect and do not refer to a prisoner's nationality. Instead, the term *tabiiyet* is used to designate national identity, whereas the terms *millet* and *milliyet* only refer to the ethno-religious and communal identity of a prisoner who is an Ottoman subject. This adheres to the traditional usage of the term according to the late Ottoman linguist, Şemseddin

Province and independent sub-division	Muslim		Ecumenical Patriarchate		Armenian		Jewish		Bulgar		Other Ottoman communities		English, German, French, and Austrian		Iranian		Greek		Other nationalities	
	Male	Female	Male	Female	Male	Female	Male	Female	Male	Female	Male	Female	Male	Female	Male	Female	Male	Female	Male	Female
Baghdad	1,397	46	0	0	4	0	76	7	0	0	172	11	1	0	15	0	0	0	0	0
Beirut	2,598	67	417	19	6	0	14	0	5	0	155	3	0	0	0	0	0	0	0	0
Bitlis	460	29	0	0	27	8	0	0	0	0	11	3	0	0	0	0	0	0	0	0
Canik	797	29	200	3	80	1	0	0	0	0	0	0	0	0	0	0	0	0	0	0
Edirne	3,828	231	2,208	80	155	15	105	4	540	24	638	30	0	0	0	0	5	0	0	0
The Hijaz	405	45	0	0	0	0	0	0	0	0	297	45	5	0	3	0	0	0	0	0
Istanbul	2,647	131	925	27	319	7	89	3	10	0	32	0	2	0	11	0	38	1	0	0
Kastamonu	873	121	30	6	1	0	0	0	0	0	0	0	0	0	0	0	0	0	0	0
Manastır	1,488	54	542	65	152	0	11	2	250	38	2	0	0	0	0	0	1	0	0	0
Mamuretil-aziz	1,268	65	5	0	227	14	2	0	0	0	0	0	0	0	0	0	4	0	0	0
Mosul	2,493	23	43	1	1	0	58	0	0	0	64	2	0	0	1	0	1	0	0	0
Yanya	785	4	561	68	2	0	1	0	0	0	7	0	2	0	0	0	0	0	21	9
Totals	19,039	845	4,931	269	974	45	356	16	805	62	1,378	94	10	0	30	0	49	1	37	9

Chart 3.7 1911–12 prisoner ethno-religious and national identity statistics.

Note Several provinces and independent administrative sub-divisions are not represented here because their results are not available to researchers. Not all available surveys provided ethno-religious and national identity data. These numbers, therefore, do not match total prison population numbers.

Source BOA, DHMBHPSM 3/36, 4/4, 4/20, 4/21, 5/1, 5/9, 6/27, and 12/70; DHMBHPS 145/2, 145/56, 145/78, 146/69, and 146/70

Sami. His definition demonstrates the evolving and dynamic nature of *millet*'s varied meanings during this period. He clearly approves of restricting the meaning of *millet* to identify groups of people based upon religious affiliation. This he claims maintained its original Quranic meaning. He does acknowledge, although disapprovingly, that *millet* was also being used to identify peoples according to language or place of origin.[86]

The 1914 version followed the same format and overall content of the 1912 questionnaire. It did, however, change the Armenian and Ecumenical Patriarchate categories for the sake of clarity and specificity. The 1914 questionnaire altered the 1912 version to read 'Ecumenical Patriarchate and Ecumenical Patriarchate Catholics and Protestants' (*Rum ve Rum Katolik ve Protestan*) and 'Armenian and Armenian Catholics and Protestants' (*Ermeni ve Ermeni Katolik ve Protestan*).[87] The original intent of the 1912 survey was to collect the statistics on all those associated with the Ecumenical Patriarchate and Armenian communities. Ottoman authorities did incarcerate orthodox Christians, but perhaps prison officials did not properly vet the titles of these two categories in the original survey.

A summation of the significant insights into CUP conceptions of difference as revealed by the 1912 and 1914 prison surveys include: 1. Difference among the Ottoman population was classified according to confessional designation, not ethno-nationalist identities. 2. Sectarian identification of Ottoman prisoners is consistent with other forms of population tabulation utilised by the CUP and previous regimes. 3. Designations of ethnicity based upon linguistic, quasi-racial, or cultural designation were generally avoided, except in the case of Ottoman Christian communities, such as Catholic and Protestant Armenians and Ecumenical Patriarchate Christians. 4. No ethnic distinctions were made among Ottoman Muslims, such as Turks, Arabs, and Kurds. 5. The only time the term *millet* does imply the meaning of 'national' is in relation to foreigner prisoners. 6. The Ottoman state did not view any Ottoman communities as distinct nations possessing some form of independent sovereign power. The Ottoman population was still seen as subjects of the state and sultan. 7. Distinctions of identity were based along monotheistic sectarian lines and all were supposedly equal before the law. 8. In the 1912 survey the term *millet* possessed multiple meanings including religious, ethno-religious, communal, and national identity. *Millet* was not a static concept during the late Ottoman period, but remained in a state of flux until well after the demise of the empire when it obtained its present meaning of 'nation' and 'national'. 9. The ambiguity of *millet* in the 1912 survey led to confusion and recording errors among prison officials. Finally, the Prison Administration attempted to solve this confusion by circumscribing the meaning of *millet* to 'ethno-religious communal identity' in a subsequent rendition of the questionnaire.

This investigation into the use and meaning of *millet* in the prison survey possesses the potential for much greater implications regarding late Ottoman 'nationalist' history – particularly in terms of the development of Turkish nationalism. It challenges the claim that the CUP was dominated by Turkish nationalists bent on 'Turkifying' the empire in order to create a Turkish state.[88] This investigation demonstrates that the CUP conceptualised difference among the Ottoman population according to sectarian lines, in part because its core goals were: to centralise and rationalise power within its hands and the Ottoman bureaucracy; to modernise and transform the empire into an efficient, powerful state; and to maintain its territorial integrity. CUP members were elitists, but not separatists. They were still actively ascribing to and promoting official Ottoman nationalism (*Osmanlılık*) until the end of the empire, even though they became increasingly suspicious of the empire's Christian subjects after the Balkan Wars and engaged in horrific acts of demographic engineering and genocide during WWI. This official Ottoman nationalism was supposed to transcend linguistic, ethnic, communal, and religious differences, even though its core constituency consisted of the empire's Muslim population.[89]

Conclusion

The 1912 prison survey provides important insights into the composition of the Ottoman prison population in terms of numbers, crimes committed, gender, age, marital status, occupation, punishment, recidivism, and ethno-religious identity. This information is vital to reconstructing the population itself and making sense of who was incarcerated at the end of the empire. These statistics reveal that the prison population stayed relatively low throughout the Second Constitutional Period, fluctuating from 21,000 to 40,000 prisoners. The Ottoman prison population, in terms of percentage of its overall population, was comparable to other contemporary states. For example, the United States' 1910 prison population was 112,362 inmates. According to the 1910 US Census, the country's total population was 92,228,496. This means that prisoners made up only 0.12 per cent of its population. The Ottoman prison population, at most, was only 0.16 per cent of the empire's entire population. Even during the height of WWI, the percentage of the Ottoman population that was incarcerated never approached 0.2 per cent. The empire, therefore, should not be characterised as a 'police state' even though it exerted tremendous efforts to transform its major penal institutions (see Charts 3.8, 3.9, and 3.10).

Province and independent sub-division	Under 14		14–20		21–30		31–40		41–50		51–60		61–70		71+	
	Male	Female	Male	Female	Male	Female	Male	Female	Male	Female	Male	Female	Male	Female	Male	Female
Baghdad	18	2	276	8	664	19	352	22	134	3	86	5	42	0	21	2
Beirut	24	0	680	9	1,362	48	784	18	225	4	51	0	26	0	11	0
Bitlis	5	0	48	6	155	8	150	20	60	41	0	0	0	0	0	0
Canik	12	0	286	14	460	15	239	5	60	0	24	0	0	0	0	0
Edirne	36	2	1,141	61	2,583	222	1,487	86	594	35	188	14	60	3	4	1
The Hijaz	0	0	97	8	218	12	109	19	29	5	19	1	4	0	2	0
Istanbul	38	3	894	62	1,767	55	936	31	293	13	100	2	35	2	7	0
Kastamonu	0	0	222	35	403	40	201	33	64	10	50	4	6	0	1	0
Manastır	70	0	471	13	1,082	62	645	44	260	14	51	3	16	2	3	1
Mamuretülaziz	0	0	158	2	485	57	477	40	200	63	59	0	0	0	0	0
Mosul	18	0	259	0	971	16	627	10	322	4	107	2	50	0	0	0
Yanya	13	0	167	11	646	45	487	38	192	11	65	15	26	2	2	0
Totals	234	7	4,699	229	10,796	599	6,494	366	2,433	203	800	46	265	9	51	4

Chart 3.8 1911–12 prisoner age statistics.

Note Several provinces and independent administrative sub-divisions are not represented here because their results are not available to researchers. Not all available surveys provided prisoner age data. These numbers, therefore, do not match total prison population numbers.

Source *BOA, DHMBHPSM 3/36, 4/4, 4/20, 4/21, 5/1, 5/9, 6/27, and 12/70; DHMBHPS 145/2, 145/56, 145/78, 146/69, and 146/70*

Prisoner's gender, marital status, and dependants/no dependants

Province and independent sub-division	Male					Female				
	Single	Married		Widowed		Single	Married		Widowed	
		Children	No children	Children	No children		Children	No children	Children	No children
Baghdad	779	642	368	81	70	8	30	13	12	15
Beirut	1,687	1,191	331	58	24	23	36	9	1	14
Bitlis	66	374	54	0	0	6	21	7	2	0
Canik	682	365	197	40	10	2	22	8	9	2
Edirne	2,881	3,941	731	178	119	51	239	52	33	29
The Hijaz	267	46	71	3	16	15	2	4	11	14
Istanbul	2,421	631	812	24	31	48	45	33	1	10
Kastamonu	305	245	43	43	25	1	92	18	12	2
Manastır	663	1,042	323	67	46	23	67	12	6	2
Mamuretülaziz	352	506	156	129	113	8	43	17	7	12
Mosul	455	630	285	0	0	0	3	0	0	1
Yanya	513	748	215	21	2	8	41	100	33	2
Totals	11,071	10,361	3,586	644	456	193	641	273	127	103

Chart 3.9 1911–12 Prisoner marital status statistics.

Note Several provinces and independent administrative sub-divisions are not represented here because their results are not available to researchers. Not all available surveys provided data on prisoner marital status. These numbers, therefore, do not match total prison population numbers.

Source BOA, DHMBHPSM 3/36, 4/4, 4/20, 4/21, 5/1, 5/9, 6/27, and 12/70; DHMBHPS 145/2, 145/56, 145/78, 146/69, and 146/70

Province and independent sub-division	Literate males	Literate females	Illiterate males	Illiterate females
Baghdad	115	0	1,425	56
Beirut	699	3	1,751	46
Bitlis	4	0	316	31
Canik	166	0	821	23
Edirne	1,134	52	5,475	455
The Hijaz	39	0	364	45
Istanbul	1,349	18	2,519	143
Kastamonu	137	2	847	125
Manastır	412	0	1,480	99
Mamuretülaziz	299	0	1,214	79
Mosul	129	0	2,066	26
Yanya	205	5	1,076	88
Totals	**4,688**	**80**	**19,354**	**1,216**

Chart 3.10 1911–12 prisoner literacy statistics.

Note Several provinces and independent administrative sub-divisions are not represented here because their results are not available to researchers. Not all available surveys provided data on prisoner literacy. These numbers, therefore, do not match total prison population numbers.

Source *BOA, DHMBHPSM 3/36, 4/4, 4/20, 4/21, 5/1, 5/9, 6/27, and 12/70; DHMBHPS 145/2, 145/56, 145/78, 146/69, and 146/70*

The vast majority of prisoners were male (32,584 out of 34,085), whereas females made up 4.4 per cent of the prison population (1,494 out of 34,085). Nearly 24,500 inmates were under the age of forty with twenty to thirty year-olds making up almost a third of the prison population (11,395). A total of 15 per cent of the population was under the age of twenty. Women and children, therefore, made up more than 19 per cent of the total prison population. Despite their relatively small numbers, Ottoman prison reformers took great interest in these segments of the prison population. Issues of female and juvenile inmates are dealt with in Chapters 4 and 6, respectively. More than 30,000 prisoners were from the lower socio-economic classes with almost 13,000 farmers, 7,191 artisans, and 4,856 labourers. Muslims accounted for nearly 20,000 inmates, more than 7,000 were Christian, and at least 372 were Jewish. The ethno-religious, communal constitution of the prison population was generally in line with overall population percentages in the empire. In other words, it does not appear that a particular population was targeted for incarceration over another. In areas that were predominantly Bulgar, Muslim, Armenian, or Ecumenical Patriarchate Christian, they were respectively the majority of the prison population, but in mixed areas, such as Istanbul, the numbers appear to be in line with overall population percentages. Regarding marital status, at least 11,400 were single, nearly 13,000 were married, and 4,400 prisoners had children. Illiteracy was rampant among the prison population. More than 20,500 inmates could not read or write while no less than 4,800 prisoners could. The most common crimes were misdemeanour 'theft' and 'assault and battery', while roughly one-third of the prison population was imprisoned for serious offences, such as homicide and violent theft. This data is very similar to that available for other European powers during the long nineteenth century, such as Great Britain, France, Germany, or Russia, even though these states, generally, had much larger prison populations.

In addition to understanding the composition of the Ottoman prison population, these prison surveys provide important insights into Ottoman sensibilities towards crime, punishment, and criminality. Prison and criminal legal reforms worked hand in hand during this period. The extensive changes made to the IOPC and to prison policy and practice reveal a vibrant agenda of increased centralisation of power in the hands of the state through the rationalisation of law and legal procedure concerning crime and punishment. The bureaucracy removed intermediaries to its power and the state took a greater role in the lives of its population in an attempt to standardise legal proceedings, law enforcement, and punishment. The correlation between the changes made to the IOPC and the 1912 prison survey demonstrate this close correlation between reform and practice. Most of the information collected on crime in the prison surveys correlated to issues of personal rights, safety, property, and honour, thus demonstrating CUP interests in maintaining social order, public rights, and rationalising punishment in line with contemporary global sensibilities.

Ottoman statistical efforts to understand the background, identity, and criminal behaviour of inmates represent an important progression in Ottoman statecraft. They also demonstrate innovative approaches to long-held Ottoman practices concerning land registries and censuses. This is much less about rupture of practice than about continuity, transformation, and expansion of long-held Ottoman administrative policies and practices. The knowledge gained by Ottoman prison officials and the Ministry of the Interior regarding the composition of the prison population facilitate the exploration of prison conditions, everyday life, and reform efforts to organise, supervise, discipline, and rehabilitate the empire's convicts. This is the topic of Chapter 4.

Notes

1. BOA, DHMBHPSM 8/3, doc. 13.
2. Foucault, *Discipline and Punish*, pp. 148–9.
3. I have previously published portions of this chapter, particularly regarding the ethno-religious, communal, and national identities of Ottoman prisoners in 'Conceptualizing Difference' and 'Identity in the Ottoman Prison Surveys'.
4. Porter, *Rise of Statistical Thinking*, pp. 3–39.
5. Foucault, 'Essays on Governmentality', pp. 99–100.
6. Karpat, *Ottoman Population*, pp. ix and 6–7.
7. Ibid., p. 20.
8. Ibid.
9. McCarthy, *Muslims and Minorities*, pp. 163–4, and Karpat, *Ottoman Population*, p. 18.
10. Ibid.
11. Karpat, *Ottoman Population*, pp. 29–30.
12. Findely, *Bureaucratic Reform*, p. 285.
13. Karpat, *Ottoman Population*, p. 30.
14. Ibid., p. 31.
15. Ibid. and Cox, *Diversions of a Diplomat*, pp. 37 and 44.
16. Karpat, *Ottoman Population*, p. 32.
17. Findely, p. 285.
18. Hanioğlu, *Young Turks in Opposition* and *Preparation for a Revolution*; and Gelvin, *Modern Middle East*, pp. 129–30.
19. Foucault, 'Essays on Governmentality'.
20. BOA, DHMBHPSM 3/5.
21. The catalogues of the Prison Administration (BOA, DHMBHPS and BOA, DHMBHPSM) contain forty-six completed 1912 prison surveys. Provincial centres generally distributed, collected, and then submitted the completed surveys to the Prison Administration. The following references are confirmation receipts that the Prison Administration received completed prison surveys from each province: BOA, DHMBHPS 143/36, 145/22, 145/28, 145/29, 145/34, 145/35, 145/38, 145/39, 145/40, 145/41, 145/42, 145/44, 145/43, 145/48, 145/55, 145/57, 145/59, 145/60, 145/61, 145/62, 145/64, 145/67, 145/68, 145/73, 145/80, 145/81, 145/83, 145/84, 145/87, 146/1, 146/2, 146/4, 146/8, 146/18, 146/20, 146/21, 146/23, 146/24, 146/30, 146/33, 146/34, 146/36, 146/41, 146/43, 146/44, 146/45, 146/51, 146/66, and 146/72. Unfortunately, the completed surveys for the provinces of Van, Sivas, and Ankara are not available.
22. BOA, DHMBHPSM 8/3, doc. 13.

23. BOA, DHMBHPSM 5/9, doc. 4. See Figure 3.1.
24. BOA, DHMBHPSM 4/4 (Istanbul); DHMBHPSM 4/21 (Baghdad); DHMBHPSM 5/9 (Beirut); DHMBHPSM 5/1 (Canik); DHMBHPSM 4/1 (Edirne); DHMBHPSM 3/36 (the Hijaz); DHMBHPSM 145/56 and 53/34 (Kastamonu); DHMBHPSM 12/70, 14/65, and DHMBHPS 145/26 (Mamüretülaziz); DHMBHPSM 6/27 (Manastır); DHMBHPS 145/2, 146/69, and 146/70 (Mosul); and DHMBHPSM 4/20 (Yanya).
25. For the total number of prisoners from 1912–20, see BOA, DHMBHPS 145/31, 149/45, 143/93, 96/54, 163/85, and 165/97; and DHMBHPSM 12/38 and 17/32.
26. The Ottoman Government collected statistics on a much larger range of possible occupations, see Karpat, *Ottoman Population*, pp. 214–18.
27. BOA, DHMBHPSM 8/3, doc. 13.
28. Karpat, p. 218, Chart IV.10 'Professions in the Ottoman State'.
29. Berkes, pp. 289–95 and 367–410 and Hanioğlu, *Preparation for a Revolution*, pp. 305–8.
30. BOA, DHMBHPSM 3/36, 4/4, 4/20, 4/21, 5/1, 5/9, 6/27, and 12/70; DHMBHPS 145/2, 145/56, 145/78, 146/69, and 146/70. According to these records prison officials did not assign occupations to 2,525 prisoners, however, it is highly unlikely that many of them were from the professional classes. Even if all 2,525 were professionals their percentage of the prison population would only be 11.8 per cent.
31. BOA, DHMBHPS 150/3, doc. 2.
32. Ibid.
33. BOA, DHMBHPSM 8/3, doc. 13.
34. Ibid.
35. Ibid.
36. BOA, DHMBHPS 145/31.
37. BOA, DHMBHPSM 8/3, doc. 13.
38. BOA, DHMBHPS 145/31.
39. Bucknill and Utidjian, *Imperial Ottoman Penal Code*, pp. 86–92.
40. The breakdown of the prison population in 1911–12 for the provinces of Istanbul, Beirut, Baghdad, the Hijaz, and for the administrative sub-division of Canik are Istanbul: 5,942; Beirut: 4,020; Baghdad: 1,740; the Hijaz: 459; Canik: 1,767; and Bitlis: 621 (BOA, DHMBHPSM 4/4, 5/9, 4/21, 3/36, 5/1; and DHMBHPS 145/78).
41. Ibid.
42. Ibid.
43. BOA, DHMBHPSM 5/1.
44. Ibid. Information regarding the socio-economic status and occupation of those pardoned for crimes against state officials was not recorded in the Canik 1912 prison survey.
45. Kansu, *Politics in Post-Revolutionary Turkey* and Quataert, *Social Disintegration and Popular Resistance*.

46. Bucknill and Utidjian, pp. 149–70.
47. BOA, DHMBHPSM 8/3, doc. 13.
48. Ibid.
49. BOA, DHMBHPSM 5/1, 4/4, 5/9, 4/21, and 3/36; and DHMBHPS 145/78.
50. Bucknill and Utidjian, pp. 165–9.
51. BOA, DHMBHPSM 5/1, 4/4, 5/9, 4/21, and 3/36; and DHMBHPS 145/78.
52. Ibid.
53. Bucknill and Utidjian, pp. 124–45.
54. BOA, DHMBHPSM 5/1, 4/4, 5/9, 4/21, and 3/36; and DHMBHPS 145/78.
55. Ibid.
56. Göçek, *Rise of the Bourgeoisie*; Toprak, *Milli İktisat*; and Berkes, *Development of Secularism*, pp. 335–7.
57. BOA, DHMBHPSM 8/3, doc. 13.
58. Hacking, *Historical Ontology*, p. 100.
59. Yosmaoğlu, 'Counting Bodies, Shaping Souls'.
60. Ibid. and Karpat, *Ottoman Population*, p. 35.
61. Yosmaoğlu.
62. Ahmad, *Young Turks*.
63. Ibid., p. 172. He served as Minister of the Interior, Grand Vizier, Minister of Justice, and Ambassador to Vienna during the Second Constitutional Period.
64. Yosmaoğlu, pp. 64–5 and 59–62.
65. Hanioğlu, *Preparation for a Revolution*, pp. 232–3.
66. Karpat, *Ottoman Population*, p. 189.
67. There is an intense debate concerning the origins and radicalisation of Turkish nationalism claimed to be the underpinning cause of the genocides, the ethnic cleansings, and the population transfers in the Ottoman Empire post-Balkan Wars and during WWI and the Turkish War of Independence. Many assume a primordial Turkish nationalism while others more convincingly argue that its development and radicalisation resulted most directly from the Balkan Wars and the 1914 Armenian reform agreement. For works on CUP demographic engineering see Akçam, *Young Turk Crimes* and Dündar, *Crime of Numbers*. The contentious nature of the debate concerning the origins of CUP ethnic nationalism is clearly demonstrated in Şükrü Hanioğlu and Feroz Ahmad's public exchange in the *AHR*, 101(5) (December 1996), pp. 1,589–90 and 102(4) (October 1997), pp. 1,301–3.
68. BOA, DHMBHPSM 3/5. *Mahkumin* literally means, 'convict'.
69. *Rum*, in this context, should be tanslated as Ecumenical Patriarchate instead of Greek Orthodox. Many scholars often incorrectly construe 'Greek' as a national identifier when discussing segements of the Ottoman Empire's Christian subjects. The word 'Greek' is not germane to the Ottoman language. The Turkish word '*Grek*' is borrowed from the West. Ottoman Turkish has a separate germane term for a Greek foreign national – *Yunanlı*, which is a derivative of the Ottoman Turkish name for the Greek nation-state – *Yunanıstan*. The Western term 'Greek' is itself a Western nationalist con-

struct that portions of the Greek-speaking, Ottoman Christian population adopted in the early nineteenth century in order to be identified as a 'separate' nation and gain independence from the empire. For these reasons, translating the term *Rum* as Greek Orthodox is confusing and misleading.

70. BOA, DHMBHPS 3/5.
71. Ercan, 'Non-Muslim Communities'.
72. Karpat, *Ottoman Population*, Statistical Appendices, pp. 108–89. In each of the empire's censuses the categories of identity all ran along confessional lines with the simplest being 'Muslim' and 'Non-Muslim'. The more detailed population surveys requested the numbers of 'Muslims, Cossacks, Greek Orthodox [Ecumenical Patriarchate Christians (*Rumler*)], Armenians, Bulgars, Wallachians, Greek [Ecumenical Patriarchate Christians (*Rumler*)] Catholics, Armenian Catholics, Protestants, Latins, Maronites, Syriacs, Chaldeans, Jacobites, Jews, Samaritans, Yezidis, Gypsies, and Foreigners'. This categorisation came from the 1905/6 Ottoman population survey (Ibid., pp. 162–3). The CUP prison survey appears to have utilised the 1905/6 format, but simplified it to include what the Prison Administration saw as the largest population groupings while combining the smaller groups under the heading of 'Other Ottoman Communities'.
73. Ercan, p. 385.
74. Karpat, *Ottoman Population*, pp. 35 and 46.
75. Ercan; and Braude, 'Foundation Myths'.
76. *Milel* is the plural of *millet*.
77. The Prison Administration never collected the 'ethnic' identity of Ottoman prisoners. Throughout Ottoman history, however, the bureaucracy did recognise differences between Muslim groups, such as Albanians, Circassians, Kurds, Arabs, and Turks, but these groups were not officially counted in population censuses, nor were they viewed as distinct racial or national groups. They were part of the Muslim subjects of the empire and depending on contingent circumstances were favoured or fouled by the central administration. The CUP collected demographic information on Kurds, Armenians, and Nestorians in Southeastern Anatolia as part of a larger demographic engineering programme aimed at resettling Muslim refugees and Ottoman Christians around the empire as a result of the Balkan Wars (Dündar, *İttihat ve Terakki*, pp. 85–6). For examples of the demographic maps produced by the CUP, see Dündar, *Modern Türkiye'nin Şifresi*, pp. 452–62.
78. BOA, DHEUMMTK 32/13 and 8/23; and Karpat, *Ottoman Population*, pp. 188–9.
79. BOA, DHMBHPSM 3/36, doc. 2.
80. BOA, DHMBHPSM 4/21, doc. 1.
81. BOA, DHMBHPSM 5/9, doc. 20 (Hayfa); DHMBHPSM 5/9 (Beirut); and DHMBHSM 4/20 (Yanya).
82. BOA, DHMBHPSM 6/27 (Manastır), DHMBHPSM 12/70, 14/65, and 145/26

(Mamüretülaziz), DHMBHPS 145/2 and 147/59 (Mosul), DHMBHPSM 4/4, DHMBHPS 147/93, and 148/4 (Istanbul).

83. BOA, DHMBHPS 150/3, docs 1–2 (front and back). See Figure 3.9.
84. Redhouse, *Turkish*, p. 488 and *Redhouse Sözlüğü*, pp. 1,075 and 1,111; Devellioğlu, *Osmanlıca*, p. 1011; and Sami, *Kamus-i Türki*, p. 370.
85. Braude, pp. 69–88.
86. Sami, p. 1400.
87. BOA, DHMBHPS 150/3, docs 1–3 (1914 survey); and DHMBHPS 8/3, doc. 13 (1912 survey).
88. The seminal works promoting the notion that the CUP was a Turkish nationalist organisation engaged in the Turkification of the Ottoman Empire are Berkes, *Development of Secularism* and *Turkish Nationalism*; Heyd, *Foundations of Turkish Nationalism*; Lewis, *Emergence of Modern Turkey*; Kushner, *Rise of Turkish Nationalism*; and Hanioğlu, *Young Turks in Opposition* and *Preparation for a Revolution*. More recent works that complicate these primordial nationalist approaches include Dündar, *İttihat ve Terakki* and *Modern Türkiye'nin şifresi*; and Ülker, 'Contextualising "Turkification"'.
89. Schull, 'Conceptualizing Difference'.
90. See www.census.gov/history/www/through_the_decades/fast_facts/1910_fast_facts.html and www.justicepolicy.org/images/upload/00-05_rep_pun-ishingdecade_ac.pdf for details regarding the 1910 US Census and prison population.

4

The Spatialisation of Incarceration: Reforms, Response and the Reality of Prison Life

From July 1909 to August 1910 Ahmed Şerif, an Ottoman journalist, travelled throughout the Balkans, Anatolia, and some of the empire's Arabic-speaking territories reporting on what he observed for the *Tanin* newspaper (the semi-official newspaper of the Ottoman Government). Of special interest to him was investigating the effectiveness of government administration in each area. As part of each of his journeys he visited each town's government buildings, courts, police, gendarme, and prison. His reports are detailed and surprisingly candid concerning administrative problems, such as corruption, nepotism, and abuse by government officials. These reports provide rich insights into the state of the empire in the early years of the Second Constitutional Period.[1]

During his visit to the district of Karaağaç (Şarkıkaraağaç) located in Konya province from 9 to 13 September 1909, Şerif investigated its prison. As he walked into the government offices he came to the door of the prison dorm room, which was across a narrow garden. A foul odour emanated from the small metal grate in the door that acted as the prison's only source of fresh air. Looking through the opening, Şerif saw a relatively large room holding about 25 prisoners who were either lying down or sitting and who were talking to one another. Their faces, however, were 'pale, death shaded, and bloodless'.[2]

As he entered the prison, he was overcome with what he would later describe as the worst stench imaginable, forcing him to cover his mouth and nose. He also found the prison to be poorly lit, with only one small lamp and no natural source of light. Conditions as he saw and felt them were extremely damp, miserable, and wretched. At the back of the room stood a government toilet (*hükümet abdesthanesi*) that emptied its contents into an open sewer and emitted a horrific stench that filled the entire room. He could not see how anyone could survive being imprisoned in such horrible conditions.[3]

With his anger kindled, he marched straight to the prison director and demanded an explanation. He received only deflecting excuses, such as a lack of funds and no authority to make changes. Şerif then proceeded to the court house to meet with the judge and other governing officials who made similar excuses in an attempt to blame their superiors at the provincial level.[4] In the end, he left Karaağaç angered that the town's administration was so inept and spineless. Throughout the rest of his visits in Konya he used the awful conditions of this district's prison as the standard to measure the conditions of all the other prisons. While conditions in each of the other prisons were still poor, none was as bad as Karaağaç.[5]

When punishment shifted from the plethora of options it had been in the early modern era to primarily incarceration in the nineteenth century, Ottoman authorities faced a series of challenges that Karaağaç prison starkly illustrates. As a 'total institution', the prison constitutes 'a place of residence and work where a large number of like-situated individuals, cut off from the wider society for an appreciable period of time, together lead an enclosed, formally administered round of life'.[6] Incarceration requires intense and continuous supervision, housing, provisioning, and health and hygienic measures that raise other logistical and disciplinary problems. With the discontinuance of incarceration in the Imperial Shipyards where prisoners were continuously employed, authorities now had a large number of convicts incarcerated together in idleness. As discussed in Chapter 2, Ottoman authorities and prison reformers spent much of the nineteenth century dealing with the unprecedented scale of problems caused by this shift to incarceration.

The CUP inherited these concerns and problems when it seized power in 1908, and solving them was a matter of high priority. During the Second Constitutional Period it addressed prison conditions, order, and discipline on three interrelated fronts: 1. Constructing new prisons and transforming existing ones, 2. Improving health and hygienic conditions, and 3. Implementing programmes to facilitate the rehabilitation of inmates, such as secular and religious education, skills training, and labour. These efforts resulted in the production of incarcerated space by physically dividing and separating the prison population according to differences in crime, health, age, and gender. Although these efforts peaked in the Second Constitutional Period, their origins can be traced to the 1880 Prison Regulation (*Hapishaneler ve Tevkifhaneler Nizamnamesi*), which the CUP implemented at an unprecedented level.

This chapter argues that through these reforms and the implementation of the 1880 Prison Regulation, the Prison Administration and the CUP engaged in what Henri Lefebvre called the 'production of space' to create well-ordered prisons and to address the awful conditions illustrated above.[7] The Ottoman administration spent a great deal of time, energy, and resources improving prison conditions. These efforts exemplify Ottoman attempts to assume greater responsibility for the welfare of its population, particularly prisoners, improving public health and hygiene, provisioning, and regulating inmate interactions. Many of these responsibilities were traditionally reserved for individuals and the family. This chapter argues that this intervention represents the expansion of Ottoman state patriarchy and the Ottoman 'nanny state'. Despite the best of state intentions, an investigation of reform implementation and the actual experiences of prisoners demonstrate the variegated and often haphazard nature of prison reform programmes, and the effects that these efforts actually had on their intended targets.

This chapter consists of three main, interrelated, sections. The first investigates the conditions and challenges facing inmates and administrators in the empire's sprawling prison network through the in-depth investigation of Karesi central prison (*Karesi merkez hapishanesi*). The second section looks at specific attempts at creating the well-ordered prison through the production of space in terms of new building projects, prison architectural designs, health and hygiene regimens, and the concrete ways the Prison Administration organised inmates. Finally, this chapter looks at Ottoman efforts to rehabilitate convicted criminals. These three sections are linked by an emphasis on the theme of state patriarchy and an evaluation of reform and reality.

Prison Conditions and Daily Life

As discussed in the previous two chapters and as illustrated above, prison conditions, including order and discipline, during the nineteenth century were woefully inadequate. Horrible conditions, relaxed regimens, dilapidated buildings, corruption, escapes, and abuse typified prison experience. The 1880 Prison Regulation was never implemented systematically or comprehensively throughout the empire until the Second Constitutional Period. In the Hamidian era, administrators built numerous prisons, but few were up to modern health, hygiene, or architectural standards. Additionally, there was a general lack of regular funding for prisons, including for their management and upkeep, resulting in the dilapidation of many of these newly built structures.[8] Periodic foreign and Ottoman inspections of the empire's prisons, such as those conducted by Ambassador Canning, Abdülhamid II's 'Commission for Expediting Initiatives and Reforms' (*Tesri-i Muamelat ve Islahat Komisyonu*), Ahmet Şerif, and the CUP Prison Administration confirm these assertions.[9]

The central prison in the provincial sub-division of Karesi is an excellent example of the problems faced by prison administrators from the 1870s through WWI. In Karesi's 1871–2 provincial budget, central Ottoman authorities allocated 40,165 *kuruş* for the construction of a new central prison. According to building reports, it cost 24,000 *kuruş* to build.[10] Three years after the Hamidian regime issued the 1880 Prison Regulation a report revealed that the prison contained three women incarcerated for serious crimes and requested that a women's prison (*kadınlar hapishanesi*) be built to house them.[11] Within months, the Council of State approved the request and allocated more than 11,000 *kuruş* to the construction of the prison.[12] In 1897, an earthquake severely damaged the government buildings, including Karesi's prisons. Its municipal council sent a request to the imperial government for funds to use to rebuild these structures and to expand the main prison to hold a maximum of 350 prisoners. It was approved, and 120,000 *kuruş* were allocated to the rebuilding of the area, including its prisons.[13]

As discussed in Chapters 2 and 3, in 1911 the newly established Prison Administration undertook a survey that included Karesi central prison and initiated a series of measures to build new prisons and repair older structures. These plans came to a screeching halt when the CUP lost power in the summer of 1912. In 1914, after its hiatus from power ended, the CUP initiated and conducted another comprehensive prison survey. This questionnaire (*sual varakası*) was distributed to every prison in the empire. It contained a series of questions regarding the state and condition of each prison facility. It is unique, because it calls for local prison administrators to write extensive comments and suggestions about the specific needs of their respective prisons.[14] To make their cases, some prison directors included photographs of their facilities demonstrating dilapidated edifices, massive overcrowding, and horrific living conditions.[15] Other administrators included proposed architectural designs of prisons that they wanted to be built in their districts.[16]

In the case of Karesi's central prison, the warden reported in the 1914 survey that there were 794 prisoners incarcerated there, including twenty-two females. The prison built in 1897 was designed to hold 350 prisoners. Needless to say, prison conditions, according to the report, were severely crowded. In fact, they were so 'narrow, dark, crowded, and unhealthy' that the warden deemed the prison to be beyond repair and proposed that a new one be built in its place. To illustrate just how dire prison conditions were, the warden included the following four photographs of the prison (Figures 4.1, 4.2, 4.3, and 4.4).[17] These photographs graphically illustrate the terrible shape of many of the empire's prisons. They also demonstrate just how much work the Prison Administration had to do if it was committed to comprehensive prison reform. Photographs from this provincial prison show that conditions were severely overcrowded. Prisoners were housed in tiny chicken-coop-esque hovels (*kümes*), make-shift tents described as 'gypsy dwellings' (*çerge baraka*), and huts that resembled dilapidated stalls in a local market. Each unit contained as many as two or even three prisoners. The roofing and walls of the prisoners' quarters were made of simple wood or canvas and were held down by rocks, bricks, and clay shingles. The structures depicted in these photographs were, in fact, additions built onto the prison in order to accommodate almost two and half times the prison's intended capacity.[18]

Generally speaking, prisons throughout the empire were located next to or within fortress compounds and other government buildings with very few being properly enclosed. These prison conditions made escape a common occurrence. According to archival records, throughout the Second Constitutional Period there were constant problems with overcrowding and prisoner escapes. In fact, in several reports sent to the Prison Administration, overcrowding, poor conditions, and lack of supervision and discipline were listed as the main reasons for prison breakouts.[19] Judging from Figures 4.2 and 4.4, escape from Karesi's central prison would have been quite easy. The walls were either non-existent or they were very low and weak, being made from materials that meant they were not structurally sound. Furthermore, the town, just outside of the prison, was easily accessed by simply climbing over the roof. As escapes were so common, the Prison Administration attempted to address this issue in April 1912 by issuing a general directive regarding prison order, discipline, and the prevention of prisoner escapes. The directive emphasised that the prevention of prisoner escapes and general prison order was the responsibility of the prison cadre and that most escapes were the result of negligence on the part of prison employees or even direct assistance from prison employees.[20]

Another way that the Prison Administration attempted to remedy the chronic problem of prison escapes was by alleviating overcrowding. With the approval of the Ministry of Justice, the Prison Administration periodically extended amnesty to prisoners who had served two-thirds of their sentence, who had been convicted of less serious offences (*cünha ve kabahat*), and who were well-behaved.[21] Authorities also transferred many inmates to less crowded facilities in adjacent sub-districts and provinces.[22]

Internal order, security, and discipline were also severely lacking. As evidenced by the Karesi prison photographs, inmates were not subject to work details, nor were they gainfully employed. In fact, during WWI, the Directorate of Prisons solicited the number of employed prisoners. Out of a total of 478 prisoners incarcerated in Karesi's central prison and jail only

Figure 4.1 'An example of the makeshift structures, tents, and shacks [located] at the walls of the central prison in Karesi Sancak' (*Karesi sancağı merkez liva hapishanesi hıvalisindeki çerge baraka ve külliyelerden birer nümune*).

Source *BOA, DHMBHPSM 10/14, doc. 12*

twenty inmates worked in some capacity inside the prison.[23] Most prisoners throughout the empire, including Karesi, sat idle all day, drinking tea, smoking, playing backgammon, and gambling.[24] Gambling was such a problem that many fights, injuries, deaths, and prisoner–guard collusions were blamed on it. In 1922, a gambling-related fight that broke out in the Istanbul penitentiary resulted in one death and seven injuries before the gendarme could suppress it.[25]

Prisoner fights and riots also resulted from a general lack of internal order, supervision, and discipline. For example, in 1913 a fight among prisoners broke out in the Siirt administrative sub-division (*sancak*) in Bitlis province that resulted in the injury of several prisoners. The fight was attributed to the smuggling of weapons (*kesici aletleri*) into the prison, which had exacerbated tensions among inmates.[26] No doubt, much smuggling occurred in Ottoman prisons with the consent of prison guards.[27] Prison fights similar to Siirt's were common place in Ottoman prisons. Archival records attest to numerous uprisings, disturbances, and

Figure 4.2 'Huts located on the eastern side of an interior section of the Karesi Sancak's central prison' (*Karesi sancağı merkez liva hapishanesinin şark cephesinde bir kısm-i dahili barakaları*).

Source *BOA, DHMBHPSM 10/14, doc. 13*

other disorderly conduct throughout the prison system and discuss the Prison Administration's continuous efforts to prevent such occurrences.[28]

Ottoman prisons and jails suffered from a general lack of supervision. In 1915, Karesi central prison employed only six male prison guards (*gardiyanlar*), who received a monthly salary of 200 *kuruş* each. It also employed one female prison guard (*nisa gardiyan*) at a monthly salary of 150 *kuruş*.[29] Considering that the previous year's prison population consisted of 772 males, it would be impossible for six guards to provide adequate inmate supervision. Judging from the photographs, it also appears that there was no separation of prisoners according to crimes committed or whether they were accused or convicted. This is not surprising since the prison was severely overcrowded.

Similar to the prisons inspected by Ahmed Şerif, inmates at Karesi's central prison also suffered from poor health conditions. Overcrowding exponentially facilitates the spread of communicable diseases, such as typhus, typhoid fever, and cholera. Add to these threats the open sewage

Figure 4.3 'A sectional view facing the entrance to Karesi Sancak's central prison'
(*Karesi sancağı merkez liva hapishanesinin medhali karşısının bir kısm-ı manzarası*).
Source *BOA, DHMBHPSM 10/14, doc. 14*

running through the prison huts, as illustrated in Figure 4.2, and it becomes obvious how easily cholera epidemics could ravage a prison.

Judging by the cooking grates and the utensils strewn about the huts and the prison compound, prisoners cooked their own food, which was usually supplied by family members or local charitable organisations. Despite directives contained in the 1880 Prison Regulation, local prisons rarely provided food to inmates apart from a few small loaves of bread on a daily basis.[30] They did, however, often hire outside contractors, such as bakers and grocers, to provide food for the prisoners.[31] As prisoners often cooked for themselves and stoves were the main heating source in dormitory-style prisons, fires regularly broke out, causing death and extensive property damage. For example, in March 1918 a fire broke out in the Beyoğlu women's jail that caused far-reaching damage. Prison officials conducted an investigation and allocated funds for the repairs. During this period, the female inmates were housed at other local prison facilities, such as the Istanbul women's penitentiary and the women's jail in Üsküdar.[32]

Figure 4.4 'A section of the chicken coop-esque huts in the southern part of Karesi Sancak's central prison' (*Karesi sancağı merkez liva hapishanesi cenub çephesindeki kümes şeklinde barakaların bir kismi*).

Source *BOA, DHMBHPSM 10/14, doc. 15*

The shocking photographs and report detailing the awful conditions and overcrowding at Karesi central prison led to an official visit by Talat Pasha (Interior Minister) in 1914. Talat Pasha declared the prison to be 'crowded, terrible, filthy, and unacceptable' and said that it would be replaced. In 1915, a new prison of approximately 14,000 m² was built on an almost two-acre (6.8 *dönüm*) wooded plot of land just outside the city fortress at the cost of about 24,000 *kuruş*. This new prison was two stories tall, had seven separate wards intended to house 300 prisoners, and had indoor toilets.[33] After the new prison had been built, conditions improved, but overcrowding persisted. In 1917, prison reports indicate that it held 417 prisoners (all of them male) and continued to employ a total of seven prison guards. It still suffered from overcrowding, but not to the extent that it had done two years earlier. The local municipality was also supplying the prisoners with proper provisions.[34] These improvements reduced the risk of fire, greatly ameliorated the spread of communicable diseases, and improved prisoner health and living conditions, despite continued over-crowding. Through the implementation of the 1880 Prison Regulation, the state assumed greater levels of responsibility for and power over its prisoners, although there were limits to its success.

This brief history of Karesi central prison provides a sense of the experiences and challenges facing both administrators and inmates. While the examples of prison conditions at Karesi and Karaağaç were extreme, poor conditions and difficult circumstances were the norm throughout the empire. For example, in 1905 officials at Istanbul's penitentiary proposed building sheds outside the prison in order to ease overcrowding and halt the spread of a disease epidemic by isolating sick prisoners.[35]

The vast majority of prisons suffered from bad sanitary conditions caused by poor ventilation and lighting, an inadequate potable water supply, and a lack of running water. Most prisons had no washing facilities and toilets consisted of a hole dug in the earth for communal use. Regimens stipulating regular cleanings of prison facilities and hygienic measures for inmates were rarely implemented. As a result, outbreaks of cholera, typhoid fever, typhus, scabies, and other communicable diseases were rampant in the squalid and fetid conditions under which prisoners languished. These conditions resulted in numerous deaths each year.[36] Issues related to poor health and hygiene, as illustrated in Figures 4.1, 4.2, 4.3, and 4.4, constituted a major source of concern and focus for the Prison Administration.[37] In fact, when announcing its first comprehensive reform programme in April 1912, it justified renovating existing prisons and constructing new ones by claiming that these reforms would bring health and hygiene conditions into conformity with the 'laws of civilisation'.[38] The existence of unsanitary conditions was also the most common justification given by local prison administrators for the construction of new prisons.[39]

Creating the Well-ordered Prison

As discussed in Chapter 2 and above, the Ottoman Ministry of Justice issued the first comprehensive prison regulation for the empire in 1880. This regulation meticulously detailed the responsibilities of all prison officials and employees. It also stipulated clear health and hygiene standards, prison labour, regimens, prison organisation, and the spatial separation of different types of prisoners.[40] This was a thoroughly modern and progressive prison regulation according to nineteenth-century standards. It attempted to implement modern concepts of time and space in order to facilitate prison health, discipline, and organisation for the maintenance of order and the rehabilitation of the incarcerated. When implemented, this regulation engaged in the 'production of space'. In the minds of prison administrators, a key to prison order and inmate rehabilitation was the 'spatialisation of incarceration'. This entailed dividing and organising the physical, mental, and social structure of the prison into specific areas and categories that facilitated proper health, order, discipline, and rehabilitation.[41]

As discussed in Chapter 2, the Prison Administration drew up new architectural designs; constructed new prisons and repaired existing ones; prepared and promulgated new regulations; and implemented new prison regimens in order to centralise power and instil discipline, order, cleanliness, and industriousness within the prison for both prisoners and employees. As early as 1910, the CUP began its attempts to remedy the awful conditions found in Ottoman prisons by establishing a commission for the purpose of producing a general plan for prison reform and the construction of new prisons.[42] This commission formulated a comprehensive prison construction programme that was initiated in late 1911.[43]

During the Second Constitutional Period, the Prison Administration viewed the design and construction of modern prisons as the remedy for poor sanitary conditions. These new prison designs incorporated the latest developments in order to facilitate standards of health, hygiene, discipline, and surveillance, and in order to promote prisoner rehabilitation through labour. Through the production of special modern spatial relationships these new prisons were supposed to remedy the problems of disorder and death that typified *ancien régime* (Hamidian era) prisons.

In order to create the environment that would bring the health and hygiene of Ottoman prisons in conformity with the 'laws of civilisation', each new prison was to include washrooms (*çamaşırhaneler*), toilets (*apteshaneler*), running water, electricity, proper ventilation, dormitory-style wards where prisoners of similar criminal convictions would be housed together, courtyards for exercise, and kitchens (*mutfaklar*). Each prison would also include a separate hospital or infirmary depending on prison capacity in order to isolate the sick from the healthy. Prison budgets and reports delineated the costs of medicines and treatments and reported them to the Prison Administration. Prison authorities also introduced new regimens regarding cleanliness, such as scheduled prison cleanings, whitewashing walls with lye, regularly changing and washing prisoners' clothing and bedding, frequent bathing, and the washing of hands before eating. Finally, each prison was required to employ a doctor. If the prison was small (on the district level), several prisons in the same area collectively employed a physician.[44] These seemingly obvious practices were initially mandated by the 1880 Prison Regulation, but their full implementation was not attempted until CUP rule. For example, in late 1913, Istanbul's penitentiary experienced an outbreak of cholera and scabies. Health measures to combat these communicable diseases and to prevent future outbreaks included the distribution of clean, new clothing to poor prisoners; introducing the practice of quarantining new inmates prior to their introduction into the general prison population; having the prison physician examine prisoners prior to their release to prevent them leaving with a communicable disease; making sure that prison bathrooms were in good repair; and ensuring that the prison hospital had access to fresh running water.[45]

Regarding the affect that these new spatial relationships had on prison order and discipline, prison administrators segregated inmates according to severity of crime (serious and less serious offenders), convicted and accused, age (children and adults), health (sick and well), and gender. In some cases, authorities allocated separate space for each of these divisions within the same prison, but often different prisons were constructed to meet these needs. For example, if there were enough female prisoners then a separate women's prison (*kadın* or *nisa hapishanesi*) was built alongside a men's prison, as was done in Karesi.

Less serious offenders with a sentence of less than three months' incarceration were usually kept on the district (*kaza*) level. Those prisoners with sentences of up to three years (either *cünha* or *cinayet*) were incarcerated at a sub-division level (*liva* or *sancak*) prison. Only serious offenders with sentences of three years or more were incarcerated in central prisons (*merkez hapihaneler*) on the sub-divisional and provincial levels. Prisoners convicted of serious crimes and sentenced to hard labour (*kürek*) of five years or more were incarcerated in penitentiaries (*hapishaneler-i umumi*) in specially designated cities around the empire, such as Istanbul, Edirne, İzmir, and Sinop.[46] Ottoman prison reformers eventually separated children from adult prisoners by releasing them to their parents or guardians or by sending them to reformatories (*ıslahaneler*). Prisoners aged from fifteen to nineteen were still incarcerated in regular prisons. They now, however, received reduced sentences in comparison with adults and were separated from them in specially designated areas within the prison.[47] New and refurbished prisons also included special quarters for prison employees, such as offices, guard rooms, and observation towers, as well as sleeping quarters. The style and capacity of prisons varied according to location, type of prisoner, and security needs. Prison capacities ranged from sixty to 1,000 prisoners.[48]

While many of these regulations were effectively implemented, as demonstrated by the number of new prisons built for male and female prisoners, these reforms did not go uncontested.[49] Prison administrators attempted to hire more guards, but war-time needs for additional troops often took precedence over staffing prisons.[50] Prisoners also complained about the new spatial divisions and organisation. For example, during an investigation into allegations of prisoner abuse and administrative corruption at the Sinop penitentiary in late 1912, one prisoner (Ismail, Fatsa'lı Hasan Ağa) took the opportunity during his questioning to express his displeasure with the prison's new system of organisation. He claimed that the prison was divided into three wards and that the prisoners were no longer allowed to walk around interacting freely with one another. In his opinion this caused prisoner distress and low morale, especially for those incarcerated in a prison fortress, such as Sinop. In response to the prisoner's assertions, the inspector (Sami Bey) argued that the Prison Administration promoted these divisions in order to prevent violence and prison escapes. Ismail rejected these rationales, claiming that no such problems would occur if greater prisoner conviviality were allowed.[51] This exchange confirms several important points. New spatial relationships and prisoner organisation were being implemented; prisoners were directly affected by these changes; and, finally, prisoners voiced their displeasure through official channels, expecting to be heard by the Prison Administration.

Gender also played an important role in the production of space in Ottoman prisons. In fact, prison authorities spent a considerable amount of time and energy creating female gendered space if one considers it in relation to the overall numbers of women prisoners. In 1917, women represented less than 6 per cent of the total prison population, at a figure of 1,249 out of 21,666 prisoners.[52] This percentage was up more than 2 per cent since 1915, when women made up about 3.4 per cent of the prison population (976 out of 28,773 inmates).[53] In 1917, the provinces of Ankara (139), Aydın (183), and Kastamonu (218) had the most female prisoners. Karesi also had a high number of incarcerated women (55). The vast majority of these female inmates (at least 80 per cent) were Muslim, single, and unemployed, and most were incarcerated for less than a year. The most common crimes committed by women were assault and petty theft. Women incarcerated for lesser offences (*kabahat ve cünha*) were held in district prisons. When there were only a few female prisoners in a particular region a room was rented for them in a government building (*konak*) or they were entrusted to local religious leaders (Christian, Jewish, or Muslim).[54] A significant percentage of female prisoners (nearly 20 per cent) were incarcerated for serious offences, such as murder, banditry, violent theft, and brutal assault. These inmates would be incarcerated in central prisons, such as Karesi, or in penitentiaries, depending on the length of their sentence.[55]

The 1880 Prison Regulation gave very clear instructions regarding the creation of gendered space within Ottoman prisons. This should be of no great surprise since gendered space is an important aspect of most prisons in the modern period. Gendered space also has deep roots in Middle Eastern and Islamic societies. These regulations stipulate that female prisoners be supervised by female guards and special provisions be made for incarcerated women who were pregnant or nursing.[56] All three of these issues (gendered space, gendered supervision, and gendered provisioning) were not adequately addressed during the Hamidian era, but they became pressing issues during the Second Constitutional Period as the CUP assumed greater control and authority over crime and punishment. One case in particular exemplifies the anxiety felt by the Prison Administration regarding female inmates and its desire to assume greater responsibility for them.

In 1913, an incident involving a male prison guard by the name of Mahmud Çavuş and two female prisoners at the women's prison in Karesi came to light. Prison officials investigated Mahmud Çavuş for running a prostitution ring from the prison. Apparently, he smuggled female inmates out of the women's prison and forced them into prostitution for his financial gain. As a result of the investigation, Mahmud Çavuş was fired from his job, fined 225 *kuruş*, and imprisoned for three months. The condition of the female inmates forced into prostitution was never mentioned in the report.[57]

Similar violations led officials within the Prison Administration to place the treatment of female prisoners under closer scrutiny and push for important reforms regarding the incarceration, supervision, provisioning, and rehabilitation of female prisoners across the empire. As a result of this closer scrutiny, specific questions arose regarding the incarceration of convicted female sex-workers and women incarcerated with small children. There was a desperate need for the creation of better and safer conditions for female prisoners. The Mahmud Çavuş incident only drew greater attention to the pressing issue of female inmate conditions and the necessity of hiring more female guards (*nisa gardiyanları*).

In early 1912, the Prison Administration issued a directive to implement fully the 1880 Prison Regulation regarding strict gendered space within all of the empire's prisons. In essence, the 1912 directive states that in areas where there are no women's prisons, budgetary allotments should be made to rent space for female prisoners and hire female guards for their supervision. In new prisons under construction, a secure, specially designated area for female inmates was to be separated completely from the male section. In districts where prisons already existed, separate secure wards were to be created for women prisoners. If it was not possible to secure a separate place for female inmates within the main prison, then they should be removed to a neighbouring district with proper facilities.[58]

This regulation led many prisons around the empire to make alterations to their facilities in order to provide separate quarters for female prisoners. Where there were only a few females or where the conditions were so crowded that a separate female area was not feasible, rooms in government buildings (*konaklar*) or police barracks were rented for female prisoners. For example, in 1914, officials in Turgutlu, a district in Aydın province, established a 'women's prison' to house Ayşe Kadın by renting space in a local government building for 60 *kuruş* a month.[59] Another example is the sub-division of Kütahya, wherein a local government building, a police barracks, and even a house were all rented in order to accommodate female prisoners.[60]

Officials also made special provisions for the gendered treatment of sick female inmates. A 1916 case involving overcrowding and health concerns in the women's wing of Istanbul's penitentiary called for the allocation of space and funding to create a special women's hospital for ill female inmates. Officials requested four separate wards (*koğuşlar*) to accommodate up to forty ill female prisoners. The directive sent by the Ministry of Justice to the Ministry of the Interior stipulated that if this space was not available in the prison itself, then the ill female prisoners should be sent to another prison hospital or to a civilian hospital or rooms should be rented in order to accommodate the gendered space necessary to care for them.[61] At this time Istanbul's penitentiary contained a total of thirty-three female inmates.[62] Perhaps this new facility was supposed to house ill female prisoners from the seven other prisons and jails located in Istanbul province. The total female prison population in these facilities, however, was only fory-eight at the time.[63]

Safeguarding female honour by separating the general female prison population from female sex-workers is another example of prison officials creating female gendered space and Ottoman state patriarchy. Separating certain types of prisoners from others, however, is not new to Ottoman prison regulations. As mentioned above, there was a requirement to separate convicted and accused persons as well as to separate serious and petty offenders. There was, however, an extensive discussion concerning separating female sex-workers (a lesser offence) from other female inmates.[64] Safeguarding the honour of women was an important responsibility assumed by the state at this time and was a common theme in public discourse.[65] There was absolutely no discussion, however, of separating male sex-worker from other male inmates. This is an unusual situation. There are no other examples of prisoners convicted of lesser crimes being separated from the general prison population unless they were sick or being punished for bad behaviour. Here is an ironic situation of the state attempting to safeguard the 'morality' of women and by extension 'the family' by shielding petty criminals from one another.

As stated in the 1880 Prison Regulation and in numerous directives issued by the Prison Administration, female prisoners were not supposed to be directly supervised by male guards. It was a lack of female guards that led to the Mahmud Çavuş incident. The CUP made it a special priority to hire more female prison guards. It viewed the prison cadre as linchpins of prison reform and prisoner rehabilitation, and the key to ending corruption, guard–prisoner collusion, as well as prisoner exploitation and abuse. This assumption applied equally to female and male prison cadre. Unfortunately, when the CUP came to power, the training and morality of prison guards was poor and the number was too few.

The need for more female prison cadre was especially critical. According to the 1880 Prison Regulation, female guards answered only to the chief prison officer (*ser gardiyan*) and the warden (*müdir*). No male prison personnel was supposed to enter the female wing of the prison, except if there was an extreme event (such as a fire or an uprising), and then only the chief prison officer could enter with a sufficient number of guards to handle the situation. The chief officer was then required to submit a report to the warden detailing the incident. Not even the warden himself was supposed to be anywhere near female inmates without a female guard present.[66] The ideal female or male prison guard would be educated, of good moral character, and familiar with penal law and regulations. Despite the great importance placed on hiring female prison guards, they were paid, at most, two-thirds of the wage of their male counterparts (50–100 *kuruş* monthly).[67] Female guards, however, were given considerable autonomy to perform their duties. They were essential to maintaining the gendered space and supervision needed to run a well-ordered prison.[68]

All prisoners were supposed to be rehabilitated in order to become contributing members of society, but special provisions were made in this regard for women and children that were not made for adult males. These included reduced prison sentences, easier pardons, and clergy supervision. Of chief concern were inmates who were pregnant, nursing, and/ or incarcerated with young children. By 1914, the Directorate of Prisons made concerted efforts to care for women who fell into these categories. It directed prisons to allocate additional food to pregnant women, nursing mothers, and women incarcerated with children under the age of six.[69] Young children were allowed to remain with their mothers during incarceration. According to local custom and Islamic law, children should remain with their mothers until at least age six. Interestingly, these documents reveal the Directorate of Prisons' concern that children incarcerated with their mothers would be adversely influenced by other female convicts. Authorities feared that children aged six and older would become maladjusted and more prone to a life of crime through their extended exposure to prison life. In response to these fears, one proposed solution called for placing the mother and child in a special area in the Istanbul *Darülaceze* (poor house or orphanage) where they would be isolated from the institution's general population. If the woman, however, had family or friends (*kimsesiz değil*) then they would be assigned guardianship of the child.[70]

Both the Prison Administration and the Directorate of Prisons made the improvement of prison conditions for women a special priority during the Second Constitutional Period. Even though women made up less than 6 per cent of the total prison population, administrators made provisions to provide separate space and special supervision and provisioning for female inmates. Therefore, Ottoman prisons became sites for gendered space, gendered supervision, and gendered provisioning wherein the state assumed greater responsibility for its female prisoners.

Prisoner Rehabilitation through Education and Labour

One of the main purposes of incarceration for Ottoman reformers, at least in the ideal, was the prisoner's rehabilitation and reintroduction to society as a productive citizen. Prison administrators and reformers viewed inmate rehabilitation as a multifaceted project that had to be implemented on a variety of fronts. These fronts included moral rehabilitation, education through instruction and productive labour, and, finally, proper discipline and supervision by competent, properly trained, and morally upright prison cadre. Similar to most prison reforms throughout world in the nineteenth century, Ottoman reformers met with relatively little success in implementing their vision of rehabilitation. Their efforts, successes, and failures do provide valuable insights into broader social and political issues.

As discussed in Chapter 2, Ottoman officials participated in international prison conferences and adapted many assumptions regarding incarceration, its purpose, and methods to the empire. One central concept was prisoner rehabilitation, which was not new to Islamic societies. The idea of reforming the wayward soul runs deep within Islamic law and practice. Punishment is seen as a key ingredient in reforming the sinner or criminal.[71] In addition to punishment, Ottoman authorities maintained that moral instruction could also rehabilitate a convict's soul.

Articles 50–2 of the 1880 Prison Regulation mandate that prisoners be allowed access to their respective religious leadership and have the freedom to practise their religions. Religious authorities (Muslim, Jewish, and Christian) should visit prisoners in their wards on a daily and/or weekly basis in order to attend to the inmates' spiritual needs. Also in the event of a death, religious authorities should be notified immediately in order to perform proper rites and rituals.[72] Article 9 of the 1880 Prison Regulation states that in addition to other staff, such as wardens, chief scribes, chief guards, and guards, prisons should also employ an imam and, if needed, clergymen of other denominations.[73] Additionally, Article 91 stipulates that 'all prisoners are required to carry out their respective religious obligations and rituals'. Likewise, Article 93 requires that all young prisoners who are on the verge of puberty (*mürahik*) and others designated by the prison warden must be given compulsory religious instruction by their respective clergy.[74] Despite these regulations, it is not clear how well the Prison Administration fulfilled all of these requirements.

Only two prisons actually employed clergy to teach, preach, and/or minister to their inmates. According to the 1916 Ottoman prison employment records only the Istanbul penitentiary and the Kastamonu central prison had clergy on their payrolls. The Istanbul penitentiary employed an imam, ecumenical patriarchate priest (*rum papası*), an Armenian priest (*ermeni papası*), and a Jewish Rabbi (*haham*). The imam received a monthly salary of 330 *kuruş* while the two Christian clergymen and the Rabbi were paid only 230 *kuruş* each. The Kastamonu prison employed an imam and preacher (*vaiz*) for its Muslim inmates at a monthly salary of 50 *kuruş*.[75] It appears that if other prisons kept the regulations stipulated in Articles 9 and 50–2 then the vast majority must have drawn upon the voluntary services of local religious authorities. Of course Article 9 also made the provision that prisons could fill any position 'according to need' (*icabına göre*), which, by extension, means that hiring was predicated on the number of prisoners in a particular facility.[76] Most central and provincial prisons had hundreds of inmates that would have justified the employment of clergymen, as stipulated in Article 9, but it appears that the local municipal councils did not see fit to expend the necessary funds.

In spite of the poor numbers of professional clergy in prisons, other provisions were made to ensure that prisoners were able to worship. Some prisons provided special areas of worship for inmates. For example, according to Charles Riggs, the Istanbul penitentiary contained a small mosque and chapel where prisoners could worship on a voluntary basis.[77] Apart from these scant pieces of evidence, there is very little data on prisoner rehabilitation through moral uplift and instruction. It can reasonably be concluded, therefore, that rehabilitation through spiritual edification was not the primary method for the Prison Administration and for its successor, the Directorate of Prisons.

Modern education was another possible method for prison rehabilitation. Apart from Article 92, which stipulates that every prison should have a select number of books available to prisoners, the 1880 Prison Regulation is surprisingly silent on this issue.[78] Apparently, the Prison Administration did not have an empire-wide inmate education programme. Prison administrators during the Second Constitutional Period, however, showed interest in inmate literacy. As discussed in Chapter 3, the 1912 prison survey collected statistics on this issue. According to the survey, literacy among prisoners was roughly 18 per cent.[79]

Archival documents indicate that individual prisons did employ instructors to provide a basic education to inmates. This was not, however, an empire-wide programme, and it seems to have been primarily confined to penitentiaries with inmates incarcerated for long periods of time (more than five years). For example, according to 1915 prison employment statistics, the Istanbul penitentiary employed two teachers (*mualim*) at a generous monthly salary of 600 *kuruş* each. In 1913, the Sinop penitentiary employed İzmid'li Hasan Efendi as a teacher. Being a prisoner himself, he received a salary of 50 *kuruş* a month and a private room near the entrance to the prison hospital. His duties included holding regular class hours each day and teaching prisoners to read and write. İzmid'li Hasan Efendi was relieved of his duties for alleged 'bad behaviour', which included not performing his teaching duties, gambling, and inciting other prisoners to rebellion. He allegedly showed up to teach each day for only fifteen to twenty minutes and then he would wander off to gamble in the various wards of the prison. The warden, Cemal Bey, reported his behaviour to Sinop's municipal school board and informed the board that he had replaced İzmid'li Hasan Efendi with another prisoner – İstanbul'lu Kemal Efendi. This new teacher was a former cavalry officer currently serving fifteen years' hard labour for homicide (*katil-i nefs*). Local municipalities controlled the hiring of prison teachers and not the Prison Administration, which may explain why every prison in the empire did not employ a teacher.[80] Apart from hiring a couple of professional teachers, allowing literate prisoners to educate their fellow inmates, and collecting statistics on prisoner literacy, it does not appear that the Prison Administration or the

Directorate of Prisons exerted much effort to rehabilitate inmates through education.[81] Ottoman prison policy, instead, appears to have focused its prisoner rehabilitation efforts on productive labour.

In addition to facilitating prison supervision by keeping inmates occupied with attention-directing labour, productive labour had other important functions for Ottoman prison reformers. First, according to the assumptions of prison reformers of the nineteenth century and the early twentieth, productive labour was an essential element to effective rehabilitation. This labour would keep them constructively occupied, thus preventing slothful behaviour through the pursuit of lascivious activities and idleness. As discussed above, idleness was a serious problem for prison administrators, because it often led to escapes, fights, and uprisings. Labour could also provide prisoners with useful occupational skills that would help them to become contributing members to society upon their release. In this way, prisoners were rehabilitated and shaped into productive members of society, thus making it possible for them to avoid recidivism.[82] Ottoman prison reformers discussed the benefits of prison labour in their report of the 1890 International Prison Conference proceedings in St Petersburg, Russia.[83]

Ottoman officials, however, did not appropriate these ideas from the West. The 1880 Prison Regulation already reflected these assumptions. Moreover, incarceration with hard labour (*kürek cezası*) in galleys of the Imperial Shipyards had already been practised in the empire since at least the eighteenth century.[84] The concept of hard labour changed over the course of the nineteenth century from that of the galleys to labour in prison workshops and factories, but it still maintained its original name (*kürek*), which means 'oar, paddle'.[85]

Articles 69–72 of the 1880 Prison Regulation stipulated that no prisoner was to 'remain unemployed' while incarcerated; that prisoners must work throughout their entire prison sentence; and that they should be paid for their labour. Part of that money should be used to offset the costs of their upkeep, another part should go to the state treasury, and the remainder should be held in reserve for the prisoner's personal use. Prison wardens were responsible for organising productive labour for the inmates.[86] They were also personally responsible for deciding which prisoners would work on what projects and for supplying the necessary tools. They were also required to inspect the quality of the final products and oversee their sale.[87] The Ministry of the Interior reaffirmed these provisions by issuing a special regulation (*talimatname*) in 1911 that called for the full implementation of the principle of prison labour and that described its benefits for reforming prisoners.[88] According to this special regulation, all prisons throughout the empire were to implement the principles of the 1880 Prison Regulation regarding work. Prison wardens were responsible for arranging the details in conjunction with local administrators, farmers, and businesses in order to get prisoners working.[89]

As a result of these regulations, many prisons established workshops that produced, on a small scale, socks, fabrics, shoes, carpets, tools, cabinets, and other carpentry items. Other prisons, especially in rural provincial areas, engaged in agricultural production where inmates would pick fava beans, chickpeas, tobacco, and other produce. Both male and female prisoners were supposed to engage in productive work, but in separate areas. Females were authorised to work in their prison dormitories on needlework, sewing, knitting socks, making and repairing clothing, bedding, towels, and carpets.[90]

In addition to the proliferation of prison workshops around the empire, the CUP developed a plan to create large-scale prison factories (*imalathaneler, sanayihaneler,* or *fabrikalar*) in 1911. It envisioned these factories as centres of industrial production in the empire's major cities. These factories would require industrial education and training for prisoners to learn how to operate the modern machinery necessary for textile mass production and other light industrial activities. In fact, a curriculum was proposed for prison factory workers that included instruction in reading, writing, arithmetic, geography, history, and Ottoman Turkish.[91]

As these types of factories required a great deal of investment and prisoner training, officials decided to locate them in penitentiaries where prisoners served sentences of at least five years.[92] There is an inherent logic to this type of restriction. Once trained, these prisoners would be able to do these jobs for an extended period of time. In the eyes of the CUP, prison factories had many possible benefits. Prison labour is inexpensive, readily available, reliable, and relatively stable. Additionally, factory space, housing, health care, worker discipline, and supervision are readily available and paid for by the state. In other words, by utilising prison labour an entrepreneur's costs are minimised, thus making it possible to gain an advantage on the open market.

As mentioned in Chapter 2, prison factories were established to help pay for prison reforms in 1911. Prison reformers, however, also justified their development as a means of 'stimulating' the economies of major urban centres, such as Istanbul, Ankara, Beirut, Damascus, İzmir, and Edirne.[93] Half of the net profits gained in the sale of these manufactured goods were to go to the Ottoman Treasury.[94] These funds would then be used for industrialisation and economic programmes in the cities where the factories were located, thus assisting the CUP in its imperial economic development programme.[95] In fact, prison factories had the dual purpose of rehabilitating both the prisoner and the economy, thus making prisons doubly effective as 'microcosms of modernity'. In other words, prison factories were viewed as an important aspect of imperial economic regeneration through industrialisation. They facilitated the development of the Ottoman industrial complex and a local Muslim entrepreneurial middle class that could compete with inexpensive, mass-produced foreign goods. Construction of these prison factories was one of the first steps of the CUP to implement its plan to create an Ottoman 'national economy' (*milli iktisat*).[96]

This plan of creating a 'national economy' was not put into full effect until after the assassination of Mahmut Şevket Pasha and the CUP's assumption of full control over the Ottoman administration.[97] Therefore, the construction of Ottoman prison factories and their use to stimulate local economies pre-dates the implementation of the CUP's plan to build a 'national economy'. This demonstrates the critical role that Ottoman prisons played as a testing ground for larger imperial projects.

The factory established in Edirne's penitentiary is an excellent example of a successful textile factory built and funded by the state. Edirne's prison textile factory actually became the model prison factory upon which others were fashioned and built throughout the empire.[98] Not all prison factories, however, had to produce textiles. Each was given leeway to adapt its production to local strengths, such as iron works, carpentry, or other appropriate products.[99]

It is not clear exactly how many prison workshops and factories existed in the empire by 1917, but there must have been at least twenty-five in operation.[100] As late as November 1917, Dr Paul Pollitz, the Inspector General of Ottoman Prisons, was still requesting and receiving funds for the construction of more prison factories and the development of prison lands for agricultural production.[101] These prison factories and farms were also incorporated into the Ottoman war effort, because they produced desperately needed items for the military and the civilian population during WWI.[102] Prison factories and farms were seen as essential elements in the creation of modern penitentiaries and prisons that benefited prisoners and the empire as a whole.

Despite state officials' idealisation of prisoner rehabilitation through productive labour and the proliferation of prison workshops and factories around the empire, inmates engaged in productive labour still represented a very small percentage of the prison population. Numerous documents, inspections, and eyewitnesses attest to this fact.[103] The 1916–17 prison survey indicates that less than 8.5 per cent of the prison population (1,812 prisoners out of a total population of 21,666) was gainfully employed in working for the 'common good', working at special jobs (*hasus işle meşgul*), or working within the prison's workshop or factory.[104] Despite the many regulations, programmes, and expenditures, the vast majority of inmates were still not gainfully employed. Instead, most prisoners were spending their sentences in idleness. Without a doubt, the small percentage of inmates working within the prison did benefit from their experiences, but most prisoners were not rehabilitated through productive labour.

Conclusion

As this chapter demonstrates, Ottoman prison reformers heavily engaged in what Lefebvre termed 'the production of space'. Officials did this through the conscious construction of an ordered, uniform physical space – the prison, jail, and penitentiary – in order to incarcerate criminals. This represents a direct response to the challenges the empire faced as it transitioned from a multifaceted system of punishments to one that primarily employed imprisonment. As a 'semiotic abstract', the Ottoman prison became a space wherein the ideals of imperial reformers, governmental aspirations, state administrators, local officials, prison cadre, charitable organisations, families, and inmates all converged, interacted, contested, and/or conformed on various levels. This convergence affected the efficacy of intention, reform, and reality in Ottoman prisons. Creating the well-ordered prison through the spatialisation of incarceration altered the everyday life of prisoners and prison officials in terms of interaction, organisation, living conditions, and self-perceptions, thus affecting the reality of imprisonment.

Ottoman efforts to create the well-ordered prison met with a great deal of success and failure. The greatest challenges included terrible prison conditions, overcrowding, dilapidated structures, poor supervision and discipline, and a lack of funding. Ottoman policies attempted to rehabilitate the incarcerated, through specific means, such as improved prison organisation, supervision, and provisioning; attempts at moral and secular education; and putting prisoners to work. These efforts epitomise nineteenth-century sensibilities regarding increased state intervention into the lives of its citizens and caring for its population, including prisoners. These efforts also demonstrate how prison reform addressed many of the most pressing questions of Ottoman modernity.

Building on the reforms of earlier regimes, the CUP oversaw the greatest improvements to prison policy implementation and the transformation of prison conditions. While many of these efforts did achieve success, others ended in failure, met resistance, or encountered problems associated with wartime constrictions. The Prison Administration and the Directorate of Prisons constantly monitored, inspected, issued directives, and exerted efforts that did have trangible results. On the other hand, war, prisoner and cadre resistance, corruption, and financial crisis undermined many of these gains. The ideal of reform must always be tempered by the reality of implementation and its limitations as various actors exert power and agency.

The CUP, the Prison Administration, and the Directorate of Prisons knew that all these rules, regulations, and modern designs were only as good as those who implemented them. This is why CUP prison reforms, first and foremost, focused on professionalising the prison cadre. In the eyes of Ottoman prison reformers, the prison cadre represented the linchpin to successful prison organisation and prisoner reformation. The next chapter investigates CUP attempts to professionalise its prison cadre as a means to combat the prevalence of guard–prisoner collusion, corruption, and inmate abuse. It also juxtaposes the ideals of these reforms with the realities of everyday prison life.

Notes

1. Şerif, *Anadolu'da*, pp. xi–xxiii. His other volume is *Arnavudluk'da, Suriye'de, Trablusgarb'de Tanin*. Ahmet Şerif's travel diaries of the Ottoman Empire are unlike European travel volumes. His observations have greater credibility, because he was an educated Ottoman subject with the knowledge, intelligence, native language capabilities, and cultural background to make sense of what he encountered and observed. His account often sharply critiques Ottoman state and local officials and provides detailed insight into local administrative affairs shortly after the 1908 Constitutional Revolution. During his travels he visited several prisons and jails throughout Anatolia, the Balkans, Syria, and Lebanon. His accounts corroborate, at least in part, European observations that Ottoman prisons were not effectively implementing the 1880 Prison Regulation. Conditions were poor at best and atrocious at worst. His travels and accounts do, however, take place just before the CUP initiated comprehensive prison reforms.
2. Şerif, *Anadolu'da*, p. 39.
3. Ibid., p. 39.
4. Ibid., pp. 39–42.
5. Ibid., pp. 42–7, 52–3, and 83. He also visited prisons in the districts (*kaza*) of Beypazarı, Beyşehir, and Ilgın in Konya province.
6. Goffman, *Asylums*, p. 4.

7. Lefebvre, *Production of Space.*
8. Yıldız, 'Osmanlı Devleti'nde Hapishane Islahatı'; and Chapter 2 of this work.
9. See FO 195/364, 226/113, and 97/418 for Sir Stratford Canning's prison inspection reports. See BOA, DHTMIKS for the inspection reports of the 'Commission for Expediting Initiatives and Reforms'. See Ahmet Şerif, *Anadolu'da* and *Arnavudluk'da, Suriye'de, Trablusgarb'de Tanin* for his inspections. See Chapter 2 in this book for an overview of the various prison inspections conducted during the Second Constitutional Period. Additionally, the Prison Administration's papers contain reports and petitions submitted by foreign officers working in the Ottoman Empire. For example, on 18 September 1907 a Russian headquarters chief (*stabsrotmeister*) by the name of Agura who was tasked with reorganising the Macedonian gendarmerie as part of the Mürzsteg Programme, submitted a petition to the Ottoman Governor of Macedonia and CUP supporter Hilmi Pasha criticising the severly overcrowded conditions of a local prison in the district (*kaza*) of Avrethisar. He claimed that thirty-four prisoners were being incarcerated in two small rooms and that the situation would only worsen because of the increasing crime and number of criminal prosecutions in the district at this time. The prisoners' situations were so bad that several of them, Christian and Muslim, begged the Russian official to intercede on their behalf, but the local Ottoman authorities apparently were very slow to heed his petitions (BOA, YEE 135/8). I would like to extend a special thanks to Milena Methodieva for translating the original document from Russian.
10. Şimşar, 'Karesi Hapishanesi', p. 68.
11. They were Emine, wife of Mehmed (serving five years), Şerife, daughter of Mehmed (serving eight years), and Hanife, wife of Kara Mehmed (serving a life sentence for murder).
12. Şimşar, pp. 68–9.
13. Ibid., p. 69.
14. The general directives for this survey are contained in BOA, DHEUMTK 13/11, 54/4, DHMBHPSM 9/59, and DHMBHPS 72/46. Each province returned these completed questionnaires: DHMBHPSM 11/84 (Adana); DHMBHPSM 11/26, DHMBHPS 57/39 and 154/40 (Ankara); DHMBHPSM 10/6 and 11/18 (Aydın); DHMBHPSM 12/75 (Baghdad); DHMBHPSM 10/19 (Beirut); DHMBHPSM 10/10, 10/31, 11/8, 11/32, 11/43, 11/71, and 13/1 (Bitlis); DHMBHPS 149/17 (Bolu); DHMBHPSM 10/4 (Canik); DHMBHPSM 9/94 (Çatalca); DHMBHPSM 12/18 and DHMBHPS 10/51 (Diyarbekir); DHMBHPS 149/6 and 149/9 (Edirne); DHMBHPSM 9/103 and 11/31 (Erzurum); DHMBHPSM 10/40 (Halep); DHMBHPS 149/12 and DHMBHPSM 11/7 (the Hijaz); DHMBHPS 149/11 (Hüdavandigar); DHMBHPSM 9/96 (Istanbul); DHMBHPSM 9/106 (İzmid); DHMBHPSM 10/13 (Kala-i Sultaniye); DHMBHPSM

10/14 (Karesi); DHMBHPSM 10/25 and DHMBHPS 152/35 (Kastamonu); DHMBHPSM 10/15 (Konya); DHMBHPSM 12/21 (Mamüretülaziz); DHMBHPSM 12/33 (Mosul); DHMBHPSM 10/52 (Sivas); DHMBHPSM 11/27 (Suriye); DHMBHPSM 11/25 and 18/62 (Trabzon); DHMBHPSM 10/5 (Urfa); DHMBHPS 149/36 (Van); DHMBHPSM 12/31, DHMBHPS 149/49, and 150/74 (Yemen); and DHMBHPSM 11/24 (Zor).

15. BOA, DHMBHPSM 10/14, docs 1 and 12–15.
16. BOA, DHMBHPSM 9/103, 10/14, and 11/84.
17. BOA, DHMBHPSM 10/14, docs 12–15.
18. BOA, DHMBHPSM 10/14.
19. See the four catalogues of the Prison Administration – one catalogue (BOA, DHMBHPSM) and three catalogues (BOA, DHMBHPS). There are nearly five hundred files containing thousands of documents on prisoner escapes during the Second Constitutional Period. A sampling of the internal documents of the administration dealing with escapes includes BOA, DHMBHPS 96/12, 101/2, 101/3, 101/4, 101/5, and 103/31, and DHMBHPSM 2/20, 5/4, 7/70, 7/95, and 43/9.
20. BOA, DHMBHPS 153/35. For the issue of guard-assisted prison escapes see Chapter 5.
21. This amnesty is discussed more fully in Chapter 6.
22. BOA, DHMBHPSM 17/35, doc. 40 is an official directive issued in February 1911 about transfering inmates in order to ease overcrowding. See also BOA, DHTMIK 45/5. In 1903, a typhoid fever epidemic broke out in the administrative sub-division of Çorum's prison, caused by overcrowding. Prison officials gave early releases to a number of less serious offenders and transferred others to less crowded facilities in order to ameliorate the epidemic.
23. BOA, DHMBHPSM 27/28, doc. 6.
24. According to Article 82, 1880 Prison Regulation, 'all types of games, intoxicants, and gambling are absolutely forbidden' (*her türlü la'biyat ve müskirat ve kumar oyunu kat'iyen memnu'dur*).
25. BOA, DHMBHPS 99/8; Griffiths, *History and Romance of Crime*, pp. 280–4; and Forder, *In Brigands' Hands*, pp. 26–35.
26. BOA, DHMBHPSM 8/68.
27. Regarding prison corruption and prisoner-guard collusion see BOA, DHMBHPS 73/33, 105/9, 89/61, 73/15, 73/25, 106/35, 99/14, 81/66, 83/15, 85/15, 149/50, 94/64, 137/18, 134/64, and 131/24. This topic is discussed in great detail in Chapter 5.
28. BOA, DHMBHPSM 8/74 is an example of prison administrators successfully preventing and minimising fights and disputes at the Trabzon Central Prison in 1913. Examples of fights (*kavgalar*) and riots (*isyanlar*) occurring in Ottoman prisons during the Second Constitutional Period include a fight in Konya's prison in 1914 blamed on crowded, constricted, and unsanitary conditions (DHMBHPS 4/29). Excessive crowding in Amasya's prison led

to a fight in 1913 (DHMBHPS 72/12). In Manisa's prison a fight resulted in the death of an inmate and several injuries in 1913 (DHMBHPS 148/35). In Konya's central prison in 1912, guard misconduct led to a fight that resulted in injuries to several prisoners (DHMBHPS 111/3). In 1912, a riot broke out in İzmir's central prison because of prisoner neglect (DHMBHPS 96/16). Finally, in 1914, prisoners in Cenin rioted in order to protest the transfer of some inmates to the Beirut central prison resulting in injuries to both prisoners and gendarme (DHMBHPSM 17/23).

29. BOA, DHMBHPS 154/14, doc. 67.
30. Forder, pp. 26–35. A. Forder was a British expatriate living in Jerusalem when the Ottomans entered WWI. He was arrested on suspicion of espionage and was imprisoned first in Jerusalem's jail and then in Damascus' jail. While much of his story is self-serving and derogatory of Middle Easterners, some of his claims match data found in Ottoman prison records concerning poor living conditions, lack of food, prisoner idleness, and overcrowding. For official Ottoman records that corroborate Forder's claims about prisoner nutrition and food rations in Jerusalem's prison, see BOA, DHMBHPS 74/39 and 75/19. In 1917 and 1918, Ottoman administrators reiterated specific articles from the 1880 Prison Regulation that stipulate the responsibilities of prison cadre concerning proper prisoner nutrition and provisioning (DHMBHPS 165/84 and 160/14).
31. BOA, DHMBHPS 72/41, 64/47, 81/12, 82/21, and 83/34.
32. BOA, DHMBHPSM 35/95.
33. Şimşar, pp. 69–70; BOA, DHMBHPS 151/5, docs 4 and 13–14; and DHMBHPSM 27/28, doc. 6.
34. BOA, DHMBHPSM 27/28, doc. 6.
35. BOA, ZB 310/82, doc. 1.
36. For instance, in 1918, a typhus epidemic hit the Yozgad prison and reportedly killed a large number of prisoners (BOA, DHMBHPS 79/17, 80/60, and 80/63).
37. Health and hygiene issues constitute the single largest number of documents found in the Prison Administration's catalogues (BOA, DHMBHPS and DHMBHPSM). For a closer look at prison sanitary conditions and prison hospitals see Daşcioğlu, 'Prison Hospitals'.
38. The exact phrase is '*kuvaid-i mediniye*'. This phrase can be interpreted as 'laws/principles or doctrines of civilisation' (BOA, DHMBHPS 145/31).
39. For example, see BOA, DHMBHPSM 10/23 from the Trabzon Central Prison that 'requests a new prison in order to prevent deaths as a result of poor sanitary conditions' (*gayrı sıhhı şartları haiz Trabzon merkez hapishanesi'ndeki ölümlerin önlenmesi için yeni bir hapishane yapılması talebi*).
40. BOA, DHMBHPSM 1/2, doc. 10.
41. This phrase from Lefebvre offers three ways to analyse space: 1. as a physical environment that can be perceived ('spatial practice'); 2. as a semiotic

abstraction that informs how ordinary people, corporations, planners, and politicians negotiate space ('representations of space'); and 3. as a medium through which the body lives out its life in interaction with other bodies ('representational spaces'). He proposes a unitary theory of space that unites the physical, mental, and social (Lefebvre, pp. 31–9). This approach to space has very useful applications to understanding Ottoman prisons.

42. BOA, DHMBHPS 142/54.
43. BOA, DHMBHPSM 1/6, 1/24, doc. 1, and 2/17; DHMBHPS 43/7; and Gönen, 'Osmanlı', p. 175.
44. BOA, DHMBHPSM 1/2, doc. 10; and Daşcioğlu, pp. 999–1,014.
45. BOA, DHMBHPS 72/26.
46. BOA, DHMBHPSM 1/2, doc. 10, Articles 2–7.
47. The topic of incarcerated children is discussed in great detail in Chapter 6.
48. See BOA, DHMBHPSM 53/37 for the blueprint of a model prison designed by state architect Mimar Kemal Bey to hold seventy-five inmates on the district (*kaza*) level. See DHMBHPS 148/116 for an architectural design of a prison containing a mosque, a church, a doctor's office, and a hospital. See DHMBHPS 148/117 for a prison architectural plan designed to hold 300 prisoners on the provincial level. For the most detailed architectural plans for a felons' jail in Istanbul designed to house 300 prisoners see DHMBHPSM 51/62.
49. Prison repairs, building reports, and their inspections constitute the second most prevalent type of document found in the catalogues of the Prison Administration (BOA, DHMBHPS and DHMBHPSM).
50. This is discussed in greater detail in Chapter 5.
51. BOA, DHMBHPS 147/19, docs 5–6.
52. BOA, DHMBHPS 144/74. These figures do not include political prisoners or those incarcerated in military prisons. Those prisoners fell under the jurisdictions of the Directorate for Public Security and the army.
53. BOA, DHMBHPS 17/32, docs 1–2.
54. BOA, DHMBHPS 144/74; Yıldız, *Mapusane*, pp. 94, 180, 359, and 383; and Kuru, *Sinop Hapishane*, p. 14.
55. The statistics in this section are culled from the 1916–17 prison survey (BOA, DHMBHPS 143/93).
56. BOA, DHMBHPSM 1/2, doc. 10, Articles 6, 28–9, 32–3, 53, and 61.
57. BOA, DHMBHPS 89/23.
58. BOA, DHMBHPS 144/74.
59. Atar, 'Turgutlu Hapishanesinin Genel Durumu', p. 92. The associated documents are BOA, DHMBHPS 44/38 and 47/42.
60. Bozkurt, 'Reception of Western European Law', pp. 284–5.
61. BOA, DHMBHPS 106/10. Ömer Şen dates this document to 1914, but this is incorrect since its Rumi date is listed as *Şubat* and *Mart* of 1331 and 1332, respectively, which correspond to February–March 1916 in the *Miladi* calendar (Şen, *Osmanlı'da Mahkum Olmak*, p. 160). While Şen touches

on many of these documents (pp. 157–61) some of his dates are incorrect. Moreover, he provides very little in the way of actual analysis.

During the nineteenth century the Ottoman Empire adopted three official calendars: *Hijri* (Islamic calendar), *Rumi* (Gregorian calendar), and *Miladi* (Christian calendar). Official documents were dated according to all three calendars.

62. BOA, DHMBHPS 143/93.
63. Ibid. Istanbul province had a total of eight prisons and jails: Istanbul penitentiary and jail, Beyoglu jail, Üsküdar prison and jail, Geğbüze jail, and Şile prison and jail.
64. BOA, DHMBHPS 96/40.
65. For an extensive scholarly discussion of the 'Woman Question' in the late Ottoman Empire, see Brummet, 'Dogs, Women, Cholera, and Other Menaces'; Kandiyoti, 'End of Empire: Islam, Nationalism, and Women in Turkey'; Frierson, 'Women in late Ottoman Intellectual History'; and Gelvin, 'Modernity, Tradition, and the Battleground of Gender'.
66. BOA, DHMBHPSM 1/2, doc. 10, Article 33.
67. BOA, DHMBHPS 154/14 contains a comprehensive breakdown of prison employment statistics for the whole empire.
68. See Chapter 5 for a detailed discussion of prison cadre, their qualifications, and roles in prison life and reform.
69. BOA, DHMBHPS 61/20, doc. 5.
70. BOA, DHMBHPS 160/82.
71. Peters, *Crime and Punishment*, pp. 30–1 and 96–102.
72. BOA, DHMBHPSM 1/2, doc. 10, Articles 50–2.
73. Ibid. Article 9.
74. Ibid. Articles 91 and 93.
75. BOA, DHMBHPS 154/14.
76. Ibid.
77. Riggs, 'Adult Delinquency', p. 342.
78. BOA, DHMBHPSM 1/2, doc. 10, Article 92.
79. BOA, DHMBHPSM 3/36, 4/1, 4/4, 4/20, 4/21, 5/1, 5/9, 6/27, 12/70, 14/65, 145/56, 53/34, DHMBHPS 145/2, 145/26, 146/69, and 146/70. These are the surviving records from the 1912 prison survey. For total literacy statistics, see Chart 3.10.
80. BOA, DHMBHPS 147/27, docs 1–3.
81. In May 1917, Dr Pollitz made a list of prison reform priorities for Istanbul province. Among them was the continuation and expansion of prisoner education (BOA, DHMBHPS 159/8).
82. BOA, DHMBHPS 143/144.
83. Demirel, '1890 Petersburg Hapishaneler Kongresi'.
84. Zarinebaf, *Crime and Punishment in Istanbul*, pp. 164–8.
85. Yıldız, *Mapusane*, pp. 225–61.
86. BOA, DHMBHPSM 1/2, doc. 10, Articles 69–72.

87. Ibid., Article 17.

88. BOA, DHMUİ 61–2/25.

89. Ibid.

90. Ibid.; BOA, DHMBHPS 142/54; Şen, *Osmanlı'da Mahkum Olmak*, pp. 58–60; and Çiçen, 'Cesaevi Islahatı', pp. 109–27.

91. Çiçen, pp. 122–3.

92. Ibid.; BOA, DHMBHPS 158/27; and Şen, *Osmanlı'da Mahkum Olmak*, pp. 61–2.

93. For basic information on the establishment of labour prisons, see Gönen, pp. 173–83.

94. BOA, DHMBHPSM 1/2, doc. 10, Article 72.

95. The prison factories in Aydın, Edirne, and Istanbul were built, respectively, to produce textiles, cabinets, and shoes. Each yielded good returns, but Edirne was especially productive (BOA, DHMBHPSM 8/3, docs 20 and 25). The 1912 prison survey collected information on prison factory production: For Istanbul, see DHMBHPSM 4/4, doc. 9 (backside) and for Edirne, see DHMBHPSM 4/1, doc. 25 (backside).

96. There is an extensive literature on the CUP's economic policies and its attempts to create a 'national economy' (*milli iktisat*) via the establishment of a Muslim bourgeois entrepreneurial class. This new industrial class would be established through 'state-interventionism' as opposed to free trade. For detailed analyses of the CUP's economic policies see the works of Zafer Toprak; Ahmad, 'Vanguard of a Nascent Bourgeoisie'; and Göçek, *Rise of the Bourgeoisie*.

97. Mahmut Şevket Pasha was Grand Vizer after the CUP countercoup in January 1913. He was not, however, a CUP member or supporter. He controlled the Ottoman military and prevented the CUP's full consolidation of power until his assassination on 11 June 1913. The CUP then gained full control over the entire Ottoman administration. See Turfan, *Rise of the Young Turks*, pp. 285–428.

98. BOA, DHMBHPSM 3/27. In this prison circular (*tamim*), Edirne's prison textile factory is labelled 'the model' for other prison factories (*Edirne Hapishanesi'nde mahkumlara yaptırılmakta olan dokuma sanayiinin suret-i tatbikinin diğer hapishanelere de tavsiye edilişi*).

99. For example, instead of producing textiles, the Istanbul prison factory specialised in carpentry items, such as desks and chests (DHMBHPS 4/4, doc. 9, backside).

100. BOA, DHMBHPS 143/93. This document shows the number of employed prisoners within the empire.

101. BOA, DHMBHPS 119/23. The CUP utilised some of the funds provided by Germany for the Ottoman war effort in WWI to pay for prison reforms. The Germans, however, were not pleased to see this money being spent on pursuits other than the Ottoman war effort.

102. During WWI, many prisoners were put to work on agricultural and road

repair projects to assist the war effort (DHMBHPS 76/20, doc. 3). The 1917 prison survey commissioned by Dr Pollitz contains a category requesting the numbers of prisoners being employed in activities for the 'common good' (*menafi-yi umumi*) (BOA, DHMBHPS 143/93).

103. For example, Konya's governor wrote a report complaining of inmate idleness and requested funds and equipment to establish a prison factory after inspecting Konya's central prison in 1916 (BOA, DHMBHPS 28/100). Johnson, 'Prison Conditions in Constantinople'; Riggs; and Forder all attest that idleness was a persistent problem.

104. BOA, DHMBHPS 143/93. This survey collected several types of data relating to prisoner employment: 1. 'Prisoners eligible to work for the common good' (total: 2,186); 2. 'Prisoners working for the common good' (total: 1,047); 3. 'Prisoners working in the prison' (total: 424); 4. 'Prisoners occupied with special work' (total: 307); and 5. 'Prisoners not working' (total: 19,772).

5

Disciplining the Disciplinarians:
Combating Corruption and Abuse through
the Professionalisation of the Prison Cadre

Usually when the topic of discipline and prisons is broached, the first items of discussion are Jeremy Bentham's prison panopticon and Michel Foucault's *Discipline and Punish*. The panopticon was designed to provide prison guards with maximum surveillance over inmates, therefore facilitating the guards' ability to control, discipline, and rehabilitate the incarcerated. This design enabled prison officials to peer into every cell and continuously supervise prisoners while remaining hidden from view. This act of unseen surveillance was supposed to instil prisoner self-discipline. For Foucault, this act represented the ultimate example of the state's ability to control and dominate society through the implementation of new instrumentalities of governance. As discussed in Chapter 4, these new methods of prison governance included new regimens, prisoner organisation and divisions, improved hygiene and health conditions, better provisioning, constant surveillance, religious instruction, and 'rehabilitating' labour. Most importantly, prison guards became the linchpins in the implementation of these reforms. According to Foucault, prison officials and especially guards are the definitive representatives of state power to prisoners who, in turn, epitomise society's disorder, unruliness, and menace to the common good.[1]

Foucault, however, fails to recognise very important aspects of the panopticon and the various roles played by guards. The panopticon's architectural design contains a dual disciplining purpose. In addition to disciplining prisoners, it is also designed to discipline the prison cadre. Foucault never acknowledges how corruption and collusion between guards and inmates adversely affects discipline and order. In other words, the state, as represented by the guards, also requires surveillance, thus breaching the supposedly impenetrable barrier and upending the unidirectional flow of power that Foucault drew between 'state' and 'society'.[2]

The origins of the panopticon can be traced to eighteenth-century Russia during the reign of Catherine the Great. Jeremy Bentham's brother,

Samuel, was the first to invent this design, but for a factory, not a prison.[3] Samuel Bentham designed his factory panopticon to facilitate discipline, order, and efficiency through maximum surveillance of the 'subject'. In addition to the workers, the 'subjects' of his panopticon also included the foremen. In fact, it appears that the supervision of the foremen was the primary purpose of his original design. If factory owners or managers could control and discipline the foremen, they could better control the labourer, thus improving factory order, productivity, and profits.[4] Foucault misses this important aspect in his analysis of the intent, power, and purpose of Jeremy Bentham's prison panopticon. He fails to see the negative affect that prison guards had on overall prison order and disorder and the need for prison guards to be supervised and disciplined as well.[5]

Disciplining the disciplinarians or the professionalisation of the prison cadre is a central aspect of prison reform that is often overlooked by penal scholars. It is, however, vital to understanding the CUP's attempts at penal and imperial reform and state centralisation of power. The stipulations, sources, and legitimation of CUP attempts to professionalise its prison cadre together with other aspects of prison administrative reform demonstrate that prison guards acted as the foundation for Ottoman penal policy and modernisation. Disciplining the disciplinarians was seen as the means of putting an end to corruption, prisoner abuse, and guard–prisoner collusion that was so prevalent in Ottoman prisons. Properly trained prison cadre would facilitate the rehabilitation of criminals by fostering a disciplined and well-ordered prison environment. The CUP's vision of the ideal prison guard also embodies its self-image as a group of elite technocrats or *savant* that would rescue the empire from ruin and destruction. The professionalisation of prison cadre and general administrative reform within Ottoman prisons also represent broader CUP attempts to centralise state power during the Second Constitutional Period and to continue the process of Ottoman modernity initiated by earlier regimes. How these reforms were formulated, legitimated, and implemented represent an Ottoman passage to modernity.

This chapter argues against a distinct rupture with the past that often pervades the discourse of modernity, be it unified, alternative, or multiple. There is much more continuity in these processes of transformation than is often acknowledged.[6] The protection of the 'weak' from the abuse of state officials had been at the core of Ottoman sultanic practice and legitimacy since the empire's inception. The Sultan's subjects from the lowest classes, including prisoners, had always been empowered to petition their ruler and expected their grievances to be heard and appropriately addressed. This 'Circle of Justice' is not a modern concept and its ideal was central to the efforts exerted by Ottoman officials to 'police' their own.[7] What is distinctly modern about these actions, however, is the level of standardisation of norms and procedures regarding the training, supervision, and requirements for the ideal prison guard. These standardisations also affect imperial oversight, inspection, and investigation of violations of these norms and practices. The goal of all of these reforms was to bring the Ottoman criminal justice system into 'conformity with the laws of civilisation'. These actions created a distinct process of Ottoman sociolegal practice that is both modern and Ottoman.

Finally, this chapter focuses on the praxis between normative legal and administrative reform and its implementation among state authorities and prisoners from 1880 to 1919. In so doing, it builds upon previous chapters and continues to expand the analysis of prison reform and reality through the prism of imperial intention, daily prison life, and the complicated interactions between local prison administrators, staff, and inmates. Therefore, this chapter focuses on examples of corruption, prisoner abuse, guard–prisoner collusion, imperial efforts to fight these problems, the effectiveness of these reforms, and local reaction by both officials and inmates.

This chapter first discusses the specific qualifications and responsibilities of local prison officials and personnel as stipulated by the 1880 Prison Regulation. It then investigates Ottoman prison reformers' vision of the role that prison officials, specifically guards, were to play in implementing the comprehensive overhaul of the empire's prisons and in rehabilitating prisoners. Finally, this chapter looks at concrete steps that the Prison Administration took to combat corruption, prisoner abuse, and guard–prisoner collusion through the detailed analysis of a 1912–13 scandal at the Sinop penitentiary and its aftermath. The explication of this and other examples of guard–inmate interactions demonstrates the reality of prison life and illuminates the murky and porous boundaries between guards and inmates, continuity and change, and state and society.

Professionalising Prison Employees

Ideally speaking, prison guards are the front line of state power, authority, discipline, and justice against the incarcerated. Guards and prisoners, however, often become common bedfellows. Within prison culture and society there exists a long history of prisoner–guard collusion. Bribes, kickbacks, sexual favours, contraband, smuggling, assisted escapes, gambling, extortion, and so forth have been and still are common within prisons around the world. Ottoman documents detail numerous incidents of rampant corruption among prison cadre, prisoner abuse, and extensive collusions between guards and inmates. These fraternisations and abuses of power blur the boundaries and moral distinctions between these seemingly oppositional entities.

As briefly described in Chapter 4, administrative corruption and official misconduct were rampant in Ottoman prisons during the nineteenth century as evidenced by guard-assisted prisoner escapes, weapons' smuggling, guard-run prostitution rings, and so on. There are numerous reports and investigations regarding the occurrence of these types of incidents involving guards and prisoners during the nineteenth century, some of which are discussed below.[8] Ottoman authorities expended much time, energy, and resources attempting to fix these problems. This section begins with a detailed discussion of the 1880 Prison Regulation's delineations of the authority, responsibilities, and organisation of local prison administration. Prison officials utilised the 1880 Prison Regulation as the template for proper prison administration and reform throughout the rest of the empire's existence.

The 1880 Prison Regulation lists the offices and responsibilities of all prison personnel. According to Article 9, prison employees consisted of:

a director (*müdir*), a chief scribe (*birinci katib*), assistant scribe (*ikinci katib*), a chief guard (*ser gardiyan*), regular guards (*gardiyanlar*), gatekeepers (*kapıcılar*), a physician (*tabib*), launderer (*çamaşırcı*), health personnel/nurse (*hastahane hademesi*), janitor/custodian (*işçi*), and an imam and/or clergyman (*imam ve iktiza eden memurin-i ruhaniyyeden*).[9]

Not every prison filled all of these positions. In fact, district-level prisons (*kaza*) often only had one guardian to run the entire prison, especially if the prison held only a few inmates. Most prisons located in provincial centres, however, were fully staffed.[10]

The Ministry of Justice appointed prison wardens (*müdir*) on the provincial, sub-division, and district levels. It was also responsible for their dismissal. Wardens were required to implement the entirety of the prison regulation by overseeing the organisation, order, security, finances, and administration of the prison. They were also in charge of organising work details, securing provisions and prisoner possessions, and overseeing prisoner admittances, releases, and discipline. The 1880 Prison Regulation also required them to submit regular reports to the respective ministries about the goings-on inside the prison and any changes to prison personnel. Wardens also had to wear special uniforms and be present twice a week for a general count of all prisoners.[11]

Prison clerks (*katib*) were responsible for keeping an accurate inventory of all prison materials, such as furniture, bedding, tools, prisoner belongings, prisoner wages and financial accounts, prison stores, provisions, and the number of prisoners. They were supposed to keep registers of all prisoners on a daily and weekly basis, something that was inspected regularly by the warden and chief guard. Additionally, they were to document prisoner behaviour and punishments, keep track of sentences, and see to it that inmates were released on time. Finally, they were ordered to regularly submit copies of their prisoner registers and bookkeeping to the Ministry of Justice, the Police Administration, and to provincial governors and judicial inspectors.[12]

Chief guards (*ser gardiyan*) were required to be literate, to know arithmetic, to be of 30 to 50 years of age, and to wear the appropriate uniform. They oversaw all guards and answered to the warden for any damage or misconduct by guards or prisoners should it not be reported immediately. They could not be employed in any other capacity outside the prison. Their responsibilities included supervision of the prison cadre, counting prisoners daily in the presence of the chief clerk, and maintaining general prison discipline, order, cleanliness, and appropriate prisoner behaviour. Additionally, they oversaw the proper storage and distribution of provisions and prisoner belongings. Chief guards were charged with conducting any investigations into prisoner or guard misconduct, wherein they would personally interrogate suspects, report their findings to the prison director, and write up any prescribed punishments. They were also responsible for the proper transfer of prisoners and for all the comings and goings at the prison. Everything and everyone entering or exiting the prison had to be inspected by the chief guard, including visitors, personnel, food stuffs, medicine, industrial products, and letters.[13]

Guards represent the front-line prison officials who interact with inmates and are subject to the supervision of the chief guard and warden. They oversee the day-to-day activities of the prison and prisoners, including basic discipline, order, and cleanliness. This was the same in Ottoman prisons. Any problems they encountered with prisoners had to be reported to their superiors or else they would be held responsible for any resulting consequences and damages. Similar to the chief guard, guards could not hold outside employment. Their families could not enter any portion of the prison or grounds where prisoners were present. Guards also could not allow any prisoners to enter their personal quarters. Male and female guards had the exact same responsibilities regarding their gender-specific charges. Guards distributed food, clothing, and other provisions as directed by the chief guard. They were responsible for supervising inmates during transfers, while on work details, caring for their personal hygiene, and receiving approved visitations. Guards were to prevent unauthorised visitations, contact between vendors/contractors and prisoners, as well as the smuggling in or out of any goods or persons. Their personal interactions with prisoners were to be strictly professional. Thus any prisoner fraternisation, such as gambling, game playing, eating or drinking with prisoners or their visitors and relatives, talk or idle chatting, accepting gifts from them or their relatives and friends, or buying from or selling anything to prisoners was strictly prohibited. Guards were also forbidden to drink alcohol or use any kind of narcotic. If they violated any of these regulations they were subject to incarceration, fines, and dismissal from their jobs.[14]

Despite this legislation, Ottoman prisons continued to maintain the reputation as legendary bastions of corruption and prisoner abuse. Tales of sadistic torture and prison cadre venality fill numerous pages of Western travel volumes and foreign reports (the vast majority of which are, at best, second-hand accounts). For example, Vahan Cardashian claimed that, during Sultan Abdülhamid II's reign, should severe beatings and brandings of 'Christian' prisoners not produce the desired information regarding political secrets then their 'hair was shaved off, incision made, and vermin placed in the skull', adding that, 'thousands upon thousands of innocent men have undergone these fiendish tortures, in one or more forms'.[15] Although the evidence is clear that many of the most salacious accounts are hyperbole – products of those with clear political agendas – corruption, prisoner abuse, and guard–prisoner fraternisation regularly occurred in Ottoman prisons. The Ministry of the Interior during the Hamidian era regularly replaced prison directors and guards for acts of misconduct (*yolsuz*), forcing them to forfeit their pensions.[16] Still, corruption, bribe taking, and prison cadre-assisted escapes remained regular occurrences. Although not completely realised during the Hamidian era, the CUP did attempt to implement the 1880 Prison Regulation to its fullest extent, particularly concerning the qualifications, duties, and responsibilities of Ottoman prison officials and employees.

Disciplining the Disciplinarians

As discussed in Chapter 2, the CUP established the empire's first centralised Prison Administration (*Hapishane İdaresi*) in May 1911. This agency was attached to the newly restructured Ministry of the Interior and immediately began collecting statistics on every aspect of incarceration. Efforts to professionalise all of the empire's officials commenced immediately with the Ministry of the Interior circulating the Regulation for the School of Civil Servants (*Mekteb-i Mülkiye Nizamnamesi*) to the Prison Administration on 14 August 1911. This regulation contains forty-two articles that stipulate the basic guidelines for conduct, character, and duties applicable to all state officials. It was the foundation of more job-specific regulations for prison personnel, such as the 1880 Prison Regulation.[17]

On 5 October 1911, the Prison Administration distributed an employee survey to each of the empire's prisons. According to the survey's directive, at the end of each month every prison had to report any changes in the employment status of its prison cadre. The information requested included the names, positions, responsibilities, dates of hire, and salaries of all prison personnel.[18] This directive exemplifies Ottoman attempts to monitor prison employment practices. During the first quarter of 1912 most of the provinces and independent administrative sub-divisions (*liva* or *sancak*) returned their completed employment statistical forms to the Prison Administration.[19]

Mosul province exemplifies the general prison employment information gathered by this survey. Its central prison employed Muhammad Nuri Efendi as warden at a monthly salary of 750 *kuruş*, a chief clerk (Muhammad Sadik Efendi) at 400 *kuruş* a month, an assistant clerk (Mahmud Efendi) at 300 *kuruş* a month, a chief guard (Rakha Bey) also at a monthly salary of 300 *kuruş*, a physician (Haziyat Efendi) at 250 *kuruş*, and eight male prison guards all at the same salary of 150 *kuruş* a month. In addition to these personnel, the prison employed a nurse and a launderer. Twelve of the sixteen employees had been working at the prison for more than a year, whereas the other four had been hired quite recently.[20] The eight guards and one chief guard were responsible for supervising 592 inmates over the course of the year. This total number included convicted, accused, and serious and lesser offenders. Ninety-six inmates were convicted of serious crimes (*cinayet*), ranging from manslaughter and murder to severe assault and highway robbery. All of them were serving sentences of incarceration with hard labour ranging from three years to life. Four others received death sentences for highway robbery. A total of 199 inmates were convicted of lesser crimes (*cünha* and *kabahat*), serving sentences ranging from twenty-four hours to three years of incarceration. This means that over the course of the year the guard–to–prisoner ratio could have been as high as 1:65 for Mosul's central prison in 1911. Most likely, the ratio was much lower, since not all of these prisoners were necessarily incarcerated simultaneously. A total of 156 prisoners served terms of three months or less and an additional 297 prisoners were awaiting trial.[21]

These employment records not only reveal very detailed information about each prison employee, but they also demonstrate that there were discrepancies in pay between prison employees in smaller administrative districts and provincial centres, between male and female personnel, and between employees who worked in penitentiaries (*hapishaneler-i umumi*), prisons (*hapishaneler*), and jails (*tevkifhaneler*). It also appears that salaries had not yet been standardised.[22] Except for the warden, all prison employees were appointed by the local municipal councils on the district, sub-district, and provincial levels. It appears that these councils decided the number, identity, and salary of those hired and, thus, possessed a great deal of local autonomy in terms of staffing prisons, especially since prison budgets came from local coffers.

A few examples illustrate these points. Most provinces only hired chief guardians for the central prison and jail in the provincial capital and on the sub-divisional level. In 1914, the province of Trabzon, however, had a chief guard for every prison and jail irrespective of whether it was at the provincial, sub-divisional, or district level. Each prison had at least two guards and one of them was always a chief guard; therefore, Trabzon employed three times more chief guards than any other province, seventeen in total.[23]

Female prison guards were generally paid at least a third less than their male counterparts. In the provinces, especially at the district level (*kaza*), most male guards received a monthly salary in the region of 100 to 150 *kuruş*, whereas female guards generally received in the region of 50 to 100 *kuruş* per month.[24] Male guards who worked in some of the provincial capitals made an additional 50 *kuruş* a month. In general, prison employees who worked in the central prisons in the provincial and major administrative sub-districts received higher wages than their district counterparts. A comparison of prison personnel salaries in the provinces of Adana and Bitlis for 1914–15 illustrates this point. Adana's guard salaries were completely standardised throughout the province from provincial prisons to district jails. All male guards received 200 *kuruş* a month and female guards received 150 *kuruş*, whereas in Bitlis provincial centre and sub-division male guards received 150 *kuruş* a month, but district level male prison-guard salaries ranged from 100 to 150 *kuruş*. Discrepancies were even greater among female guards, who on the provincial level received a monthly salary of 100 *kuruş*, but on the divisional level, received pay ranging from 100 to 150 *kuruş*, which was similar to the male guards in the same sub-division (*muş*). On the district level, however, monthly salaries for female guards were very erratic, ranging from 40 to 80 *kuruş*. Since local municipal councils set salaries and hiring practices, large pay discrepancies existed from one province to another and even within the same province.[25] Such low wages for employees often led to acts of embezzlement and prisoner extortion, as discussed below.

The Prison Administration and later the Directorate of Prisons constantly issued directives to prison employees defining acts of misconduct, warning against them, and delineating the punishments that violators would incur. These directives provide important insights into what types of misconduct and criminal behaviour prison officials were engaging. For example, stealing prisoners' food was one of the most prevalent kinds of misconduct committed by officials as attested to by numerous reports and eyewitness accounts.[26] Prison guards often stole state-allocated prisoner rations for their own personal gain, especially during wartime.[27] In 1915, a case of corruption involving prisoner bread came to the attention of the Directorate of Prisons. A combination of prison official negligence and private contractor corruption led to the purchase and distribution of spoiled bread in Jerusalem's central prison. The contractor was punished and prison officials were reprimanded for their actions.[28] Both the Prison Administration and the Directorate of Prisons repeatedly issued directives reasserting the official policy regarding proper food purchase, storage, and distribution. A 1911 directive specifically details the proper distribution of prisoner provisions with the unspoken purpose of preventing misappropriation of foodstuffs by prison cadre.[29] In 1916, 1917, and again in 1918 the Directorate of Prisons reissued the specific articles governing prisoner food found in the 1880 Prison Regulation.[30] Prison regulations also empowered several different commissions at different times to combat the issues of misappropriation of prisoner food, negligence regarding the purchase of food, and poor prisoner nutrition.[31]

Other examples of directives warning against corruption and misconduct include the ones issued in December 1912 and May 1913. Both reiterated official policy that prison-cadre misconduct must be properly investigated and could result in the loss of salary, pension, and employment.[32] On 19 March 1914, the Directorate of Prisons issued another directive reaffirming the illegality of selling smuggled intoxicants and other items by government officials. These sorts of violations also had to be properly investigated, judged in a court of law, and given appropriate punishments.[33] Then in August 1916, the Ministry of the Interior reissued part of the prison regulation that discussed the fines and punishments meted out to employees who engaged in misconduct, such as embezzlement and dereliction of duty.[34] A similarly worded, but expanded, directive was reissued six months later in February 1917.[35]

This continual dissemination of regulations and official policies regarding proper conduct and prison-cadre responsibilities reflect CUP interests in ending the rampant corruption occurring in the empire's prisons. Reminders of official policy and the consequences of its violation were not the only ways prison administrators addressed the problems of corruption and prisoner abuse. They also emphasised prison personnel professionalisation.

While the 1880 Prison Regulation discusses only rudimentary qualifications for the chief prison guard, such as an age requirement and the ability to read, write, and carry out basic computations, it is entirely silent concerning the qualifications of other prison officials. On 4 January 1912, the Prison Administration issued a directive entitled 'Concerning the Selection and Appointment of Prison Officials and Employees' (*Hapishaneler Memurin ve Mustahdeminin İntihab ve Ta'yini Hakkında*). This directive delineated in abundant detail the criteria, qualifications, and selection process for prison officials and employees.[36] The directive was also unambiguous about the source, goals, and justification of the newly announced standards.

The directive begins by extolling the virtues, efficiency, and discipline of European prison employees. According to the directive, European prison cadre paid careful attention to the social and spiritual welfare of their prisoners and preformed their duties with such exactitude, diligence, order, and discipline that they were able to transform 'vile and wicked' prisoners into individuals who possessed 'moral character' by the end of their incarcerations.[37] The directive also indicated that the Prison Administration shared the same goals as other European countries regarding prison conditions and prisoner rehabilitation. It clearly linked the employee's qualifications and attributes with the effective implementation of penal policy. The calibre of Ottoman prison cadre needed to match that of their European counterparts. If Ottoman prison guards did not possess the necessary qualifications or were found negligent in their duties, they would be discharged from service without a pension or any monetary compensation.[38]

The directive clearly delineates the new selection process for prison employees and the necessary qualifications, characteristics, and skills ideal prison guards would possess. In addition to emulating the model European prison guard, the properly qualified Ottoman guard needed to possess the ability to read and write Ottoman Turkish, needed to have good oral communication skills, and needed to demonstrate an adequate knowledge of criminal law as assessed by an exam. Guards also had to possess the attributes of order, discipline, virtue, and good moral character, in addition to being ethical people with job-related experience. Ideal candidates, therefore, were former military and gendarme officers.

Finally, the directive concludes that prison cadre possessing these stipulated qualities would act as 'the foundation for the implementation of general Ottoman prison reform'.[39]

This directive reflects the Prison Administration's view of the role that guards and other officials were to play in prison reform and prisoner rehabilitation. First, European prisons were seen as models of proper administration, discipline, and order. This, in turn, enabled them to rehabilitate their prisoners successfully.[40] It also demonstrates that one of the primary goals of CUP prison reform was to bring discipline, progress, and order to Ottoman prisons and facilitate the 'rehabilitation of the criminal's soul'.[41] This would, in turn, make former prisoners productive members of society upon their release, because they would now possess good 'moral character'.[42]

Additionally, the directive reveals ideological connections the CUP made between prisons and the military in terms of committee members' shared assumptions and practicality. As discussed in Chapter 2, Comtian Positivism was at the core of CUP ideology and the centralisation of power was its chief aim.[43] The Positivist members of the CUP identified themselves as the *savant* of the empire. Their self-identification was due to the fact that most of the CUP inner circle consisted of low-level bureaucrats and junior military officers educated according to European standards in the military and professional academies of Sultan Abdülhamid II. Preserving the empire and transforming it through the centralisation of its administration and bureaucracy was their chief priority.

Many CUP members had been military officers who planned and participated in the 1908 Constitutional Revolution.[44] This connection between the military and imperial reform has a long imperial tradition. Most reforms associated with defensive developmentalism focused first on the military. For these reasons it is natural that the CUP should want military officers to run its prisons. Former military personnel were ideal prison employees as a result of their training, discipline, and experience in a 'total institution' similar to the prison. Since the inception of the modern conscript army, it has been the military's responsibility to take untrained peasants and workers and turn them into disciplined soldiers. In the minds of CUP members, former military officers were the most qualified to train, supervise, discipline, and 'rehabilitate' society's miscreants.[45] Military and gendarme officers, trained according to European standards, were the prison guards of choice. The CUP considered them the advanced guard of administrative reform that would purge the Ottoman bureaucracy of Abdülhamid II's nepotistic, corrupt, and sycophantic cronies, thereby ensuring professional advancement based on merit and efficiency.

Since much of the top leadership of the CUP was trained in military academies and/or were former military officers, they wanted to use the best of their kind as the leaders of their penal reform programme. And since the prison was a microcosm of imperial transformation, the CUP wanted to place its 'best and brightest' in control of its prisons. By disciplining the disciplinarians, the CUP inserted the cream of the crop into the centre of their imperial reform programme. Former military officers were the Ottoman harbingers of modernity. They were the vital, front-line players who were supposed to bring order, discipline, progress, and reason not only to prisons, but to the entire empire. They were the key to imperial transformation, administrative centralisation, and prisoner rehabilitation.

There were more than a thousand prisons and houses of detention within the empire when the CUP created the Prison Administration in May 1911. In order to fulfil the requirements of this directive, the Prison Administration would need to hire an enormous number of guards with military experience. Also according to a documented exchange between the Istanbul penitentiary and the Prison Administration dated 10 and 15 January 1912 (just six days after the directive regarding prison-cadre qualifications was issued) the ratio of guards to prisoners was supposed to follow the European standard of roughly 1:7 or fifteen guards for every 100 prisoners.[46]

Despite the ideology and the directives, this ratio was never achieved according to prison employment and prisoner statistics collected in 1915 and 1917.[47] The total prison population in 1914–15 was 28,773 inmates, but the total number of guards (including chief guards, male and female guards) was only 1,782. This makes the overall guard-to-prisoner ratio 1:16. The female guard-to-female inmate ratio, however, was significantly lower at less than 1:6. The male-guard-to-male-inmate ratio was 1:18, making this ratio significantly higher than what the 1912 directive mandated.[48] This stark difference in ratios between males and females can be attributed to the requirement that every prison employ a female guard, even if there were only a few female inmates. Since women only made up 3 to 6 per cent of the prison population, in many cases one female guard was supervising just a handful of prisoners.

The overall guard-to-prisoner ratio became even higher as WWI progressed. By 1917, the guard-to-prisoner ratio nearly doubled to 1:30. The prison system employed only 719 guards to supervise a prison population of 21,666 inmates. Unfortunately, the breakdown of male and female guards is not available, but the overall numbers are staggering. In just a couple of years, the prison population dropped by more than 7,000 convicts, while the number of guards plummeted by almost 60 per cent.[49]

This sharp decrease in prison cadre and inmates can be attributed to wartime mobilisation efforts. Many prison guards were actually reserve military personnel who were activated for military duty during WWI.[50] Additionally, many prisoners were mobilised for military duty as part of an amnesty programme in 1917 that allowed male prisoners of good behaviour, convicted of lesser crimes (*cünha*), and with six months to a year left of their sentences to enter military service in lieu of completing their prison terms.[51]

Guard–Prisoner Relations: Breaking down the State–Society Divide

As mentioned above, officials exerted great amounts of effort and resources professionalising the prison cadre, fighting prisoner abuse, and preventing cadre corruption, with mixed results. While the Prison Administration and later the Directorate of Prisons never eradicated these problems, officials undertook extensive investigations into prisoner allegations; punished prison officials, cadre, and prisoners for misconduct; and standardised prison administration, oversight, and accountability to an unprecedented degree. This was all accomplished despite the numerous challenges the empire faced in its final decade of existence. In this case, Samuel Benthan's panopticon model acts as an effective double metaphor for Ottoman efforts to discipline both prisoners and prison cadre. The concrete reforms taken by the Prison Administration and Directorate of Prisons represent a form of surveillance over local prison officials and cadre. Together they enacted clear regulations concerning conduct and responsibilities; established and empowered inquiry commissions to oversee and investigate prison employee conduct, thus holding them accountable for their actions; and allowed inmates to petition central authorities with complaints of ill-treatment. Many of these petitions resulted in official investigations and disciplinary action.

While the archives provide numerous cases of corruption and abuse that Ottoman authorities investigated and attempted to resolve through punishments to both prisoners and prison officials, one stands out as epitomising administrative efforts and illustrating the dual metaphor of the panopticon. It also demonstrates the types of events and malpractices that characterised prison life and the interactions between prison cadre and inmates.[52] In October 1912, the Prison Administration initiated an investigation into allegations of corruption and abuse against Sinop penitentiary's warden, Cemal Efendi, and his staff.[53]

According to the investigative reports, on 28 October 1912 a male inmate by the name of Ismail submitted a formal complaint (petition) to the Ministry of Justice claiming that the recently appointed prison warden (Cemal Efendi) had obtained his position through nepotism. (His brother was the vice-general prosecutor for the Kastamonu province.) The complaint accused the warden of poor character, of possessing no merit as an administrator, and that all of his decisions were based on self-interest. Ismail went on to allege that the warden was making a huge profit from his involvement in a prison-wide weapons' smuggling ring. He warned that if the ministry did nothing then the situation in the prison would worsen, because of the traffic in illegal weapons.[54]

These allegations are very serious, but what is most significant about Ismail's petition is the language he uses in an attempt to move the ministry to action. He asserts that the warden's actions 'go against the age of prison reform wherein prisons are supposed to be schools of reform and places of rehabilitation'. Likewise, he asserts that 'in the end your ministry's clean conscience will never be content with this state of affairs and with my loyalty to the state, I humbly submit this information'. Finally, he signs the petition as 'Ismail from among the prisoners'.[55] Calling upon authorities to administer justice and to protect the weak while asserting one's loyalty is nothing new to Ottoman culture or politics. Nor is it unusual that petitioners would themselves appear as one of the masses ('Ismail from among the prisoners'). What is interesting is that as a convicted criminal he uses the language of prison reform to justify action against the warden. This indicates that the CUP's rhetoric of reform did not stay within the realm of the elite, but had reached the masses. Prisoners knew their rights, petitioned for them, and couched their complaints in the ideals and rhetoric of the day, thus demonstrating their exercise of agency by appropriating certain concepts for their own benefit. In the end, petitioning prisoners became part of the Prison Administration's system of cadre surveillance and assisted in disciplining the disciplinarians.

In response to these allegations, another prisoner, by the name of Cemal, wrote a letter of support for the prison warden to the Kastamonu provincial office of the Ministry of Justice dated 20 February 1913. He denied all of Ismail's accusations. In his petition he claimed that the penitentiary was being terrorised by a gang of tyrannical inmates who were intimidating the well-behaved prisoners and slandering the warden and guards. He requested that these 'bad' prisoners be transferred as a way to remedy the situation. Cemal also denied that guards were abusing these prisoners. He asserted that they only punished these prisoners according to regulations, because of their constant infractions. Interestingly, he also claimed to speak for all the prisoners.[56]

The Ministry of Justice forwarded Ismail's petition to the Ministry of the Interior with instructions that the matter be investigated. The Ministry of the Interior took the allegations very seriously and assigned Behçet Bey, a state inspector (*mülkiye müfettişi*), to oversee the case. It charged him with conducting a thorough and meticulous investigation into the allegations.[57] This is exactly what he and Sami Bey (the other state inspector assigned to the case) did, judging by the documents they produced and the punishments carried out. In the end, this investigative team worked with local officials from the municipal council and other provincial offices to take depositions from numerous individuals including the warden, prison guards, gendarme officers, and several prisoners.[58] The way this investigation was conducted and its findings provide rich insights into prison life, reform, and administrative oversight in the late Ottoman Empire.

The first thing the investigative team did was contact the local municipal council to request the personnel file for Cemal Efendi (the warden) in order to ascertain his background and employment history. Personnel files usually included the employee's date of birth, place of origin, family history, education, and previous state appointments. It also contained information on past disciplinary actions or investigations taken against the employee. According to his file, Cemal Efendi was born, raised, and educated in Trabzon and had held various governmental positions including district governor (*kaymakam*) and tax collector. He had been previously under investigation for refusing to assume an assigned position as a village mayor (*nahiye müdürü*), but appeared to then have been appointed as warden of the Sinop penitentiary, instead, where he had served for the last four months.[59]

The next portion of the investigation looked into the official records submitted by the Sinop prison cadre regarding disciplinary actions taken against the prisoners in question. The inspectors requested follow-up information about these cases from the warden and chief guard. According to the official records, several prisoners were punished for violating prison rules and engaging in dangerous behaviour. These violations included attacking guards, intimidating other prisoners, bad conduct, not fulfilling their responsibilities, making and smuggling weapons, and trying to escape. The first prisoner, Çorumlu Şakir, confessed to making skewers (*şişler*) from the legs of gas stoves in the prison in order to sell them to other inmates. As a result he was sentenced to twenty days of solitary confinement, according to Article 85 of the Prison Regulation.[60] The next two prisoners, Tikveşlu Hakki and Arslan, hid behind a door in the third ward of the prison and attacked a prison guard (Bekir Çavuş) with clubs when he opened the door. The two prisoners claimed they had been angry with the guard because he opened their ward late. These prisoners were punished with twenty-one days' solitary confinement, placed in chains, and fed reduced rations. Supposedly this punishment was in accordance with Article 81 of the 1880 Prison Regulation. Punishment with chains (*prangabendlik*), however, had been outlawed since the 1850s.[61] Another prisoner, Kastamonulu Şükrü, was sentenced to forty-two days of solitary confinement in chains for stealing the iron from window frames and walls in order to manufacture weapons. Previously, he had stolen similar items from the prison factory, thus the harsher sentence.[62] Sami Bey, the state inspector, summarised most of these actions in his own report and had it verified by the chief guard of the Sinop penitentiary, Ahmet Hamdi.[63]

In addition to these inmate misdeeds and punishments, Sinop penitentiary records discuss three other important events that took place on 23 October 1912. All three are central to the investigation of the prison warden and his cadre, resulting from Ismail's petition. According to the official records, the first event concerns an attempted escape by several prisoners who allegedly broke the lock on the main door of the third prison ward and attempted to rush the main gate. It just so happened that this attempted escape coincided with a prison search conducted by the gendarme in the presence of the vice-governor, vice-prosecutor, and gendarme commander. The search resulted in the discovery and confiscation of eighty-three daggers (*kama*), knives (*bicak*), and files (*eğe*) used for weapons making. All prisoners involved in the attempted escape were thrown into chains and sentenced to solitary confinement for 21 days.

The second event involved a prisoner by the name of İzmid'li Hasan Efendi who lost his position as prison teacher for not performing his duties and for suspicion of aiding and abetting the trafficking of weapons.[64] Finally, ten other prisoners of various religious, ethnic, and linguistic backgrounds, such as nomadic, Kurdish, Shiite, Armenian, Sunni, and Albanian, were accused of planning to escape from the prison by building a ladder, breaking a hole in the ceiling, and fleeing through the attic of the prison's third ward. The accused were each sentenced to 21 days of solitary confinement in chains.[65]

Finally, the warden Cemal Efendi submitted his own report stating his version of events. He simply reiterated what the official documents said about the prison search for weapons and punishments handed out to the prisoners involved. He also revealed that he took disciplinary action against seven of the prison cadre (five guards and two supervisors). They were all dismissed from their positions for weapons' smuggling and owing debts to prisoners (implying that they engaged in prisoner fraternisation and gambling).[66] This is a significant number of prison personnel to be fired all at once, especially since at the time Sinop penitentiary incarcerated more than 700 prisoners and employed only thirty-one guards (that being one chief guard, eight supervisory guards, two gatekeepers, and twenty regular guards).[67]

After investigating the official records and questioning the prison officials, the state inspectors began questioning some of the inmates. The interviews were recorded word for word, according to what the prisoner said in the first person, thus preserving colloquialisms, poor grammar, and so on. These interviews give a very different version of events. The main prisoners questioned were Fatsa'lı Hasan Ağa (Ismail of the original petition), İzmid'li Hasan Efendi, and Reşit Efendi. They claimed that there had been no attempt to escape the day of the prison inspection that uncovered the contraband weapons. In fact, they asserted that prisoners had gathered together (including the three of them) to protest the treatment of one of their own who they claimed had been unjustly punished by the cadre. This protest occurred after Ismail (Fatsa'lı Hasan Ağa) wrote his petition and submitted it to the warden who, in turn, purposefully delayed forwarding it to the Ministry of Justice until after the search for weapons had been conducted. The prisoners who congregated to protest were bound in chains and placed in solitary confinement for five days. The inmates denied that any of their friends were trying to escape through the ceiling of the third ward, but that they had somehow been framed by the warden and the guards and then falsely accused.[68] The warden denied that Fatsa'lı Hasan Ağa and İzmid'li Hasan Efendi had ever been placed in solitary confinement, but claimed that İzmid'li Hasan Efendi had been removed from his teaching position on suspicion of smuggling weapons and not performing his teaching duties.

Finally, Fatsa'lı Hasan Ağa, İzmid'li Hasan Efendi, and Reşid Efendi all claimed that the warden and the guards were the ones behind a weapons smuggling scheme. The warden had allegedly awarded a monopoly over the production and sale of prison-manufactured goods to a prisoner named İpsiz Recep. He was the only prisoner allowed to import raw materials to the prison, such as wood, mother of pearl, and fabric, and sell them to the prison factory craftsmen at high prices or on credit so that they could produce their goods. He was also permitted to monopolise the sale of these manufactured goods outside of the prison. In other words, Fatsa'lı Hasan Ağa, İzmid'li Hasan Efendi, and Reşid Efendi all claimed that the warden allowed İpsiz Recep to control the flow of goods in and out of the prison in order to get a cut of the profit. The latter came mainly from smuggling weapons into the prison and selling them to inmates at exorbitant prices. The three prisoners claimed that skewers and knives usually costing 10 *kuruş* at the local market were being sold to prisoners for 1 to 2 lira! They also contradicted the warden's story that only eighty-three weapons had been found during the inspection. Instead, they claimed that the guards actually uncovered more than 200 weapons, but only eighty-three had been reported and turned over to the gendarme commander. Their overall story implicitly claims that the search for weapons had been staged as a means to counteract Ismail's petition and cover up the prison cadre's corruption and prisoner abuse. They also claimed that the guards, gatekeepers, and chief guards were all complicit in the warden's corruption by not doing their duty and allowing these weapons to be smuggled into the prison.[69]

As a result of this investigation, Kastamonu province, the Ministry of Justice, the Ministry of the Interior, and the Prison Administration took measures to restructure Sinop penitentiary's cadre. The situation had become so unruly that the gendarme was called in to restore prison order and aid in its reorganisation in May and June 1913. Additionally, the prison warden, Cemal Efendi, was relieved of his duties and replaced.[70] The above-mentioned ministries also authorised and implemented the complete restructuring of the prison personnel in order to streamline the chain of command and standardise prison positions and titles throughout the empire. In so doing, they increased the wages of all prison personnel with the exception of the warden. Prior to these changes, Sinop penitentiary employed a cadre consisting of a warden (salary: 1,000 *kuruş*/mo.), a clerk (300 *kuruş*/mo.), a chief guard (300 *kuruş*/mo.), eight guard supervisors/*gardiyan çavuş* (200 *kuruş*/mo.), two gatekeepers/*kapıcı* (160 *kuruş*/mo.), and 20 regular male guards/*gardiyan nefri* (150 *kuruş*/mo.). After the restructuring, it employed a warden (1,000 *kuruş*/mo.), a clerk (400 *kuruş*/mo.), a chief guard (400 *kuruş*/mo.), an assistant chief guard/*ser gardiyan maafi* (300 *kuruş*/mo.), two gatekeepers/*kapıcı* (250 *kuruş*/mo.), and 19 male guards/*gardiyan* (200 *kuruş*/mo.).[71]

By taking these actions and implementing change the Prison Administration attempted to improve prison discipline and organisation in order to stamp out corruption and prisoner abuse. The cooperation among various ministries on the imperial, provincial, and local levels to investigate this case and the concrete steps that were taken to rectify the situation all reflect the state's commitment to disciplining its disciplinarians. This commitment did have a real effect on order, discipline, and conditions throughout the empire's prisons. Despite these efforts, however, corruption, guard–prisoner collusion, prisoner abuse, and breakdowns in order and discipline still continued to occur.

The Sinop case also vividly illustrates the realities of prison life and the interactions between prison officials and inmates and among the prisoners themselves. Rivalries, alliances, collusions, abuse, allegations, and exploitations abounded within Ottoman prisons causing serious problems for the Prison Administration in terms of order, discipline, security, and prisoner rehabilitation. Understanding the realities of prison life and administration clearly explicate the blurred boundaries between convict and cadre.

Conclusion

Professionalising the prison cadre was a central focus for the Ottoman administration, CUP, and prison reformers. These entities viewed the prison cadre as the linchpins to creating a progressive, modern, and civilised penal system that was standardised, disciplined, ordered, and able to rehabilitate and transform the empire's miscreants into productive moral citizens. This vision did not stay in the ethereal realm. Officials translated it into concrete programmes for improvement of prison administration, personnel supervision, and accountability.

Samuel Bentham's intended subject of his factory panopticon acts as an effective metaphor for Ottoman prison reforms intended to discipline the disciplinarians. As demonstrated by the central government's response to the Sinop penitentiary scandal, the Prison Administration took concrete actions to supervise and discipline its local prison personnel. These included taking prisoner petitions seriously, conducting robust investigations into corruption and abuse allegations, punishing guilty officials, and implementing real change concerning prison chains of command, wages, new standards of employment, and increased employee oversight. This vision and these actions, however, did not stamp out corruption, abuse, or collusion in the Ottoman prison system.

One of the most significant findings of this investigation into prison corruption and attempts to professionalise prison personnel concerns the porosity of the boundaries between state officials and societal actors, especially guards and prisoners. In other words, personal agency often blurs the rigid lines that social scientists tend to establish between the reified entities labelled 'state' and 'society'. This investigation also demonstrates the intricate interactions between ideal, reform, implementation, and reality. The involvement of so many individuals, from visionaries, officials, and reformers to local actors, such as cadre and inmates, disrupts and often upends the top–down methodology repeatedly used to describe late Ottoman reforms. Local realities and actors affected reform programmes much more than the scholarly literature often acknowledges.

Resistance to and appropriation of these visions of reform affected the reality of prison life in many unexpected ways. The question should not be whether these reforms failed or succeeded, but how they affected the reality of lived experience. Ottoman visions of the well-ordered prison staffed by former military officers acting as harbingers of penal reform never came to full fruition. Its attempted implementation, however, did change the power dynamics within the prison as individuals, such as Ismail, other prisoners, and various prison personnel exercised their own agency to work within and against the system in an attempt to reshape it to their own advantage. The Ottoman prison provides a vivid illustration of this dynamic.

Continuing with this theme of reform and reality and the state's assumption of greater responsibility for its population, Chapter 6 investigates the situation of incarcerated children. It looks closely at the efforts of Ottoman legislators, governmental officials, and the Prison Administration and Directorate of Prisons to change the very definition of childhood and to care for the empire's most vulnerable segment of its population. These reforms and their implementation provide additional insights into late Ottoman views about childhood, punishment, law, criminal accountability, and state patriarchy.

Notes

1. Foucault, *Discipline and Punish*, pp. 195–230 and 'Essays on Governmentality', Chapter 4.
2. For an important critique on the debate regarding the artificially rigid divide between 'state' and 'society' created by Foucault and social scientists, see Mitchell, 'The Limits of the State'.
3. Werret, 'Potemkin and the Panopticon'.
4. Ibid. Similar to the penitentiary, military, hospital, and asylum, the factory can also be classified as a 'total institution', because it employs modern technologies of surveillance and discipline to control nearly every aspect of a person's life. 'Total institutions' are quintessential examples of the modern nation-state, whose development is essential to state consolidation of power (Goffman, *Asylums*, p. 4).
5. Foucault, *Discipline and Punish*, pp. 195–230.
6. See Anonymous, 'AHR Roundtable'.
7. Darling, pp. 157–87.
8. A sampling of these cases can be found in BOA, DHMBHPS 73/33, 105/9, 89/61, 73/15, 73/25, 106/35, 99/14, 81/66, 83/15, 85/15, 149/50, 94/64, 137/18, 134/64, and 131/24. DHMBHPS 131/24 is especially rich. It consists of more than 200 pages of investigations and reports concerning numerous cases of corruption within Ottoman prisons during the Second Constitutional Period.

9. BOA, DHMBHPSM 1/2, doc. 10, Article 9.
10. BOA, DHMBHPS 154/14 contains the 1915–16 employment statistics for the Prison Administration.
11. BOA, DHMBHPSM 1/2, doc. 10, Articles 11–19 and 21.
12. Ibid. Articles 20–1, 84–5, and 94–7.
13. Ibid. Articles 14, 21–44, and 47.
14. Ibid. Articles 14, 23–44, 82–4, and 87.
15. Cardashian, *Ottoman Empire*, pp. 105–6.
16. See BOA, DHTMIK 42/3 for an example of action taken against a corrupt official during the Hamidian era. The warden of Sinop prison was dismissed from his duties, lost his pension, and was replaced for unspecified misconduct in the spring of 1903. Also see Yıldız, *Mapusane*, pp. 400–2.
17. BOA, DHMBHPS 53/6. In early 1917, after Dr Pollitz became Inspector General of the Directorate of Prisons, the Ministry of the Interior published a special directive entitled 'Instructions for Departmental Directors and Personnel' (*daire müdir ve müstahdemini hakkında talimatname*) that spelled out in five sections and thirty-two articles the responsibilities and duties of all directors and employees working in the various departments in the Ministry of the Interior (BOA, DHMBHPSM 25/73).
18. BOA, DHMBHPSM 8/3, doc. 10/b, 11/1, and 11/2.
19. This is a list of completed employment statistical forms for 1911–12: BOA, DHMBHPSM 2/108 (Adana); DHMBHPSM 3/30 (Ankara); DHMBHPSM 3/28 (Aydın); DHMBHPSM 3/16 (Basra); DHMBHPSM 5/25 (Bitlis); DHMBHPSM 5/18 (Canik); DHMBHPSM 4/16 (Cezair-i Bahr-i Sefid); DHMBHPSM 3/8 (Diyarbekir); DHMBHPSM 7/57 (Edirne); DHMBHPSM 8/11 (Halep); DHMBHPSM 4/3 (Hüdavendigar); DHMBHPSM 3/20 and 4/16 (Istanbul); DHMBHPSM 2/112 (İşkodra); DHMBHPSM 3/18 (İzmid); DHMBHPSM 3/15 (Kaseri); DHMBHPSM 3/23 (Kosova); DHMBHPSM 3/34, 5/28, and DHMBHPS 86/29 (Mamüretülaziz); DHMBHPSM 2/114 (Manastır); DHMBHPSM 5/13 (Mosul); DHMBHPSM 2/89 and 3/11 (Selanik); DHMBHPSM 7/106 (Trabzon); DHMBHPSM 3/4 (Urfa); DHMBHPSM 5/29 (Van); and DHMBHPS 6/3 (Yemen).
20. BOA, DHMBHPS 5/13, doc. 2.
21. BOA, DHMBHPS 146/69, doc. 2.
22. See endnote 19 of Chapter 5.
23. BOA, DHMBHPS 154/14, docs 40–1.
24. 'According to F.D.E., Système des Mesures, pp. 23–9, the basic unit of Ottoman coinage was the *piastre* or *kuruş*. The gold *lira* (*livre*) = 100 *piastres* (*kuruş*); the silver *medjidié* = 20 *piastres*; and 1 *kuruş/piastre* = 0.22 francs. This source noted that legally the *medjidié* = 19 *piastres* and 1 *piastre* = 38 *para*, but, for convenience sake, the convention was: 1 *medjidié* = 20 *piastres* (*kuruş*); a double *piastre* (*ikilik*) = 80 *para*; and 1 *piastre* = 40 *para*.' The above is quoted directly from Brummett, 'Dogs, Women, Cholera', endnote 20.

25. For a comprehensive comparison of the different salaries for every prison employee in the Ottoman Empire in 1911–12 see the references listed in endnote 19 of this chapter. For employment statistics for 1914–15 and 1916–17 see DHMBHPS 154/14 and DHMBHPS 143/93. Generally speaking, in provincial capitals, prison employees received the following monthly salaries: director (*müdir*) 1,000 *kuruş*, chief clerk (*katip*) 500 *kuruş*, physician (*tabib*) 250 *kuruş*, chief guard (*ser gardiyan*) 400 *kuruş*, male guard (*gardiyan*) 200 *kuruş*, female guard (*nisa gardiyan*) 150 *kuruş*, and various types of prison workers and servants, such as hospital attendants and janitors (*hademe*) 150 *kuruş*. Compare these salaries with employees who worked in jails (*tevkifhaneler*) and made significantly less than their prison counterparts, except at the lowest levels. They were paid according to the following scale: director (*tevkifhane memuru*) 350 *kuruş*, clerk (*katip*) 300 *kuruş*, chief guard (*ser gardiyan*) 300 *kuruş*, male guard (*gardiyan*) 200 *kuruş*, female guard (*nisa gardiyan*) 150 *kuruş*, and various servants (*hademe*) 150 *kuruş* (BOA, DHMBHPSM 7/57, doc. 35).
26. See Riggs, 'Adult Delinquency' and Forder, *In Brigands' Hands* about the frequency of prison officials appropriating prisoners' food.
27. BOA, DHMBHPS 71/51 discusses guard misappropriation of prisoner rations for their own personal gain during the Ottoman-Italian and Balkan Wars.
28. BOA, DHMBHPS 74/39.
29. BOA, DHMBHPSM 8/7 and 9/13.
30. BOA, DHMBHPS 160/14, 78/81, and 165/84.
31. BOA, DHMBHPS 71/51, 81/18, and 83/34.
32. BOA, DHMBHPS 8/59.
33. BOA, DHMBHPSM 11/59.
34. BOA, DHMBHPSM 25/50.
35. BOA, DHMBHPS 27/18.
36. BOA, DHMBHPSM 8/3, docs 19 and 23/a.
37. Ibid.
38. Ibid. and BOA, DHMBHPSM 17/35, docs 12/a and 12/b issued in 1913.
39. Ibid. This directive was subsequently reissued in 1913 with the same general stipulations and guidelines (BOA, DHMBHPS 8/13).
40. Of course research on nineteenth and early-twentieth-century European prisons has proven otherwise. For example, see O'Brien, *Promise of Punishment*, pp. 190–225.
41. See BOA, DHMBHPSM 8/3, docs 10/a, 25, and 26 regarding the importance the Prison Administration placed on rehabilitating prisoners.
42. The Ottoman phrase found in the directive concerning the selection of prison employees is '. . . *ifayi vasifa eden müstahdeminin mesa'i cediyesi semeresile hapishaneye dahul eden bir şahs-ı şerir bile hıtam-ı müddet-ı mahkumiyetinde sahib ahlak ve sıfat olduğu halde huruç eylemektedir*' (BOA, DHMBHPSM 8/3, doc. 19).

43. Hanioğlu, *Young Turks in Opposition* and *Preparation for a Revolution*. See also Gelvin, *Modern Middle East*, pp. 129–30.
44. For a useful study of the relationship between the military and Ottoman society and its development, see Turfan, *Rise of the Young Turks*.
45. It must be noted here that the CUP did not necessarily want the *Alaylı* military officers to run the prisons or be prison guards. In fact, the CUP blamed them for many of the inefficiencies and overall ineptness of the Ottoman military. An *Alaylı* officer was one who rose up in the ranks from enlisted personnel and was not the recipient of a modern military education so crucial to the CUP's vision of a modern military force. Their training and discipline were substandard and they were unprepared to handle modern weaponry and military tactics. Their promotion from the ranks of enlisted soldier was supposedly based upon loyalty to the sultan and not due to merit, training, or ability. Subsequently the CUP purged a large number of these military officers from its ranks. Turfan indicates that out of an officer corps of 26,310 in December 1908 only 16,121 remained by January 1911. As a result of several purges and enacted laws over ten thousand *Alaylı* officers were expunged from the Ottoman Army (Turfan, pp. 155–65, endnote 115).
46. Regarding the January 1912 exchange between Istanbul's *hapishane-yi umumi* and the Prison Administration, see BOA, DHMBHPS 85/23, docs 1–2.
47. For the 1914–15 prison employee statistics broken down by province and prison, see BOA, DHMBHPS 154/14. See BOA, DHMBHPS 17/32 for the number of prisoners incarcerated in 1914–15 and for the total number of prison guards and the 1916–17 prison population, see BOA, DHMBHPS 143/93.
48. In 1915, 131 chief guards (all male), 1,480 male guards, and 171 female guards were employed in the empire's prisons.
49. BOA, DHMBHPS 143/93.
50. Even Dr Pollitz's personal assistant and translator, Nizar Bey, was called up for military duty during WWI. The Inspector General was successful in preventing his assistant from being activated for military service (BOA, DHMBHPS 80/22). Many prison employees were reserve military officers required to serve during the war as witnessed by the numerous archival documents discussing their military pay and leave requests. For examples see BOA, DHMBHPS 74/42, 74/44, 78/25, 91/1, 91/28, 91/32, 91/47, 93/20, 93/31, 93/34, 151/20, 151/34, 153/57, 154/60, 156/69, 157/49, DHMBHPSM 9/98, 12/54, 13/21, 14/68, 18/49, 18/51, 28/53, and 46/110.
51. BOA, DHMBHPS 79/38, doc. 71.
52. The Ottoman archives hold literally thousands of cases of abuse and corruption that various ministries investigated. BOA, DHMBHPS 131/24 alone contains more than 217 documents associated with investigations into cases of employee misconduct and corruption (*yolsuz ve suistimalat*) within the Prison Administration throughout the Second Constitutional Period.

53. All of the documents relating to this case contained in the Ottoman Prison Administration's catalogues are BOA, DHMBHPS 147/5, 147/12, 147/16, 147/17, 147/18, 147/19, 147/21,147/23, 147/24, 147/25, 147/26, 147/27, 147/28, 147/29, 147/30, 147/31, and 147/47.
54. BOA, DHMBHPS 147/5, doc. 2.
55. Ibid.
56. BOA, DHMBHPS 147/29.
57. BOA, DHMBHPS 147/5, doc. 2.
58. BOA, DHMBHPS 147/24.
59. BOA, DHMBHPS 87/44, doc. 6.
60. BOA, DHMBHPS 147/16, docs 1–2.
61. BOA, DHMBHPS 147/17. Concerning outlawing the use of chains in punishment (*prangabendlik*) see Saner, 'Osmanlı'nın Yüzlerce Yıl Süren'.
62. BOA, DHMBHPS 147/12, 147/23, and 147/30.
63. BOA, DHMBHPS 147/30.
64. BOA, DHMBHPS 147/21, 147/25, and 147/27, docs 1–3.
65. BOA, DHMBHPS 147/25 and 147/26.
66. BOA, DHMBHPS 147/21, docs 1–4 and 147/47, docs 1–3.
67. BOA, DHMBHPS 89/17, doc. 2.
68. BOA, DHMBHPS 147/19, docs 1–3.
69. BOA, DHMBHPS 147/19.
70. BOA, DHMBHPS 96/33.
71. BOA, DHMBHPS 89/17.

6

Creating Juvenile Delinquents: Redefining Childhood in the Late Ottoman Empire

According to the results of the 1912 Ottoman prison survey, Beni Saab's prison in Beirut province contained 447 prisoners – two females and 445 males. The local *nizamiye* court convicted 373 prisoners of less serious offences (*cünha ve kabahat*), and the other seventy-four individuals were awaiting trial. Among the 373 sentenced inmates, three males were convicted of deviant sexual behaviour (*fi'il-i şeni*).[1] In modern Turkish this term refers almost exclusively to sodomy, but in late Ottoman times it also included any action considered to be 'deviant' sexual behaviour not allowed under Islamic law, including prostitution.[2] It also implies consensual participation by all involved. Violent, deviant sexual behaviour (*cebren fi'il-i şeni*) had its own category in the prison questionnaire and was considered a serious offence (*cinayet*), carrying with it a more severe punishment.[3]

In the case of these three male prisoners incarcerated for 'deviant sexual behaviour' at the Beni Saab prison, all were sentenced to incarceration from three to six months. It is very likely that they committed their crimes together based upon several interrelated pieces of information gleaned from the administrative organisation of Beni Saab, geography, and the prison survey. Beni Saab was located on the eastern-Mediterranean coast between the port towns of Yafa (Jaffa) to the south and Hayfa (Haifa) to the north on the Plain of Sharon. As a district (*kaza*) it possessed a minimum security prison for criminals convicted of minor and lesser crimes from the local area. In 1850, Beni Saab consisted of twenty-seven villages (*köyler*).[4] According to population records in 1914, the sub-district's total population was 35,951: breaking down into 35,929 Muslims, eighteen Ecumenical Patriarchate (*Rum*) Christians, and four Samaritans.[5] The town of Tulkarem was the largest urban area in Beni Saab having a population estimated at 5,000 in 1916.[6] The bulk of the district's population consisted of farmers who lived in small villages. In fact, 204 of the 447 prisoners were listed as farmers on the prison survey with another 114 listed as land owners.[7] More concretely, the prison survey indicates that all three of the aforementioned prisoners were artisans (*esnaf*) and Muslim. One was between twenty and thirty years old and the other two were under the age of fourteen.[8] It is not, therefore, unreasonable to speculate that the two minors were working under the supervision of the adult prisoner. The two children and the man with whom they most likely perpetrated their crime were incarcerated together. They all shared a common religion, social class, profession, regional identity, and criminal conviction for which they would spend the next three to six months incarcerated together in a dormitory-style prison with the adult having full access to both minors.

Circumstances permitting, Ottoman prison authorities at the time separated inmates according to the gravity of their crimes, whether they were convicted or accused, and by gender. Juvenile prisoners, however, were not separated from adults. In the case of Beni Saab, there were no serious offenders incarcerated in its prison. The less serious offenders found in this prison, however, would not have been separated according to their particular crimes. During the day prisoners milled around together with little supervision, and at night they all slept together in open wards. Prisoners were not separated according to differences in age, and, therefore, all prisoners, whether they would be considered children or not by twenty-first-century standards, were incarcerated together, slept together, and had complete access to one another at all times.

It does not take a vivid imagination to picture the treatment these boys may have experienced. Circumstances similar to those at Beni Saab helped motivate Ottoman officials to reform prison conditions and introduce laws regarding children convicted of criminal offences. In fact, the CUP-led government implemented numerous reforms to the empire's criminal justice system regarding the status and treatment of children. These reforms included altering the legal definition of childhood, promulgating new laws establishing the age of criminal culpability, and consolidating the state's authority over Islamic criminal law in relation to minors. Additionally, these reforms created a gradated system of punishments for individuals aged from fourteen to nineteen, separated children from adult inmates, expanded the purpose of 'reformatories' (*ıslahhaneler*) to accommodate juvenile delinquents, and established the practice of early release for minors who met particular specifications.

The interest in incarcerated children and corresponding actions taken by the CUP provide important insights into Ottoman views concerning the nature and definition of childhood. They also demonstrate the importance of children and childhood in Ottoman society's imagination about its own national future. These concerns and reforms, however, do not constitute a case of rupture whereby Ottoman views simply conformed to those of the West. Instead, they represent a process of continuity and change over the course of the nineteenth century whereby the state gradually assumed more responsibility for the welfare of the empire's children. CUP reforms regarding juvenile delinquents, when viewed in the context of the development of state-mandated child reformatories, public primary education, health and hygiene regulations, and the establishment of scouting and other youth organisations, demonstrate the state's increasing intervention into the lives of its citizens. Children became associated with the future prosperity, pride, and protection of the Ottoman 'nation'. The health and welfare of children and their legal status moved from the private sphere of the family to the public sphere as determined and controlled by the state. The Ottoman administration thus assumed the position of chief power-broker, at least in large urban areas, regarding a child's legal status and welfare.

Children and Childhood in the Middle East

There is no universal definition of childhood. Class differences, socio-economic status, levels of education, religion, and cultural norms and mores all influence opinions regarding the purpose and definition of child-hood. The Middle East is no exception in this respect. The vast number of religious, linguistic, ethnic, and socio-economic communities in this region makes it particularly difficult to distil a commonly held notion of childhood. There are, however, some ideal commonalities that help to illustrate generally held societal views of childhood in the Middle East prior to the sweeping changes brought about by modernity, particularly among the majority Muslim population.

According to Elizabeth Warnock Fernea, the 'cultural ideal' of child-hood in the Middle East prior to the onset of modernity consisted of several elements, such as the importance of sons, and values associated with honour, religion, morality, hospitality, and respect for elders. Social practices such as religious traditions, discipline, education, and division of labour helped to impose notions of 'proper' masculinity and 'proper' femininity and the superiority and dominance of men over women. Social norms and mores emphatically stressed loyalty to family and family honour, and viewed the family as society's most fundamental unit, as well as the main source of protection, support, instruction, control, and social standing.[9] This 'ideal' view of children and childhood in the pre- and early modern Middle East closely parallels the view in Europe. According to Ariès, in medieval Europe childhood was a fairly short period that ended 'as soon as the child could live without the constant solicitude of his mother, his nanny or his cradle-rocker'.[10] Of course, historical, cultural, and social specificities augment this 'ideal' view depending on context and circumstances. It is, however, useful for analysing the changes that took place in the Ottoman Empire over the long nineteenth century (especially during the Second Constitutional Period) in terms of the state's newly assumed role regarding child welfare.

Present-day assumptions characterising children as innocent, malleable, dependent, and vulnerable have relatively recent origins. They are the result of the dislocation and breakdown of the 'traditional' rural family structure over the course of the late eighteenth and nineteenth centuries. In Western Europe, phenomena such as the Industrial Revolution, the development and spread of capitalist market relations, urbanisation, imperialism, and the inception and spread of modern methods of governance caused greater centralisation of state power and authority concerning the welfare of its population. Child labour, the awful living conditions in tenements, the spread of communicable diseases, the promotion of education, the development of national identities, and the population becoming the state's object of rule all led to a heightened interest in the welfare of the nation's future, namely children.[11]

One of these crucial changes in perceptions and treatment of children concerned their discipline and punishment in penal institutions. David Garland argues that, beginning in the mid-nineteenth century, 'our modern conceptions of youth and childhood began to restructure the laws and practices of punishment in . . . ways we now take for granted'.[12] Prior to this transformation in Western Europe and North America it was common for children under the age of fourteen who were guilty of serious crimes to receive the same corporal punishment as adults, including execution.[13] Over the course of the nineteenth century, the harsh penal practices that state authorities carried out against children began to offend contemporary cultural perceptions of childhood. They functioned as the impetus for extensive reform campaigns aimed at creating new legislation that established 'special reformatories, juvenile courts, and a more welfare-orientated approach to young offenders'.[14]

Many of these sensitivities regarding children, however, were not new to the Ottoman Empire. For example, the mandate to care for the poor, the needy, and especially the orphan and the widow are long-standing requirements of Islam. Child welfare, particularly caring for the poor and the orphaned, has been a part of Islamic law and society dating back to the earliest community. Ottoman commitments to Islamic norms and mores, such as child welfare, were foundational to the dynasty's ruling legitimacy.

During the nineteenth century Ottoman officials placed greater emphasis on protecting and providing for those who were in dire need. While widespread industrialisation may not have occurred in the Ottoman Empire, as it did in Western Europe, the forced migrations and ethnic cleansings of millions of Muslims by Czarist Russia and several Balkan states caused massive dislocation and upheaval to Middle Eastern families during the second half of the nineteenth century.[15] Nazan Maksudyan argues that the presence of overwhelming numbers of orphaned refugee children on the streets of Istanbul and other Ottoman cities compelled officials to formulate and implement numerous reforms aimed at bettering the welfare of these children. The establishment of poor houses, vocational orphanages, and public education were among the attempted solutions to reduce the suffering of these children, secure the safety of urban areas, and fashion children into productive citizens.[16]

Changing Western concepts of childhood and the state's relationship to its youngest citizens did affect Ottoman perceptions, but to cast Ottoman reforms as Western-driven is a gross overstatement. Ottoman actions are much better described as responses to a combination of internal crises and European encroachment. These responses adapted some Western practices to long-standing Ottoman institutions and policies, thus creating new hybrids distinct to Ottoman modernity. Ottoman penal reforms regarding children were not any different, although they did lag behind other Ottoman reforms affecting children, such as the creation of 'reformatories' and attempts at expanding public education.

Two of the earliest attempts by Ottoman officials to improve the conditions of incarcerated children are Article 90 of the 1880 Prison Regulation and the empire's participation in and ratification of the proceedings of the 1890 International Prison Congress in St Petersburg, Russia. Article 90 states that 'incarcerated children under the age of nineteen shall be kept separate from other prisoners both night and day in a place specially designated for them'.[17] Prison officials in the Hamidian era did not fully implement Article 90. Similarly, the motions ratified at the 1890 International Prison Congress were also set aside, even though they included detailed regulations regarding the treatment of incarcerated minors with a focus on their rehabilitation through work and education.[18] Widespread attempts at implementation of these provisions did not occur until the Second Constitutional Period. In this period prison administrators and Ottoman lawmakers implemented many of these laws and viewed it to be within the state's mandate to care for and rehabilitate juvenile delinquents, as well as the orphaned and the indigent. One of the first areas in which the CUP affected change concerned a child's legal status.

Shari'a, Childhood and the Age of Accountability

Since the mid-eighteenth century, penal studies have extensively debated the legal status of children in terms of criminal culpability and incarceration.[19] In the Ottoman Empire, the issue of incarcerated minors was no different, but very few tangible reforms were carried out. Reasons for this lack of action are twofold: first, the Ottoman Government's lack of a centralised prison administrative apparatus prior to 1911 and, second, the power and autonomy held by Islamic legal institutions to determine the age of accountability for one's actions and to adjudicate in criminal matters. The issues surrounding the concept of childhood in the Ottoman Empire and its change during the Second Constitutional Period are intimately connected with Islamic law.

According to Islamic law, criminal culpability for one's actions begins with the onset of puberty.[20] Therefore, prior to the physical manifestation of puberty (that is, nocturnal semen discharge for males and the commencement of menses for females), perpetrators of criminal offences cannot be held accountable for their actions as long as they have not completed their fourteenth year. In other words, prior to the onset of puberty, offenders are 'presumed not to be aware of the unlawfulness of their actions and lack criminal intent'.[21] Minors do not possess a *mens rea* or 'guilty mind', because they are deemed unable to comprehend the full implications of their actions. The various schools of Islamic theology, with the exception of Shi'ism, set a minimum and a maximum date for the onset of puberty. For females, according to the Hanafi tradition (that is, the official Islamic school of law for the empire since the sixteenth century) puberty begins as early as nine, but no later than age fifteen. For males, the Hanafi tradition holds that puberty starts sometime between the ages of twelve and fifteen.[22] Lawmakers adopted these Islamic legal concepts for juvenile criminal culpability into the 1858 IOPC.[23] In other words, girls as young as nine and boys as young as twelve theoretically could be tried, convicted, and incarcerated as adults.

Article 40 of the original 1858 IOPC reads as follows:

An offender who has not attained the age of puberty is not liable to the punishments prescribed for the offence which he has committed and if he is further not a person possessed of the power of discernment he is given up to his father, mother or relatives by being bound over in strong security. In case no strong security is produced by the father, mother or relatives he is put in prison for a suitable period through the instrumentality of the police for self-reformation.

But if such offender who has not attained puberty is *murahiq* [that is, on the verge of puberty, between the ages of nine and fifteen and still not having shown the physical signs of puberty] that is if he has committed that offence deliberately by distinguishing and discerning that the result of his action and deed will be an offence, if his offence is of the category of Jinayets [serious crimes] calling for the punishments of death or perpetual kyurek [permanent incarceration with hard labour] or confinement in a fortress or perpetual exile he is put in prison for a period of from five years to ten years for self-reformation; and if it is an offence necessitating one of the punishments of temporary kyurek or temporary confinement in a fortress or temporary exile he is likewise put in prison for a period equal to from one fourth up to one-third of the period of the punishment called for by his offence; and in both these cases he may be taken under police supervision for from five years to ten years; and if his offence necessitates the punishment of deprivation of civil rights he is similarly imprisoned for reformation for from six months to three years; and if his offence is one necessitating a punishment less severe than the punishments mentioned he is similarly imprisoned for reformation for a definite period not exceeding one-third of such punishment.[24]

Article 40's legal definition regarding the age of accountability was mitigated and clarified for procedural purposes by a Ministry of Justice directive circulated on 26 March 1874. This circular states:

> Males and females who have not completed the age of thirteen years shall be regarded as infants whilst offenders who are just over the age of fifteen if their puberty cannot be established shall be deemed to be *murahiqs* [on the verge of puberty] with discernment.[25]

However, the original Hanafi interpretation of the age of accountability was re-established with the creation of the *Mecelle* in 1877. As mentioned in Chapter 1, the *Mecelle* was the Ottoman Empire's official civil law code consisting of a combination of Hanafi interpretation of *shari'a* and Western civil law.[26] According to the *Mecelle*, the age of puberty and, thus the beginning of accountability and adulthood, is as follows:

> Art. 985. The time of puberty is proved by the emission of seed in dreams and the power to make pregnant, and by the menstrual discharge and power to become pregnant.
>
> Art. 986. The beginning of the time of arrival at puberty is, for males, exactly twelve years of age and, for females exactly nine years, and the latest for both is exactly fifteen years of age. If a male, who has completed twelve, and a female who has completed nine, has not reached a state of puberty, until they reach a state of puberty, they are called '*murahiq*' and '*murahiqa*' [on the verge of puberty].
>
> Art. 987. A person in whom the signs of puberty do not appear, when he has reached the latest time for arrival at puberty [fifteen years old] is considered in law as arrived at the age of puberty.[27]

In other words, everyone who has commenced puberty is considered criminally culpable and punished as an adult, even if she is only nine years old. If a child has reached the minimum age of the commencement of puberty, but has not shown its signs, she or he is considered 'partially responsible' and is subject to punishment. This punishment, however, is at a reduced level from that of an adult. Additionally, if a person has reached the age of fifteen, but he or she has yet to produce evidence of puberty, he or she is criminally culpable and subject to full punishment under the law. It is theoretically possible, therefore, according to Article 40, that children even under the age of nine (girls) and twelve (boys) could be placed in jail alongside adults if there was no relative to whom the child could be 'bound in strong security'.

Determining the criminal culpability of a minor was very convoluted in the nineteenth century. Consequently, it was open to vast differences of interpretation and opinion. This complicated definition of criminal culpability allowed Islamic court judges incredible latitude in determining accountability on a case-by-case basis. Each child's accountability was subject to issues of age, sex, and puberty instead of a simple age threshold. Having the parameters for accountability more clearly delineated for the first time in the 1858 IOPC and the *Mecelle* constitutes a vast improvement over previous practice since it standardised the rules for criminal culpability and limited them to Hanafi guidelines. Even though the empire was officially Hanafi in its Islamic traditions, various regions of the empire were allowed to maintain alternate Islamic interpretations and local judges possessed the liberty to follow those customs as long as they did not contravene Sultanic decree. For these reasons, the new codifications should be considered a major rationalisation of Islamic law and practice within the empire. Islamic judges and courts, however, still possessed great autonomy in implementing these laws. The CUP considered this autonomy contrary to its desired outcome of a standardised, rationalised, and centralised criminal justice system. This issue, therefore, became a major focus of reform.

Adopting a Concrete Definition of Childhood

These legal statutes determining the age of accountability remained intact until the Second Constitutional Period. On 4 June 1911, the Ottoman Parliament repealed Article 40 of the 1858 IOPC and replaced it with this new version:

> Those who have not completed the age of thirteen years [who are not fourteen years old] at the time of committing an offence are deemed to be devoid of the

power of discernment and are not responsible for the offence they commit, but are given up to their parents or relative or guardian by judgment of a Junha Court [Court of Less Serious Criminal Offences] and by way of taking recognisance from them, or they are sent to a reformatory [*ıslahhane*] for training or detention for a period not to extend beyond their age of majority. If opportunity is afforded through negligence in care or supervision to children given up to their parents or relative or guardian by recognisance, to commit an offence before completing the age of fifteen years, a fine of from one Lira to one hundred Liras is taken from those charged with their care.

With regard to those who, at the time of committing an offence, have completed the age of thirteen years but have not finished the age of fifteen years [who are not sixteen years old] punishment is ordered with regard to them, on account of the offence committed by them, in the following manner:–

If his offence is of the category of Jinayets [serious offences] calling for the punishments of death, perpetual kyurek [life sentence with hard labour] or confinement in a fortress, or perpetual exile he is put in prison for self-reformation for from five years to ten years; and if it is an offence necessitating the punishments of temporary kyurek, temporary confinement in a fortress, or temporary exile he is likewise put in prison for self-reformation for a period equal to from one-fourth up to one-third of the period of the punishment called for by his offence, and in both these cases he may be taken under police supervision for from five years to seven years; and if his offence necessitates the punishment of deprivation of civil rights he is likewise put in prison for self-reformation for from six months to three years. If it necessitates a punishment less severe than the punishments mentioned he is likewise put in prison for self-reformation for a definite period not exceeding one-third of the period of that punishment. If it calls for a fine, half of it is deducted. Those who, at the time of committing an offence, have finished the age of fifteen years but have not completed the age of eighteen years [who are not nineteen years of age] are put in prison for self-reformation for from seven years to fifteen years in cases calling for the punishments of death or perpetual kyurek or perpetual confinement in a fortress or perpetual exile; and in cases calling for the punishments of temporary kyurek or temporary confinement in a fortress or temporary exile they are likewise put in prison for self-reformation for from one-half to two-thirds of the period of the original punishment, and in both cases they may be taken under police supervision for from five years to ten years; and if the offence is one necessitating a punishment less severe than the punishments mentioned, punishment of imprisonment is ordered after deducting one-fourth of the original punishment.[28]

A comparison of the original Article 40 with its successor reveals a number of important changes in the legal status of children and definition of childhood. In fact, the 1911 version represents a fundamental shift in the 'official' nature, definition, and view of childhood in the late Ottoman Empire, at least in terms of criminal culpability. It shifts from a flexible

Islamic legalistic view to one that is standardised and consequently closed to individual interpretation, particularly concerning the age of accountability, when childhood ends, and the 'rehabilitation' of juvenile offenders.

The 1911 revisions establish the age of accountability and the ability to discern between right and wrong as being fourteen years of age. No longer is accountability based on the attainment of puberty, but solely on a specific age regardless of gender or puberty. This represents a closer adherence to the 1810 French Penal Code, which states in Article 66 that those accused under the age of sixteen are not capable of knowing the difference between right and wrong (*sans discernement*). However, the new Article 40 preserves a version of the concept of *mürahik* by making provisions for lesser punishments for those who are fourteen and fifteen years old, thus preserving Islamic interpretations of accountability at the latest possible age prior to the manifestation of puberty and melding this with Western conceptualisations of criminal culpability. This demonstrates an interesting example of Ottoman adaptation of European norms and mores to its specific cultural context that does not represent what many scholars have deemed Ottoman 'secularisation'.[29]

This change also represents an example of continuity and ideological manifestation. The CUP and the Ottoman Parliament during the Second Constitutional Period built upon continuous attempts by various Ottoman governments to centralise bureaucratic, administrative, and legal power within the hands of the state. This is evident in the progression and development of the legal statutes determining the age of discernment, which progressed from a strictly Islamic legal interpretation as witnessed by the promulgation of the 1858 IOPC and the *Mecelle* to the combination of Islamic legal definitions and age designations in 1874 to accountability being determined solely upon an established age in 1911. In addition to being an example of continuity and change, the 1911 Article 40 is a manifestation of the CUP's ideological goals and pragmatic style of rule.

One of the core facets of CUP pragmatism and ideology or 'shared set of attitudes' was the creation of a more rational, centralised, efficient, and regulated system of government in all of its multifarious actions and responsibilities.[30] By placing a concrete standard for the age of accountability, the CUP circumscribed the power of Islamic courts and judges. It also rationalised the process for determining accountability and removed the ambiguity that existed under previous legal interpretations. When combined with other changes to the IOPC discussed in Chapter 1, these actions further established the state as the central powerbroker over its population in terms of crime and punishment.

Access and Reconfiguration

Through the appropriation of increased authority at the expense of 'traditional' Islamic legal institutions, the CUP gained more access to the private sphere, specifically the family. One of the quintessential characteristics of the modern era is the attempt by states to intervene into the lives of their populations in order to harness social power. From time immemorial, the family is the most recognised unit of the private sphere, where individuals, specifically fathers and husbands in patriarchal societies, have the greatest amount of autonomy over their dependants in terms of social behaviour, finances, education, living arrangements, and marriage.[31] With the commencement of the early modern period and absolutism, rulers attempted, in a more systematic way, to remove intermediaries and gain greater access and control over the resources of their domains, including the family. Starting in earnest in the late eighteenth century, rulers and states assumed progressively greater amounts of authority over the family, so much so that traditional patriarchy had been replaced by 'state patriarchy'.[32] In other words, the state assumed the role of the familial patriarch in an attempt to shape and control society on its most fundamental level. This was done through education, concerns for child safety and welfare, the promotion of women's rights and freedoms, and even issuing marriage licences and promulgating inheritance laws. The CUP's appropriation of the power to determine the age of accountability demonstrates a culmination of Ottoman bureaucratic efforts over the nineteenth century to create a level of 'state patriarchy'.

The Ottoman administration's penetration into the lives of its subjects, particularly at the level of the family, is further illustrated by the nature and potency of an important vagrancy law passed by the CUP-led Ottoman Parliament in 1909, entitled The Law on Vagabonds and Suspected Persons (*Serseri ve Mazanna-ı Su-i Eshas Hakkında Kanun*). This law provided the police with incredible latitude and discretion in controlling what the Ottoman administration viewed as the most volatile and threatening segment of the population: single, adult, unemployed males, who lived alone. Parliament passed stringent laws restricting and controlling their movements, housing, ability to find work, and leisure activities. Authorities justified these measures by claiming that vagrants and vagabonds were immoral, lazy, and lecherous individuals who threatened civil order because they did not pursue 'family life'. The state assumed the responsibility to protect the family from these dangerous individuals, because it viewed the family as the foundation of national identity and civil society's well-being.[33]

Ottoman lawmakers did not formulate and pass the 1909 vagrancy law in a vacuum. This law built upon legislation passed in the 1890s that increasingly restricted the occupation of begging and highlighted vagrancy as a threat to public order. These were not laws, but 'regulations' (*nizamnameler*), crafted in direct response to the break down in public order in urban areas resulting from a huge influx of refugees to the empire from the Balkans, the Crimea, and the Caucasus. They did not, however, target vagrants in such a direct way as did the law of 1909.[34] The roots of this law can be traced even further back to the late eighteenth century. Sultan Selim III decreed harsh anti-vagrancy laws and adopted extensive surveillance practices in response to social disorder caused by a sharp increase in rural migration to Istanbul.[35]

Throughout the nineteenth century Ottoman sultans and administrators established many youth organisations associated with athletic, educational, and military institutions in order to expand state patriarchy and further intervene into the life of the family.[36] For example, the CUP adopted and promoted boy scouting in the empire. Scouting originated in Great Britain and quickly spread to the United States during the first decade of the twentieth century. The first scouting organisation established in the Ottoman Empire was The Turk's Strength (*Türk Güçü*) in 1913 with the support of CUP members such as Ziya Gökalp. It was organised with the purpose of promoting morality and vitality among the empire's youth, particularly among male Muslim Turks.[37]

In May 1914, the Minister of War, Enver Pasha, hired Harold Parfitt, an Englishman and founder of the first boy scout troop in Belgium, to establish a new scouting organisation (*İzcilik Dernekleri*) in the Ottoman Empire. This was a state-sponsored organisation connected to the Ministry of War and founded to prepare young males for military service. It was a completely voluntary organisation whose membership comprised of young males aged from eleven to seventeen.[38]

Within a month of the establishment of *İzcilik Dernekleri*, Enver Pasha and the Ministry of War established another scouting organisation, the Ottoman Strength Associations (*Osmanlı Güç Dernekleri*). This organisation was compulsory for all young males aged seventeen and above attending public schools. Consequently, the *İzcilik Dernekleri* was subordinated to the *Osmanlı Güç Dernekleri*, and the *Türk Güçü* was disbanded. In addition to founding the *Osmanlı Güç Dernekleri*, the Ministry of War also directed and funded it, thus making it a distinctly paramilitary organisation mandated to prepare male youth for military and national service. This purpose is clearly illustrated by the following Ministry of War declaration:

In this era, for every nation which wants to survive, to defend its homeland (*vatan*), its virtue (*ırz*), and its honour (*namus*) in the face of its enemies, [it] must become a 'nation-in-arms' (*millet-i müsellah*) . . . From now on when our homeland is in danger, those who are true men will not loiter in the streets, but will run and take up arms to defend our Ottoman honour and homeland, which has been entrusted to us by God . . . The Ministry of War is concerned about this vital issue more than anyone else, therefore, it took upon itself this responsibility and founded the Ottoman Strength Associations (*Osmanlı Güç Dernekleri*).[39]

This notion of a 'nation-in-arms' was further reinforced by the outbreak of WWI and by mobilisation of the Ottoman full military (*seferberlik*). All of the nation's assets and resources had to be mobilised, including its children for protection and self-defence. The connection between scouting and the 'nation-in-arms' concept continued to strengthen and evolve during the war, especially as a result of German military influence.[40] Scouting is a clear example of state attempts to train, influence, and gain greater access to children, which had traditionally been the primary concern of the family.

The combination of the CUP's newly established graduated system of punishments for minors and the establishment of scouting organisations represents the entrenchment of the concept of adolescence in the Middle East. These legal and social developments helped establish a grey area between childhood and adulthood for male inhabitants of the empire. Adolescence became a critical period for young males to gain education, training, and experience, thus preparing them for adulthood and service to their national family.[41]

In addition to giving the state more access to the private sphere, these regulations and laws also enabled the CUP to reshape and secure state control over the public sphere, at least in terms of consolidating and centralising its control over the adjudication of criminal matters. Building on the legal reforms of the nineteenth century, particularly the adoption of the 1858 IOPC and the promulgation of the *Mecelle*, the creation of *nizamiye* courts, and the adoption of the 1879 Code of Criminal Procedure, the CUP intensified Ottoman bureaucratic efforts to whittle away the relatively independent authority of the empire's Islamic legal institutions. This process culminated in 1917, when the CUP-controlled parliament passed the Law of *Şeriat* Court Procedure and the Law of Family Rights. These two laws effectively unified Ottoman judicial procedure by finishing the codification process of Islamic law started during the Tanzimat and fully centralised the state's power over the judiciary. The combination of the processes of codification and procedural delineation standardised Ottoman judicial practice and procedure in both criminal and civil matters. The state assumed complete control over all judicial authority by completely bringing both *shari'* and *nizamiye* courts under its authority.[42]

The consolidation of state power over criminal law and its adjudication are partial fulfilments of the CUP's stated goals. When addressing the Grand Assembly (Ottoman Parliament) in 1910, the Ottoman Grand Vizer, İbrahim Hakki Pasha, declared:

> A constitutional government cannot govern according to the methods of an authoritarian regime [that is, Abdülhamid II's *ancien régime*]. A constitutional government cannot accept or allow one law to be valid in one part of the country and not in another, or that soldiers are recruited from one portion of the population and not from another, or that a portion of the population would pay certain taxes while another portion is exempt.[43]

The ambiguity caused by utilising puberty to determine one's age of accountability could not remain unchanged according to the ruling philosophy of this new constitutional government and administration. All facets of life, law, religion, and politics had to be harmonised and uniformly applied. This CUP agenda appears to be equal parts pragmatism and idealism.

Rehabilitating the Delinquent Child: Islahhaneler *(Reformatories)*

The 1911 version of Article 40 places great emphasis on the 'rehabilitation' of juvenile delinquents. It significantly augments the gradation of punishment according to the age stipulations set forth in the original article. In 1911, prisoners aged from fourteen to nineteen were not considered 'full' adults, and therefore, deserved lighter sentences than their adult counterparts. New provisions stipulate measures for the betterment, welfare, training, and 'rehabilitation' of the accused under the age of fourteen. Most significantly, however, these rehabilitative provisions were to be determined by newly established *'Cünha'* (minor criminal offence) courts. Court judges no longer automatically entrusted parents or guardians of the child to supervise and rehabilitate their under-aged juvenile delinquent. Special courts were designated to determine the proper procedure for the 'correction' and 'rehabilitation' of the child. Unlike its original version, the revised Article 40 stipulated that children under fourteen be placed in reformatories (*ıslahhaneler*).

Ottoman reformatories originated in the Tanzimat period (1839–76) and were first established by the famous Ottoman bureaucrat and reformer,

Midhat Pasha, during his governorship of the Danube and Niş provinces in the 1860s. Midhat Pasha originally intended these institutions to be special training and vocational schools for orphaned and indigent children in the above-mentioned provinces. They soon spread throughout the empire in order to assist in the manufacturing sector of the Ottoman economy. Separate reformatories were established for girls and boys and some were employed to make uniforms for the army and to train young artisans after the disbanding of the guilds. Still others were used to develop a new cadre of trained technicians to run the sultan's factories. These modern schools and factories served technical, economic, and charitable purposes.[44]

Midhat Pasha specifically commissioned these first reformatories as a means of assisting in the relief of poor, orphaned juvenile refugees who were flooding the empire's urban areas as a result of recent wars in the Balkans and the Crimea. He legitimised these institutions by claiming to draw their name from a Quranic verse that calls for the improvement and reformation of orphans. During the reign of Sultan Abdülhamid II, the Ottoman administration continued to utilise these reformatories, but changed their name from *ıslahhaneler* (reformatories) to *Hamidiye Sanayi Mekteb-i Alisi* (Sultan Abdülhamid II's Vocational School for Industry) in order to marginalise Midhat Pasha and take control of these institutions.[45] It is important to point out that at their inception and for the first fifty years of their existence these nineteenth-century *ıslahhanes* were not centres of punishment or reform for juvenile delinquents. Even during the Second Constitutional Period, Ottoman journalists referred to the Tanzimat and Hamidian era reformatories as 'orphanages' instead of juvenile criminal correctional facilities.[46] In fact, the only provisions made for children convicted of criminal behaviour prior to the Second Constitutional Period entailed either placing them under the strict supervision of their parents/ guardians or in prison.

The CUP's prison reform programme for children under the age of fourteen consisted of two interrelated policies. The first required the complete separation of juveniles from adult criminals and the second called for a focus on their rehabilitation. Reformatories (*ıslahhaneler*) were the key to achieving both of these priorities. The Prison Administration reintroduced *ıslahhaneler* into the Ottoman bureaucratic vernacular, but transformed them into centres of reform and rehabilitation for juvenile delinquents as detailed in a new penal regulation entitled Regulations for Reformatories (*Islahhaneler Nizamnamesi*), promulgated in the fall of 1911. Officials circulated this new regulation concurrently with the 1911 IOPC changes, the drafting of the comprehensive prison survey, and the creation of the Prison Administration.

The first article of this regulation referenced the 1911 version of IOPC Article 40, especially the portions stressing the rehabilitation of children, thus reinterpreting and expanding the role of the *ıslahhane*. In fact, the first article of the newly written Regulations for Reformatories justified this transformation based upon the non-existence of a 'suitable place within the Ottoman Empire' to reform and rehabilitate juvenile delinquents under the age of fourteen as mandated by the revised Article 40. Ottoman officials created these reformatories for the sole purpose of reforming juvenile criminal offenders and, therefore, they should not be conflated with existing institutions for the orphaned and indigent.[47]

The Prison Administration designed these new *ıslahhaneler* as places where juvenile delinquents under the age of fourteen would be separated from adult criminals, could serve their sentences in a healthy environment, obtain an education and suitable upbringing (*terbiye*), and would come to possess 'proper character'. Juvenile delinquents would stay in these institutions until they reached the age of majority (eighteen years old).[48] Ideally, these reformatories would be built far from cities in open-air locations with a preference given to agricultural areas. They were to accommodate both boys and girls, but were to separate the sexes into specially designated buildings. Their education would consist of special studies and training in modern curriculums grounded in the science of child development. These curriculums included lessons in reading and writing, proper behaviour, and industrial training so they could learn a trade and work in the empire's factories. Both the reformatory's director and instructors were required to be specialists in childhood development. Other regulations required each reformatory to implement proper health and hygiene practices, and keep a physician and chemist on staff. All employees, including staff, doctors, and teachers, were required to submit regular reports of their observations to the director. Daily routines for the children were to follow normal prison regulations and to consist for all inmates of lessons, work, and opportunities for religious worship. Their food was to be hot and prepared on site. Finally, off-site visitations with parents/guardians or other relatives were prohibited.[49]

Children were rewarded for industriousness and for good behaviour, but they were punished for bad behaviour. If a child was a repeat offender then the punishments meted out became steadily more severe. Repeat offenders were first placed in isolation, in the place of which they would lose privileges, such as correspondence and on-site visits. If infractions continued, then the child's clothing would be withheld (for a maximum of three days). If the behaviour persisted then food and water would be withheld (for a maximum of three days). Finally, as the ultimate punishment, their food, water, and clothing would all be withheld (for a maximum of three days). In the course of these punishments the physician was instructed to keep close watch over the juvenile to ensure his or her safety. These regulations, however, repeatedly stressed that the aim of these punishments was the child's rehabilitation.[50] The end goal of these reformatories was to provide delinquent children with a safe environment where they would be housed, educated, trained, disciplined, and rehabilitated. Similar to their nineteenth-century namesakes (that still existed), these reformatories rehabilitated delinquent children by teaching them vital life skills and by providing them with modern educations, thus turning them into contributing members of society.

While the process of establishing these reformatories began in 1911, major progress was not made until 1916 when the CUP hired Dr Paul Pollitz as Inspector General of Prisons and Penitentiary Establishments for the Ottoman Empire. As mentioned in Chapter 2, Dr Pollitz continued, expanded, and oversaw a massive Ottoman prison reform campaign during WWI. Using IOPC Article 40 he successfully pressed for the expanded use of *ıslahhaneler* throughout the empire until his dismissal in 1919. In addition to advocating for the construction of more reformatories, he also called for renting appropriate spaces for these institutions until suitable edifices could be built.[51] Prior to his appointment, there appears to have been built only one reformatory for juvenile delinquents in the empire (Istanbul).[52] By 1919 the Prison Administration had completed or was building sixteen reformatories in major population centres throughout the empire.

Reformatories, however, only dealt with those juvenile delinquents under the age of fourteen. There existed a still larger population of incarcerated children aged from fourteen to nineteen addressed by provisions in Article 40. In lieu of reformatories, Dr Pollitz implemented a pardoning campaign for incarcerated children aged from fourteen to eighteen that ended up releasing nearly half of those inmates early from prison.

Counting and Pardoning Juvenile Delinquents

Situations similar to those described above at Beni Saab prison were exactly what CUP prison reformers attempted to address by reforming IOPC Article 40, creating a centralised Prison Administration and commencing sweeping prison reforms in 1911–12. The 1911 changes to Article 40 were immediately reflected in the 1912 prison survey. The section of the questionnaire requesting a prisoner's age contained similar categories to that found in Article 40; the first two categories, for example, requested the number of prisoners who were aged fourteen and younger and those aged from fourteen to twenty, respectively, in addition to six other categories recording a prisoner's age grouped according to ten-year increments.[53]

In the period from 1912 to 1917, the number of children under the age of fourteen in Ottoman prisons dropped significantly. In 1911–12, Ottoman prisons incarcerated at least 241 children under the age of fourteen: 234 males and seven females (see Chart 3.8). By 1917 only a handful of inmates under the age of fourteen remained in the prison system. It appears that CUP efforts to remove this age category of children from prison were largely successful. This fact is confirmed by a special prison survey taken in 1917.[54]

As discussed in Chapter 2, Dr Pollitz organised an extensive prison survey (*izahat*) beginning in late December 1916. Part of this survey concerned the total number of the empire's juvenile prisoners who were under the age of nineteen. Prison officials completed this survey and tabulated its results by March 1917.[55] The total number of people under the age of nineteen incarcerated in Ottoman prisons in 1916–17 was 1,676 out of a total prison population of 21,666. The vast majority of these juvenile delinquents were male. According to the survey, Ottoman prisons incarcerated only forty-nine female juveniles.[56] This represents an enormous drop in the number of incarcerated young people according to statistics gathered in 1912. Ottoman prisons incarcerated at least 5,169 inmates under the age of twenty, 236 of whom were female, in 1911–12 (see Chart 3.8). Notwithstanding this precipitous decline in juvenile inmates over this five year span, Dr Pollitz still wanted to reduce further the number of incarcerated children within the empire's prison system.

As early as 3 March 1917, Dr Pollitz wrote directly to the Grand Vizier, Talat Pasha, requesting the pardon of certain types of inmates as a way to ease overcrowding. He offered two specific proposals. The first called for the release of juvenile inmates (both male and female) under the age of nineteen who were well behaved, of good character, and who had served two-thirds of their sentences (regardless of whether they committed a felony or misdemeanour). Second, he proposed the release of adult prisoners, both male and female, who had between six months to a year left of their sentences. These prisoners also had to be well behaved and of good character. Only those incarcerated for lesser offences (*cünha*), however, were eligible for early release provided that they agreed to enter military service.[57] Dr Pollitz waived this requirement for pardoned juvenile inmates.[58]

With the approval of the Grand Vizier, the Ministers of the Interior,

Justice, Finance, and War, and the head of Parliament, Dr Politz organised and oversaw a special prison survey to gather specific information on each juvenile delinquent incarcerated in the empire's prisons. The survey commenced in mid-March 1917 and concluded on 26 April 1917 with the arrival of Beirut province's statistics. The Ottoman Prison Administration quickly tabulated all the statistics into a master list.[59]

In order to determine which particular juvenile inmates qualified for early release, this survey collected data that went far beyond simple numbers. The grand survey (*izahat*) of Ottoman prisons completed in March 1917 only requested overall figures. The special survey, however, collected the children's names, ages, dates of incarceration, time served, time remaining, and crimes committed.[60] For example, in Istanbul penitentiary (*Dersaadet hapishane-yi umumi*), prison officials recorded the above-mentioned details for a total of ninety inmates. All of these prisoners were male and all but eight were incarcerated for theft. The others were serving time for crimes ranging from assault and homicide to kidnapping and indecent sexual behaviour. Sentences ranged from sixty-seven days to seven years of incarceration. Of the ninety minors, only four were under the age of fourteen – two were thirteen years old, one was twelve, and one was eleven. All four were incarcerated for theft (*sirkat*) and their sentences ranged from sixty-seven days to two years. These juvenile inmates hailed from various imperial and international locations, such as Mosul, Diyarbekir, and Trabzon, as well as Iran and Greece. For example, the eleven year-old inmate, Hasan bin Rasul, was given the designation of *Iranlı* (Iranian).[61]

According to the sources, Ottoman officials pardoned almost 45 per cent of all of the empire's incarcerated juveniles (745 out of 1,676) as reported by the 1917 prison survey (*izahat*). These 745 inmates were not pardoned all at once, but they were released over a period that stretched from May 1917 to December of that year.[62] This juvenile pardoning occurred simultaneously to the pardoning of adult inmates who met the afore-mentioned stipulations. For example, on 15 July 1917 the CUP Government, including the Grand Vizier, various cabinet members, heads of ministries, and the leader of Parliament pardoned ninety prisoners from the Istanbul penitentiary. Sixty-nine prisoners were adults and the remaining twenty-one were people under the age of nineteen.[63] On 13 December 1917 the same Ottoman officials authorised the pardon of 480 additional prisoners from various provinces and independent sub-divisions, including Beirut, Antalya, İzmid, Mecca, and Haleb. The pardoned inmates included 346 adults and 124 children, all of whom met the stipulated criteria for early release.[64] By the end of 1917, the empire only had 931 inmates who were eighteen years old or younger in its prisons. This represents an enormous reduction in juvenile prisoners compared to 1912 figures.

Conclusion

In addition to removing large numbers of young people from prison through pardons and the construction of more reformatories, Dr Pollitz strove to improve juvenile education, health, nutrition, and living standards.[65] Neither Dr Pollitz, the Directorate of Prisons, nor the Ministries of the Interior and Justice viewed juvenile delinquents in the same light as they viewed adult inmates. As they saw it, it was imperative that the two groups be separated from each other so that adult criminals would not corrupt or physically harm the young people. The Ottoman administration and society both agreed that juvenile delinquents should be reformed and made into contributing members of society.[66] Dr Pollitz continued to change the nature and definition of childhood in the Ottoman Empire that built upon the efforts of the CUP and earlier administrations. He was not the harbinger of penal progress and Western standards of penology to the Ottoman Empire any more than Stratford Canning had been in the 1850s. The empire already had its own long tradition of criminal justice and was in the midst of its transformation prior to either of these two individuals' efforts. What Dr Pollitz did was re-invigorate and better integrate current Ottoman prison programmes and policies in order to help bring them to fuller fruition. This is exactly the case for the empire's juvenile delinquents. Nothing he implemented was of his own making; he simply enforced and expanded existing Ottoman standards and programmes, some of which dated back to the 1850s. With his assistance, juvenile delinquency was more clearly delineated and differentiated from adult criminality and both penal codes and practices reflected broader Ottoman sensibilities regarding childhood and punishment.

Today in the Republic of Turkey and other Middle Eastern successor states of the Ottoman Empire, adulthood or the age of majority, at least in the eyes of the state, begins at age eighteen. At this age, youths commence university studies or full-time employment, submit to military service, assume full accountability for their actions before the law, and, where available, obtain voting rights. The roots of this notion of the end of childhood and the commencement of accountability can be traced to the late Ottoman Empire, particularly the Second Constitutional Period. During this era, the CUP, the Prison Administration, the Directorate of Prisons, and Dr Pollitz successfully implemented many reforms regarding the welfare and legal status of children. These penal reforms, in conjunction with the establishment of scouting organisations and public education programmes, changed the nature and definition of childhood in the empire. In state-controlled legal terms, criminal culpability was no longer dependent on the commencement of puberty, but set at a fixed age.

These developments introduced a grey area – adolescence – between the innocence of childhood and full maturation, during which a person was partially accountable for her or his actions. Ottoman officials viewed adolescence as an important time of learning, growth, development, and preparation, so that once adulthood was reached, the individual would be ready and able to build, defend, and serve the nation. The CUP's assumption of power over the legal standing of children and its rationalisation of Islamic criminal law and procedure also reflect its desire and ability to intervene more fully into the lives of the members of its population, especially at the individual and family levels. It was during the Second Constitutional Period that notions of state patriarchy, adolescence, and childhood became intimately linked to national survival within the modern Middle East.

Notes

1. BOA, DHMBHPSM 22/43, doc. 12.
2. Peters, *Crime and Punishment*, pp. 59–62.
3. Sir James Redhouse translates *fi'il-i şeni* as 'indecent assault' and translates *şeni* as 'bad, infamous, abominable; vile, immoral' (Redhouse, *Redhouse Sözlüğü*, pp. 373 and 1,056). This definition of *fi'il-i şeni* is problematic. *Fi'il* literally means 'action' or 'act', and 'assault' is not part of its meaning. As a serious offence (*cinayet*) listed in the Ottoman prison survey, *fi'il-i şeni* is modified by the word *cebren*, which means 'by force, under constraint, compulsorily' (Redhouse, p. 218) and implies the meaning of 'assault'. Therefore, *cebren fi'il-i şeni* more accurately stands for 'indecent assault' or 'sexual assault' and *fi'il-i şeni* means 'indecent sexual behaviour'.
4. Doumani, *Rediscovering Palestine*, p. 48 (Table 1).
5. McCarthy, *Population of Palestine*, p. 53 (Tables A1–15).
6. Collins and Steichele, *Ottoman Post and Telegraph Offices*, pp. 44–7.
7. BOA, DHMBHPSM 22/43, doc. 12.
8. Ibid.
9. Fernea, *Children in the Muslim Middle East*, p. 11. Other useful works on childhood in the Middle East include Fernea, *Remembering Childhood in the Middle East*; Gil'adi, *Children of Islam*; Barakat, 'Arab Family'; Mohsen, 'New Images, Old Reflections'; and Rugh, *The Family in Contemporary Egypt*.
10. Ariès, *Centuries of Childhood*, p. 128.
11. Concerning the development of current conceptions of childhood, see Stone, *Family, Sex and Marriage in England*; Ariès; and Gillis, *Youth and History*.

12. Garland, *Punishment and Modern Society*, pp. 201–2.
13. On juvenile justice see Sutton, *Stubborn Children*; and Platt, *Child Savers*.
14. Garland, pp. 201–2.
15. For a detailed discussion of the ethnic cleansing of Ottoman Muslims, see McCarthy, *Death and Exile*.
16. Maksudyan, 'Orphans, Cities, and the State'.
17. BOA, DHMBHPSM 1/2, doc. 10, Article 90 states, *'Onsekiz yaşını tekmil etmemiş olan çocuklar mevkuf bulundukları hade gece ve gündüz sa'ir mahbusinden bütün bütün ayrı bir mahalde ikamet ettirileceklerdir'* (Convicted children under the age of nineteen must be housed, day and night, in a place that is completely separate from the other inmates).
18. Demirel, '1890 Petersburg Hapishaneler Kongresi'.
19. Howard, *State of Prisons in England and Wales* and *Account of the Principle Lazarettos*.
20. Outside of criminal culpability, Islamic legal discourse also debates the issues of when children begin to obtain rational thought and discernment concerning religious truth and the difference between right and wrong. Eyal Ginio looks at how Islamic court judges and scribes determined the appropriate age when a child could legally convert to Islam in seventeenth-century and eighteenth-century Ottoman Salonika. Two prominent eleventh-century Islamic thinkers and jurists, Al-Ghazali and Al-Sarakhsi, divided childhood into three general time periods: '(1) the total absence of reason; (2) imperfect reason following the development of discernment; and (3) the full possession of reason when the child approaches maturity' (Ginio, 'Childhood, Mental Capacity, and Conversion', pp. 100–1). Salonika Islamic court jurists assigned specific ages to these periods. 'The Lasonican scribes registered three different categories of minors when dealing with conversion to Islam: Children under the age of seven [the undiscerning child]; children . . . age . . . seven to ten; and adolescents above [ten]' (Ibid., p. 101). There is a significant difference, however, between age-appropriate conversion to Islam and criminal culpability. While Ginio's analysis demonstrates that childhood was subject to different Islamic-based legal interpretations, the age of criminal accountability is very clear (as demonstrated below).
21. Peters, *Crime and Punishment*, p. 20.
22. Ibid., pp. 20–1.
23. Bucknill and Utidjian, *Imperial Ottoman Penal Code*, pp. 26–30.
24. Ibid., p. 27.
25. Bucknill and Utidjian, p. 28. For the original text of the circular, see Nazif Bey, *Kavanin-i Ceza'iyeh Mecmuᶜası*, p. 16.
26. Messick, *Calligraphic State*.
27. Tyser, Demetriades, *et al. Mejelle*, pp. 154–5.
28. Bucknill and Utidjian, pp. 29–30.
29. Berkes, *Development of Secularism*, pp. 347–410.
30. According to Zürcher, the CUP leadership 'shared [a] set of attitudes rather

than a common ideological programme'. These shared attitudes included nationalism, Positivism, a great faith in the power of education to elevate the masses, an implicit belief in the role of the state as the prime force in society, and a powerful belief in progress and change (Zürcher, *Turkey*, p. 132).

31. For a discussion on patriarchy, its origins, and development, see Lerner, *Creation of Patriarchy*.

32. Hatem, 'Economic and Political Liberation in Egypt'.

33. Ergut, 'Policing the Poor'.

34. 'Tese'ülün men'ine dair nizamname, 13/Ş/1313 [29 January 1896]', *Düstur, Birinci Tertip*, vol. 7, pp. 48–9.

35. Başaran, 'Remaking the Gate of Felicity'.

36. For an overview of these organisations see Aktar, 'Tanzimat'tan Cumhuriyet'e Gençlik' and Toprak, 'II. Meşrutiyet Döneminde Paramiliter'. For a detailed discussion of youth sporting movements and nationalism during the Second Constitutional Period, see Cora, 'Constructing and Mobilizing'.

37. Cora, 'Constructing and Mobilizing', pp. 45–61; Üstel, *İmparatorluktan Ulus Devlete*; and Toprak, 'II. Meşrutiyet Döneminde Paramiliter' and 'İttihat ve Terraki'nin Paramiliter'.

38. Cora, pp. 47–8.

39. 'Güç Dernekleri', *Tanin*, 11 Haziran 1330 [24 June 1914], No. 1,977, p. 4 and 'Güç Dernekleri', *İkdam*, 11 Haziran 1330 [24 June 1914], No. 6,229, p. 2. This is a modified translation of the quotation in Cora, p. 51.

40. Cora, pp. 51–8.

41. The modern Turkish word for the concept of 'youth' (*gençlik*) may trace its origins to this time period.

42. Berkes, *Development of Secularism*, pp. 416–19, and Peters, *Crime and Punishment*, p. 133. While both authors consider these changes as proof of Ottoman/Turkish secularism and Westernisation, their interpretations are difficult to substantiate. The Ottoman state had always been the chief authority in judicial matters, but it never exercised direct centralised control over them. Analytically separating religion and state contradicts the historical fact that both were intimately intertwined during the empire's long history. For a more nuanced analysis of the intent and effects of the 1917 Code of *Şeriat* Procedure, see Hardy, *Blood Feuds*, pp. 52–61. He effectively demonstrates that the 1917 Code of *Şeriat* Procedure did not abrogate *shari'* court authority to adjudicate in criminal matters, particularly regarding blood money.

43. MMZC 1/3 1: 275.

44. Özen, 'II. Meşrutiyet'e Kadar Islahhaneler'; Kornrumpf, 'Islahhaneler'; and Maksudyan.

45. Maksudyan, pp. 494 and 507, endnote 6. Abdülhamid II saw Midhat Pasha as a threat to his attempts to centralise power in his own hands.

46. Ibid., p. 507, endnote 6.

47. BOA, DHMBHPS 151/83. This regulation consists of twenty-five articles detailing the authority, purposes, goals, and responsibilities of these reforma-

tories. It also stipulates that reformatories must provide incarcerated children with education and professional training.

48. Ibid. Article 2.
49. Ibid.
50. Ibid. Articles 20–3.
51. BOA, DHMBHPS 76/5, 158/37, 78/36, and DHMBHPSM 34/97.
52. BOA, DHMBHPS 78/36.
53. BOA, DHMBHPSM 8/3, doc. 13.
54. For example, see 1917 prison survey results for Istanbul (BOA, DHMBHPS 158/17), Aydın (BOA, DHMBHPS 158/2), Suriye (DHMBHPS 160/69), and Adana (DHMBHPS 158/66). These surveys list the ages of all inmates under the age of nineteen. Among these provinces only Istanbul and Aydın had any children under the age of fourteen. Istanbul had four children of ages eleven and twelve and two who were thirteen years of age. All of the children were incarcerated for theft (*sirkat*). The remaining eighty-six juvenile inmates were of age fourteen to eighteen. Aydın had two thirteen year-old inmates out of a juvenile prison population of 110. These two provinces generally had the highest number of juvenile and adult prisoners in the empire and serve as good barometers concerning fluctuations in the prison population.
55. BOA, DHMBHPS 143/93.
56. Ibid., doc. 2. This master list breaks down inmates under nineteenth years old according to province (*vilayet*) and independent administrative sub-division (*sancak*). The breakdown by province (children/adults) is Istanbul: 90/967, Edirne: 47/604 (2 girls), Adana: 104/1,049, Ankara: 103/1,385 (21 girls), Aydın: 310/2,843 (17 girls), Bitlis: 7/96 (not all districts reported), Beirut: 51/1,251, Halep: 39/664, Hüdavendigar: 48/849, Diyarbekir: 63/1,128, Suriye: 31/1,149, Sivas: 143/1,214, Trabzon: 23/183 (not all districts reported), Kastamonu: 55/1,255, Konya: 75/985, Mamuretülaziz: 23/234, and Mosul: 14/505 (not all districts reported), independent administrative sub-divisions of Urfa: 17/285, İzmid: 24/279, İçil: 13/85, Eskişehir: 22/164, Bolu: 26/502, Teke: 22/215, Canik: 34/289, Cebel-i Lübnan: 18/275, Çatalca: 3/19 (not all districts reported), Zor: 0/102, Kudüs (Jerusalem): 54/643, Karesi: 73/757, Kala-i Sultaniye: 23/151, Kayseri: 52/255, Karahisar-ı sahib: 7/302, Menteşe: 28/248, Maraş: 8/366 (6 girls), and Niğde: 30/368 (3 girls).
57. Although not stated explicitly, the military service stipulation only applied to male prisoners, but records indicate that female prisoners were still released as a result of Dr Pollitz's proposal. For example, his proposal resulted in the early release of six women from prisons in Adana province (BOA, DHMBHPS 108/31).
58. BOA, DHMBHPS 79/38, doc. 71.
59. BOA, DHMBHPS 159/5 contains the tabulated statistics from this campaign. The only provinces and independent sub-provinces whose totals were not included in this compilation were Istanbul, Aydın, Antalya, Cebel-i Lübnan, and Bolu.

60. For the numbers and names of incarcerated children in most of the empire's provinces and independent administrative sub-divisions for 1916–17, see BOA, DHMBHPS 158/66 (Adana); 159/2 (Ankara); 158/2 (Aydın); 159/12 (Beirut); 159/33 (Bitlis); 117/6 (Canik); 158/9 (Diyarbekir); 158/68 (Halep); 159/7 (Hüdavendigar); 158/17 (Istanbul); 158/57 (Kastamonu); 158/63 (Konya); 159/4 (Mamüretülaziz); 159/10 (Mosul); 158/69 (Sivas); and 160/69 (Suriye).

61. BOA, DHMBHPS 159/16. While this file does not specifically state that these prisoners are from the *Dersaadet hapishane-yi umumi*, when it is cross-referenced with BOA, DHMBHPS 108/13 there is an overlap in prisoner names that makes it clear that DHMBHPS 159/16 refers to the Istanbul penitentiary.

62. For the documents associated with the pardoning of juvenile offenders, numbers, and the requirements for their releases, see BOA, DHMBHPS 108/13, 108/16, 108/19, 108/27, 108/31, 109/49, 116/41, 159/05, 159/16, and 159/36.

63. BOA, DHMBHPS 108/13.

64. BOA, DHMBHPS 108/31.

65. Documents related to Dr Pollitz's reform programmes are as follows – Reformatories: BOA, DHMBHPS 76/5, 158/37, 78/36, and DHMBHPSM 34/97; Children of Incarcerated Women: DHMBHPS 160/82 and 61/20; Children's Health in Prison: DHMBHPS 158/43; New Regulations for the Punishment of Children: DHMBHPS 158/49; and Regarding the Establishment of Prison Schools for Incarcerated Children: DHMBHPS 39/20.

66. BOA, DHMBHPSM 35/91.

Conclusion

When British Ambassador to the Ottoman Empire, Sir Stratford Canning, submitted his 'Memorandum on the Improvement of Prisons in Turkey' to Sultan Abdülmecid I in 1851, he summarised his observations of Ottoman prison conditions and administration accordingly:

> In Turkey where prisons exist in every city and town of a certain extent, and where little attention has hitherto been paid to the science of constructing and administering them, there is ample room for improvement without any considerable out lay. Much unnecessary bodily suffering, much of the evil resulting from moral contagion and from a corrupt and cruel exercise of authority not contemplated by the law, may be removed at once by a few judicious regulations and corresponding arrangements. Even the adoption of these indispensable preliminaries to a more complete system of improvement could hardly be effected without some additional expense. But in the present advanced state of human knowledge and public opinion no government which respects itself and claims a position among civilised communities can shut its eyes to the abuses which prevail, or to the horrors which past ages may have left in that part of its administration which separate the repression of crime and the personal constraint of the guilty or the accused.[1]

His report makes it clear that prison conditions were very poor and that administration was corrupt and inefficient, but he noted that most problems could be solved relatively easily and conditions improved.

Flash forward almost seventy years to 1919 and it appears that little had changed concerning Ottoman prison conditions and administration. A few months after the Ottoman Empire's unconditional surrender to the *Entente* Powers in the autumn of 1918 and their occupation of Istanbul, British officials undertook an inspection of the city's prison facilities. As mentioned in the Introduction, the purpose of this commission was to gain propaganda to use against the 'Turks' in the upcoming Paris Peace Conference. The commission hoped to reveal the Ottomans' barbaric and uncivilised nature and, therefore, demonstrate their unfitness for self-rule. Many authorities were also looking for propaganda to vilify the empire's image and undermine its status and prestige among India's Muslim population. The British reports painted a graphic picture of Istanbul prison conditions.[2]

Two British military officers (Commander Heathcote-Smith and Lieutenant Palmer) together with the newly appointed Director of the Ottoman Directorate of Public Security (Husni Bey) conducted the first prison inspections on 7 December 1918 and filed their report four days later.[3] The report described horrific scenes of prisoner ill-treatment, malnourishment, facility degradation, corruption, and woeful sanitary conditions, although Commander Heathcote-Smith notably reported that he did not consider overcrowding to be a serious problem. He wrote that 'a considerable number [of prisoners] were recently released, and for a Turkish prison [it] is not unduly crowded'.[4]

According to the report, there were no prison uniforms or bedding. Prisoners slept on the floor, and the prison lacked discipline. Prisoners freely moved about the prison during the day, inside and out, and spent their time in idleness. At night, however, guards rounded up the prisoners and made them sleep in their assigned wards. Prisoners claimed that their treatment by the prison cadre was deplorable and that they were routinely beaten.[5] They also complained of terrible health and hygiene conditions. Vermin were everywhere, because the prison was rarely cleaned and inmates had access to washing facilities only once every three or four months. Although separate sick wards were available, the ill received little treatment. The report also claimed that over the past several months, three or four prisoners, on average, died weekly.[6]

Regarding nourishment, prisoners were left mostly to fend for themselves. The state was supposed to provide food rations consisting of six ounces of bread and three ounces of a coarse wheatmeal soup (*bulgar*) per day. These rations, according to the prisoners, rarely reached them, because the prison director, Hussein Fuad, routinely stole the food and profited from its sale. The report describes the prisoners as 'merely a mob of half naked, lousy human beings with shrunken wasted bodies and ravenous eyes, gradually dying of starvation, cold and disease brought on by neglect'.[7]

The women's ward was little better, despite the presence of several inmates with infants. There was utter disregard to the inmates' nourishment, and sick female prisoners were neglected. For example, one female prisoner had a severe case of typhus, but was not adequately quarantined and thus posed an infectious threat to the other inmates. The report claimed that thirty-two female prisoners had died over the last two and a half months.[8]

As a result of this inspection it was proposed that allied military commanders visit all prisons throughout the empire in order to ascertain their respective conditions. Additionally, the entire prison system was placed under the direction of General Milne to whom orders had recently been given to oversee issues pertaining to the empire's police and public sanitation.[9] Commander Heathcote-Smith and Admiral Webb, therefore, undertook a subsequent inspection of the same prison in late January 1919 in order to ascertain whether or not the Ottoman Government had addressed any of the concerns that were expressed in their initial report.[10] Admiral Webb reported that 'with the exercise of a considerable amount of moral pressure, and in the face of the usual Turkish evasiveness and procrastination, some reforms have at length been carried out.'[11] Conditions, however, still remained horrendously poor. According to Webb:

Maison D'Arret [Sultanahmet Jail (*Tevkifhane*)] . . . is the place where men are confined while awaiting trial . . . In an old tumbled-down building with a small, ill-paved courtyard, I found imprisoned 186 Moslem and Christian Ottoman Subjects. These were distributed among a variety of rooms each of which I visited in turn . . . On the ground which had been laid bare by the removal of the boards was an indescribable collection of excrement and filthy cast off rags of prisoners, the whole being a breeding place for vermin of all kinds. The prisoners were lying about on the boards and sometimes even on the bare earth, and none of those had any covering other than the filthy rags which still clung round them. The squalor and filth of these dens, the indescribable stench arising from them, the gloom even at mid-day relieved by tiny windows high up near the ceiling, and the total lack of ventilation, all these features formed a scene which I am not likely to forget.

Of the miserable creatures lying or sitting about on the ground and floors, subsequent medical examination showed that between 80% and 90% were suffering from the mange (Scabies). Quite a number have become consumptive through starvation and malnutrition, and many forms of illness, chiefly Typhus and Syphilis were raging among them. There was not even pretence of their being given any medical attention. Their diet, which consisted of a very coarse and indigestible bread, is augmented once daily by a cupful of so-called soup, so repulsive in taste and smell that even the prisoners in their ravenous hunger often turned away from it in disgust. I smelt it and the stench was overpowering; to taste it was impossible.

The sanitary arrangements, or rather the lack thereof, are best left to the imagination. Baths were, of course, practically an unknown quantity, and even drinking water was so stinted that they clamoured loudly to be given some . . . What made the horror of these places even worse was that all were still awaiting trial; a great majority had been there for over 4 months, many from 6 to 12 months, and some as much as 21 to 25 months. It is difficult to understand how any human being could survive 21 months or even 12 months of such treatment, and of course the mortality has been extremely high . . . [T]he Turkish Government has at last been persuaded to take action in the matter. The whole system is so honeycombed with bribery and corruption that it is hopeless to expect any real improvement while the Turks remain their own masters.[12]

As a result of these inquiries the Ottoman Grand Vizier Damad Ferid Pasha sent a letter assuring British authorities that all steps were being taken to remedy the awful situation that existed in these prisons. Namely, he related that new prison buildings were under construction and would be opened within the next few months; all inmates would be transferred to these new prisons; and, finally, the method of detention currently in existence at the Istanbul Jail (*Maison D'Arret*) would be discontinued.[13]

These claims appear to have been carried out, as confirmed by two inspections conducted on 29 March 1919 and 3 April 1919 by Allied powers, with the presence this time of both French and British personnel.[14] The report written by the British High Commission of Constantinople dated 6 April 1919 claims that 'regarding the appalling conditions prevalent in the Turkish prisons here, I have the honour to record that an improvement is now visible'.[15] The *Maison D'Arret* was decommissioned and in the process of being torn down.[16]

Admiral Webb summed up his remarks by stating:

> [T]he actual conditions of life for the prisoners were distinctly better; the food was more nourishing and almost palatable; the accommodation in use was somewhat cleaner, and the prisoners themselves had lost that haunted look which was so marked previously. It may reasonably be said, therefore, that the prison problem in Constantinople has temporarily ceased to be an acute one . . . In conclusion I may say that a great, if spasmodic, step forward has been taken in prison reform here, but I am more than ever convinced that were we to relax our vigilance the old state of things would inevitably recur.[17]

Despite these improvements, it appears that within less than a year conditions worsened yet again. In February 1920, allied authorities filed two additional reports, in French, about conditions in Ottoman prisons. The Internal Commission for the Inspection of Anatolian Ottoman Prisons submitted its report on 7 February 1920, whereas on 23 February 1920 a delegation of French, British, and Italian Military *Attachés* and High Commissioners submitted their prison inspection report directly to the Ottoman Minister of the Interior. Both reports claimed that Ottoman prisons suffered from poor conditons. The second report, however, described the state of Istanbul's penitentiary as one of a 'reign of anarchy' caused by severe overcrowding, poor hygiene, and tremendous prisoner suffering. It claimed that sustained prison improvement was not a priority for the post-war Ottoman government.[18] Some prisoners attempted to take advantage of the *Entente* occupation by petitioning Greek officials to intervene on their behalf for changes and relief that specifically favoured Ecumenical and Armenian Christian inmates.[19]

Conclusion

According to all of these inspections, sanitary and general living conditions were so deplorable that it appeared that little had changed since the 1850s. It is, therefore, easy to conclude that the Ottomans spent little time, effort, or resources on prison reform during the nineteenth century, despite repeated reprimands and urgings by Western powers to make reforms. Perhaps the stereotypes concerning the 'Turkish' prison and 'Turkish' barbarity and venality were well-deserved. This is, however, simply not the case. Conditions in 'total institutions' rapidly deteriorate if the institution is neglected and not adequately provisioned. These enclosed institutions, including prisons, hospitals, and asylums, completely depend on the outside world for care and upkeep. With the loss of the war, the occupation of Istanbul, the expulsion of the CUP from power, and the commencement of the Turkish War of Independence, there was a general breakdown in all social services. The Ottoman Government, economy, military, police, and population were in complete disarray. Prisons became low priority for the new government. Funds were directed elsewhere and Dr Pollitz was relieved of his duties and sent back to Germany. This all resulted in the rapid deterioration of prison conditions and, thus, explains what the foreign inspectors found in 1918 to 1921.[20] In fact, Charles Riggs, an American researcher living in Istanbul, wrote an article entitled 'Adult Delinquency' that detailed Istanbul's criminal activities, courts, and prisons in 1920–1.[21] His report substantiates the *Entente* inspections, but instead of blaming 'Turkish venality' for the poor conditions and high crime rates, he clearly attributes these conditons to the grave effects of war and occupation.[22]

In contrast to the prejudiced and orientalist claims of British, French, and other foreign inspectors, this book demonstrates that Ottoman authorities exerted enormous efforts to transform the empire's prisons and criminal justice system over the course of the nineteenth century in order to meet the challenges the empire faced as a result of internal crises and European encroachment. These efforts aimed at transforming the empire into a modern powerful state that possessed a monopoly on the use of force, particularly in terms of its military, policing, and the punishment of criminal offenders. Ottoman efforts to transform its criminal justice system and centralise its power over the adjudication of criminal matters, especially punishment, were not systematically progressive throughout the second-half of the nineteenth century. Each regime, however, built upon the efforts of its predecessors, thus making prison reform a key part of imperial transformation, shared ideals of civilisational progress, and of modern nation-state construction.

Ottoman prison reform culminated in the Second Constitutional Period, specifically during WWI. In the face of massive starvation, population transfers, civil war, total war mobilisation, economic ruin, ethnic cleansings, genocide, pandemic disease, insurrections, military campaigns, and imperial dismemberment, the CUP continued its prison reform campaigns until its expulsion from power. The effort, time, resources, and energy expended on criminal justice reform by various regimes during the nineteenth century demonstrate the importance of prisons to overall imperial transformation. Notwithstanding these seemingly progressive reforms, they were also accompanied by devastating social engineering programmes that resulted in human atrocities comparable with contemporary colonial and 'civilisational' projects around the world, such as those waged against Native-Americans, Congolese, various South Asian populations, Australian and Oceania Aborigines, and Black South Africans, to name only a few. This is the dark side of nation-state construction and modernity. This is the barbarity of the 'civilised' world to which the Ottoman Empire belonged.

Prisons do indeed act as prisms into broader nineteenth-century Ottoman politics, culture, and society. They are microcosms of imperial transformation wherein many of the pressing questions of Ottoman modernity played out. Prison reformers addressed key imperial issues, such as administrative centralisation, the introduction of modern methods of governance, new concepts of time and space, industrialisation and economic development, profesionalisation of government personnel, issues of gender and childhood, the rationalisation of penal law and practice, concepts associated with ethno-religious national identity, public health and hygiene, and the state's assumption of greater responsibility for the welfare and supervision of its population. These efforts provide important insights into Ottoman sensibilities towards crime, punishment, and the role of the state in maintaining public order and rehabilitating criminals.

Ottoman efforts to transform the empire's criminal justice system, however, do not constitute a process of secularisation and Westernisation. Penal reforms in the Ottoman Empire appropriated new approaches to governance and adapted them to existing norms, institutions, and practices. This hybridisation process created an entirely new dynamic of criminal justice and penality that was both fully modern and Ottoman. This new dynamic is manifest by the empire's codification of Islamic criminal law, the adoption of incarceration as the primary form of criminal punishment, the abrogation of *qadi* and local administrative punitive autonomy, and the standardisation of juvenile criminal culpability. Each of these new phenomena was grounded in Ottoman and Islamic cultural norms and sensibilities that were, in turn, reinterpreted and reconfigured to meet the challenges of the modern age.

Conclusion

This study represents an interpretive endeavour concering the role that penal institutions played in Ottoman state construction that tests the applicability of Western approaches and methodologies. Similar to the development of Western European and North American states, the development and centralisation of modern penal institutions were central aspects of modern state construction in the late Ottoman Empire in terms of social control and discipline. This study argues, however, that Ottoman penal institutions represent much more than just apparatuses for imposing social control and discipline. Not only do prisons act as windows into Ottoman modernity from a state ideological and administrative perspective, but they also juxtapose these reform efforts with the everyday experiences of the incarcerated and prison cadre. When taken in aggregate, the reform and reality of prison life offer unique perspectives into prisoner agency, state ideology, and how state efforts are altered, adapted, and resisted by the objects of those reforms.

Ottoman prison reforms in the nineteenth and early twentieth centuries achieved much. Efforts to remove children from prisons were largely efficacious. Officials eased overcrowding, improved overall health and hygiene conditions, built new prisons, and aggressively prosecuted and punished corrupt and abusive officials. Despite these improvements, prison officials and inmates still faced enormous challenges, such as dilapidated facilities, poor provisions and conditions, limited funds, continued overcrowding, escapes, breakdowns in discipline and order, corruption, and prisoner abuse. This close examination of Ottoman prison life demonstrates the convoluted and complex nature of state and societal relations at its most basic level.

The collocation of reform and reality in Ottoman prisons overcomes the overly deterministic state-centric narrative of late Ottoman efforts at modernisation. In its place, a new narrative emerges revealing the dynamic created by the intersection of reform and the exercise of personal agency, wherein individuals accept, reject, appropriate, and augment various aspects of Ottoman modernity for their own interests. Ottoman attempts at reform should not necessarily be judged with moralistic labels of 'success' or 'failure'. Instead, scholars should focus on how attempts at transformation affected human interactions and relationships, state policies and practices, and everyday life within the empire.

In 1926, Clarence Richard Johnson, a professor of sociology at Bucknell University in the United States who spent three years living, teaching, and researching in Istanbul after WWI, published an insightful article in the *Journal of Applied Sociology* entitled 'Prison Conditions in Constantinople'. His article makes two very important observations concerning Istanbul's prisons. First, Mustafa Kemal Atatürk did not continue the progressive prison reforms of the late Ottoman era in the immediate post-war period. Johnson's article describes Istanbul's prisons as lacking internal order and discipline. Prisoners were poorly clothed, improperly provisioned, and not separated according to severity of crime. Most prisoners slept in open dorms with no beds and sat in idleness all day. No efforts were made to rehabilitate prisoners through education and productive labour. Crowded conditions persisted, leading to sickness, disease, and vermin infestations. Fights, smuggling, weapons making, and gambling were routine occurrences. In his opinion, however, the biggest threat to prison order was the prevalence of opium addiction and drug use in Istanbul's prisons. He clearly states that the newly founded Republic of Turkey did not implement the regulations it inherited from its Ottoman predecessor.[23]

Second, Johnson's article asserts that Istanbul's prison conditions are comparable to those of seemingly more 'civilised' and progressed countries, especially the United States. In fact, while lamenting the awful conditions found in the new republic's prisons, he actually claims that they are better than those in the United States:

> If we go to them [Istanbul's prisons] having visited prisons in America, knowing something of the disgrace which all prisons are to our twentieth Century, if we try to see these prisons exactly as they are in the light of the whole prison problem, then one can say that on the whole the prisons of Constaninople are not so bad as one would expect them to be in a poverty-stricken country like Turkey. The nerve breaking, straight jacket system of many of our American prisons, where men are mere machines, and where prison officials seek to break the spirit of the inmates, seems to be happily lacking. Our American prisons are responsible for much insanity – never can I forget the horrible cries of the insane men in solitary confinement which I heard in an American prison. The prisons of Constantinople need to be reformed and they need it badly, but so do the American prisons, and the prisons in Constantinople are not such a disgrace to Turkey as American prisons are to the United States.[24]

These are remarkable words of national introspection coming from an American professor of sociology about the state of prison conditions throughout the world in the early twentieth century and about their comparability across cultures and borders on a global scale.

Ottoman prison conditions and reform efforts are indeed comparable to those found in other countries in the nineteenth century and in the early twentieth century. As various states across Latin America, Africa, Asia, Europe, and North America appropriated and adapted modern methods of governance and became incorporated into the Modern World System, penal institutions became critically important for modern nation-state construction and transformation. European characterisations of penal practices outside of its borders as despotic, oriental, and barbaric must be tempered by reform efforts and prison realities in their own countries. They must also be qualified by comparative work on 'Western' prison conditions and those in other global regions that allow for historical and regional specificity. Some work has already been done in the field of penal comparative research on a global scale, but more work is needed that integrates prisons and punishment into broader global criminal justice transformations in policing, courts procedures, and penal codes. More work must also be done that integrates these reform efforts with the realities of lived experience as individuals shaped, interacted with, utilised, and resisted modern criminal justice policies, practices, and institutions.

As mentioned above, many of the prison reforms discussed in this work do not appear to have been continued by the successor states of the Ottoman Empire. Similar to numerous reform programmes, idealism appears to have collided with pragmatism, financial constraints, and 'national' self-interest. Ethnic nationalisms have dominated Middle Eastern and South-eastern European states since the empire's dismemberment and placed a premium on the punitive qualities of penal institutions for social control and discipline. It appears that efforts at prisoner rehabilitation, proper provisioning, and care have been mostly forgotten in contemporary Middle Eastern states. Ottoman efforts at criminal justice and penal reform, however, did lay an important foundation for the penal institutions, codes, and practices adopted by many states that emerged in the wake of the Ottoman Empire's dismemberment and collapse. Any study of modern penal institutions and practices in former Ottoman territories must take this foundation into account.

Notes

1. BNA, FO 195/364, pp. 1–32.
2. BNA, FO 608/114/3, 608/114/4, and 608/52/13.
3. BNA, FO 608/52/13, pp. 238–43.
4. Ibid.
5. Ibid., pp. 239 and 241.
6. Ibid., pp. 239–41.
7. Ibid., p. 240.
8. Ibid., p. 241.
9. BNA, FO 608/52/13, p. 243.
10. BNA, FO 608/114/4, pp. 120–6.
11. Ibid., p. 120.

12. Ibid., pp. 120–6.
13. BNA, FO 608/114/3, pp. 140–3.
14. Ibid., p. 151.
15. Ibid., p. 153.
16. Ibid., p. 154.
17. Ibid., pp. 154–6.
18. See BOA, DHMBHPSM 41/32 and 41/38.
19. In March and April 1921 a group of Ecumenical and Armenian Ottoman Christians incarcerated in Istanbul's prisons petitioned Greek occupying officials to intervene on their behalf in order to secure their release. Their petition described very poor living conditions and the abuses they were subjected to by prison officials claiming that their poor treatment resulted from their Christian faith. The petitioners also pointed out that none of the guards or prison officials overseeing the prison were Christians and this needed to be remedied in order to protect Christian rights. The petition is an interesting example of inmates exercising their agency to exploit *Entente* prejudices and interfaith rivalries in order to secure special privileges and better conditions (BOA, DHMBHPS 45/75). I would like to thank Elektra Kostopolous for translating this petition from the original Greek.
20. For a detailed discussion concerning problems and poor conditions in Istanbul's prisons during the *Entente* occupation of Istanbul, see Yıldıztaş 'Mütareke Döneminde Suç Unsurları', pp. 35–83.
21. Riggs, 'Adult Delinquency', pp. 323–67.
22. Ibid., pp. 336–53. Riggs was a member of a team of professional researchers who undertook a comprehensive social study of Istanbul in 1920.
23. Johnson, 'Prison Conditions in Constantinople'. For a less scholarly discussion of the poor conditions in Istanbul's Sultanahmet jail in about 1926 by an Italian citizen, see Zaccagnini, *Ricordi di Constantinopoli*, pp. 119–28. I wish to express my thanks to Jonathan McCullom for translating this section from the original Italian.
24. Johnson, 'Prison Conditions in Constantinople', p. 274.
25. For example, see Dikötter and Brown, *Cultures of Confinement*, and Bernault, and Roitman, *History of Prison and Confinement in Africa*.

Bibliography

Primary Sources

ARCHIVAL SOURCES

Başbakanlık Osmanlı Arşivi (BOA), Istanbul, Turkey
  Dahiliye Nizareti, Emniyet-i Umumiye Müdiriyeti, Tahrirat Kalemi Belgeleri (DHEUMTK)
  Dahiliye Nezareti, Mebani-i Emiriye ve Hapishaneler Müdiriyeti Belgeleri (DHMBHPS)
  Dahiliye Nezareti, Mebani-i Emiriye ve Hapishaneler Müdiriyeti Belgeleri Müteferrik (DHMBHPSM)
  Dahiliye Nezareti, Muhaberat-ı Umumiye İdaresi (DHMUİ)
  Dahiliye Nezareti, Tesri-i Muamelat ve Islahat Komisyonu (DHTMIK)
  Yıldız Esas Evrakı (YEE)
  Zaptiye Belgeleri (ZB)
The British National Archives (BNA), London, UK
  The British Foreign Office (FO)

OFFICIALLY PUBLISHED GOVERNMENT PAPERS

Düstur: Birinci Tertip (Code of Laws: 1st Series), Istanbul: 1876–7, 4 vols
Düstur: İkinci Tertip (Code of Laws: 2nd Series), Istanbul: 1908–18, 10 vols
Levayıh ve Tekalif-i Kanuniye ve Encumen Mazbataları (Law Proposals and Records of Legislative Commissions), Istanbul: 1908–12, 4 vols
Meclis-i Mebusan Zabıt Ceridesi (MMZC), Istanbul: 1908–20, 36 vols

LAW CODES

Akgündüz, Ahmet, *Mukayeseli İslam ve Osmanlı Hukuku Külliyatı*. Diyarbekir: Dicle Üniversitesi Hukuk Fakültesi Yayınları, 1986.
——, *Osmanlı Kanunnameleri ve Hukuki Tahlilleri*. Istanbul: FEY Vakfı, 1990.
Bucknill, John A. Strachey and Haig Apisoghom S. Utidjian, *The Imperial Ottoman Penal Code: A Translation from the Turkish Text*. London: Oxford University Press, 1913.
Gökçen, Ahmet, *Tanzimat dönemi Osmanlı ceza kanunları ve bu kanunlardaki ceza müeyyidleri*. Istanbul: Ahmet Gökçen, 1989.

Mueller, Gerhard O. W. (ed.), *The French Penal Code*. South Hackensack, NJ: Fred B. Rothman & Co., 1960.

Nazif Bey, *Kavanin-i Ceza'iyeh Mecmu'ası [A Collection of Penal Laws]*. Constantinople: Garabed's Printing Office, 1902.

Tyser, C.R. and D.G. Demetriades, *et al.* (eds), *The Mejelle: Being an English Translation of Majallah El-Ahkam-i-Adliya and a Complete Code on Islamic Civil Law*. Kuala Lumpur, Malaysia: The Other Press, 2001.

Young, George, *Corps de Droit Ottoman*, 7 vols. Oxford: The Clarendon Press, 1905–6.

NEWSPAPERS

İkdam, Istanbul, Turkey
Tanin, Istanbul, Turkey
The New York Times, New York, United States

OTHER PRIMARY SOURCES

Forder, A, *In Brigands' Hands and Turkish Prisons, 1914–1918*. London: Marshall Brothers Limited, 1919.

Griffiths, Major Arthur, *The History and Romance of Crime: From the Earliest Times to the Present Day, Vol. xii, Oriental Prisons*. London: Cassell, 1910.

Johnson, Clarence Richard, 'Prison Conditions in Constantinople', *Journal of Applied Sociology*, X(1) (January–February 1926), 264–74.

Riggs, Charles Trowbridge, 'Adult Delinquency', in Clarence Richard Johnson (ed.), *Constantinople To-day or The Pathfinder Survey of Constantinople: A Study in Oriental Social Life*. New York: MacMillan Company, 1922, pp. 323–67.

Sami, Şemseddin, *Kamus-ı Türki*. Istanbul: Çağrı Yayınları, 1996 [1899].

Şerif, Ahmet with preparation by Mehmed Çetin Börekçi, *Anadolu'da Tanin, I Cilt*, Ankara: Türk Tarih Kurumu, 1999a.

——, *Arnavudluk'da, Suriye'de, Trablusgarb'de Tanin, II Cilt*, Ankara: Türk Tarih Kurumu, 1999b.

Zaccagnini, Giuseppe, *Ricordi di Constantinopoli*. Rome: Marche, 1926.

Secondary Sources

Adak, Ufuk, 'XIX. Yüzyılın Sonları XX. Yüzyılın Başlarında Aydın Vilayeti'ndeki Hapishaneler', MA thesis, Ege University, 2006.

Adams, Bruce F, *The Politics of Punishment: Prison Reform in Russia, 1863–1917*. DeKalb, Ill: Northern Illinois University Press, 1996.

Agmon, Iris, *Family and Court: Legal Culture and Modernity in Late Ottoman Palestine*. Syracuse: Syracuse University Press, 2006.

Bibliography

Ahmad, Feroz, *The Young Turks: The Committee of Union and Progress in Turkish Politics, 1908–1914.* Oxford: The Clarendon Press, 1969.
——, 'Vanguard of a Nascent Bourgeoisie; The Social and Economic Policy of the Young Turks (1908–1918)', in Osman Okyar and Halil Inalcik (eds), *International Congress of the Social and Economic History of Turkey (1071–1920).* Istanbul: Haci Teppe Universitesi, 1977, pp. 329–50.
——, 'Unionist Relations with the Greek, Armenian, and Jewish Communities of the Ottoman Empire, 1908–1914', in Bernard Lewis and Benjamin Braude (eds), *Christians and Jews in the Ottoman Empire: The Functioning of a Plural Society.* New York: Holmes & Meier Publishers, Inc., 1982, pp. 401–34.
——, 'The State and Intervention in Turkey', *Turcica* 16 (1984), 52–64.
——, 'War and Society under the Young Turks, 1908–1918', in Albert Hourani, Philip Khoury, *et al.* (eds), *The Modern Middle East: A Reader*, 2nd edn. London: I. B. Tauris, 2005, pp. 125–44.
Akbayar, Nuri, *Osmanlı Yer Adları Sözlüğü.* Istanbul: Tarih Vakfı Yurt Yayınları, 2001.
Akçam, Taner, *Young Turk Crimes against Humanity.* Princeton: Princeton University Press, 2012.
Akman, Mehmet, *Osmanlı Devleti'nde Ceza Yargılaması.* Istanbul: Eren, 2004.
Aktar, Yücel, 'Tanzimat'tan Cumhuriyet'e Gençlik', in *Tanzimat'tan Cumhuriyet'e Türkiye Ansiklopedisi*, vol. 2. Istanbul: İletişim Yayınları, 1985, pp. 518–30.
Anonymous, 'AHR Roundtable: Historians and the Question of "Modernity"', *AHR*, 116 (3) (June, 2011), 631–751.
Appadurai, Arjun, 'Number in the Colonial Imagination', in Carol A Breckenridge and Peter van der Veer (eds), *Orientalist and the Post Colonial Predicament: Perspectives on South Asia.* Philadelphia: University of Pennsylvania Press, 1993, pp. 314–39.
Arai, Masami, *Turkish Nationalism in the Young Turk Era.* Leiden: E. J. Brill, 1992.
Ariès, Philippe, *Centuries of Childhood: A Social History of Family Life.* New York: Vintage Books, 1962.
Arnold, David, 'The Colonial Prison: Power, Knowledge, and Penology in Nineteenth Century India', in Ranajit Guha (ed.), *A Subaltern Studies Reader, 1986–1995.* Minneapolis: University of Minnesota Press, 1997.
Atar, Zafar, '20. Yüzyıl Başlarında Turgutlu Hapishanesinin Genel Durumu', *Sosyal Bilimler Dergisi*, 9/1 (March 2011), 87–102.
Avcı, Mustafa, *Osmanlı Hukukunda Suçlar ve Cezalar.* Istanbul: Gökkubbe, 2004.
Baer, Gabriel, *Studies in the Social History of Modern Egypt.* Chicago: The University of Chicago Press, 1969.
——, 'The Transition from Traditional to Western Criminal Law in Turkey and Egypt', *Studia Islamica*, 45 (1977), 139–58.
Barakat, Halim, 'The Arab Family and the Challenge of Social Transformation',

in Elizabeth Warnock Fernea (ed.), *Women and the Family in the Middle East: New Voices of Change*. Austin, TX: University of Texas Press, 1985, pp. 27–48.

Başaran, Betül, 'Remaking the Gate of Felicity: Policing, Social Control, and Migration in Istanbul at the End of the Eighteenth Century, 1789–1793', PhD dissertation, University of Chicago, 2006.

Beaumont, G. and Alexis de Tocqueville, *On the Penitentiary System in the United States*. Carbondale: Southern Illinois University Press, 1964 [1833].

Beccaria, Cesare, *On Crimes and Punishments*. New York: Macmillan, 1963 [1764].

Bentham, Jeremy, *An Introduction to the Principles of Morals and Legislation*, Oxford: The Clarendon Press, 1879 [1789].

Berkes, Niyazi, *Turkish Nationalism and Western Civilization: Selected Essays of Ziya Gökalp*. Westport, CT: Greenwood Press, 1959.

——, *The Development of Secularism in Turkey*, New York: Routledge, 1998.

Bernault, Florence and Jannet L. Roitman (eds), *A History of Prisons and Confinement in Africa*, Portsmouth, NH: Heinemann, 2003.

Bilbaşar, Serpil, 'Hapis cezasının örgütsel ve hukuksal gelişimi', *Birikim*, 136 (Aug 2000), 44–8.

Bingöl, Sedat. *Tanzimat Devrinde Osmanlı'da Yargı Reformu: Nizamiyye Mahkemeleri'nin Kuruluşu ve İşleyişi 1840–1876* (Eskişehir: Anadolu Üniversitesi, 2004).

Botsman, Daniel V, *Punishment and Power in the Making of Modern Japan*. Princeton: Princeton University Press, 2005.

Bozkurt, Günihal, *Batı Hukukunun Türkiye'de Benimsenmesi*. Ankara: Türk Tarih Kurumu Basımevi, 1996.

——, 'The Reception of Western European Law in Turkey (From the Tanzimat to the Turkish Republic, 1839–1939)', *Der Islam*, 75/2 (1998), 283–95.

Bozkurt, Nurgül, 'XX. Yüzyıl Başlarında Kütahya Hapishanesinin Genel Durumu', *Uluslararası Sosyal Araştırmaları Dergisi*, 5/21 (Spring 2012), 261–77.

Braude, Benjamin, 'Foundation Myths of the *Millet* System', in Bernard Lewis and Benjamin Braude (eds), *Christians and Jews in the Ottoman Empire: The Functioning of a Plural Society*. New York: Holmes & Meier Publishers, 1982, pp. 69–88.

Brown, Carl, *International Politics and the Middle East: Old Rules, Dangerous Game*. Princeton: Princeton University Press, 1984.

Brummett, Palmira, 'Dogs, Women, Cholera, and Other Menaces in the Streets: Cartoon Satire in the Ottoman Revolutionary Press, 1908–11', *IJMES* 27/4 (Nov 1995), 433–60.

——, *Image and Imperialism in the Ottoman Revolutionary Press, 1908–1911*. Albany, NY: SUNY Press, 2000.

Byrne, Leo Gerald, *The Great Ambassador: A Study of the Diplomatic Career of the Right Honourable Stratford Canning, K.G., G.C.B., Viscount Stratford de Redcliffe, and the Epoch During which he Served as the British Ambassador* to the Sublime Porte of the Ottoman Sultan. Columbus, OH: Ohio State University Press, 1964.

Cardashian, Vahan, *The Ottoman Empire of the Twentieth Century*. Albany, NY: J. B. Lyon Co., 1908.

Collins, Norman J. and Anton Steichele, *The Ottoman Post and Telegraph Offices in Palestine and Sinai*. London: Sahara Publications, 2000.

Cora, Yasar Tolga, 'Constructing and Mobilizing the "Nation" through Sports: State, Physical Education and Nationalism under the Young Turk Rule (1908–1918)', MA thesis, Central European University, 2007.

Cox, Samuel, *Diversions of a Diplomat in Turkey*, New York: C. L. Webster and Co., 1887.

Cunningham, Allan, 'Stratford Canning and the Tanzimat', in William Polk and Richard Chambers (eds), *Beginnings of Modernization in the Middle East, the Nineteenth Century*. Chicago: The University of Chicago Press, 1968, pp. 245–64.

Çiçen, Ahmet, 'II. Meşrutiyet Dönemi Cesaevi Islahatı', MA thesis, Afyon Kocatepe University, 2010.

Damaška, Mirjan R, *The Faces of Justice and State Authority: A Comparative Approach to the Legal Process*. New Haven: Yale University Press, 1986.

Darling, Linda, 'Do Justice, Do Justice, for that is Paradise: Middle Eastern Advice for Indian Muslim Rulers', *Comparative Studies of South Asia, Africa and the Middle East*, 22/1&2 (2002), 3–19.

——, *A History of Social Justice and Political Power in the Middle East: The Circle of Justice from Mesopotamia to Globalization*. New York: Routledge, 2013.

Daşcioğlu, Kemal, 'Documents on Prison Hospitals and Sanitary Conditions of the Prisons in the Ottoman Empire', in Aysegül Demirhan Erdemir (ed.), *1st International Congress on the Turkish History of Medicine, 10th National Congress on the Turkish History of Medicine Proceedings Book*. Istanbul: Cilt II, 2009, pp. 999–1,014.

Davison, Roderic, *Reform in the Ottoman Empire, 1856–1876*. Princeton: Princeton University Press, 1963.

Deal, Roger, *Crimes of Honor, Drunken Brawls and Murder: Violence in Istanbul under Abdülhamid II*. Istanbul: Libra Books, 2010.

DeMause, Lloyd, 'The Evolution of Childhood', in L. DeMause (ed.), *The History of Childhood*. New York: Psychohistory Press, 1974, pp. 1–73.

Demirel, Fatmagül, '1890 Petersburg Hapishaneler Kongresi', *Toplumsal Tarih*, 89 (May 2001), 11–14.

Deringil, Selim, 'Legitimacy Structures in the Ottoman State: The Reign of Abdulhamid II (1876–1909)', *IJMES* 23 (1991), 345–59.

——, *The Well-protected Domains: Ideology and the Legitimation of Power in the Ottoman Empire, 1876–1909*. London: I. B. Tauris, 1999.

Devellioğlu, Ferit, *Osmanlıca-Türkçe Ansiklopedik Lugat*, Ankara: Aydın Kitabevi Yayınları, 2004.

Dikötter, Frank and Ian Brown (eds), *Cultures of Confinement: A History of the Prison in Africa, Asia, and Latin America*. Ithaca, NY: Cornell University Press, 2007.

Dikötter, Frank, *Crime, Punishment and Prisons in Modern China: 1895–1949*. New York: Columbia University Press, 2002.

Dostoevsky, Fyodor, *Memoirs from the House of the Dead*. London: Oxford University Press, 1862.

Doumani, Beshara, *Rediscovering Palestine: Merchants and Peasants in Jabal Nablus: 1700–1900*. Berkeley: California University Press, 1995.

Durkheim, Émile, 'Two Laws of Penal Evolution', *Annèe sociologique* 4 (1902).

——, *The Division of Labor in Society*, trans. G. Simpson. New York: Free Press of Glencoe, 1964 [c. 1933].

——, *Moral Education: A Study in the Theory and Application of the Sociology of Education*. New York: Free Press of Glencoe, 1961.

Dündar, Fuat, *İttihat ve Terraki'nin Müslümanları İhsan Politikası, 1913–1918*. Istanbul: İletişim Yayınları, 2001.

——, 'The Settlement Policies of the Committee of Union and Progress, 1913–1918', in Hans-Lukas Keiser (ed.), *Turkey beyond Nationalism: Towards Post-nationalist Identities*. London: I. B. Tauris, 2006, pp. 37–42.

——, *Modern Türkiye'nin Şifresi: İttihat ve Terakki'nin Etnisite Mühensidliği, 1913–1918*. Istanbul: İletişim Yayınları, 2008.

——, *Crime of Numbers: The Role of Statistics in the Armenian Question, 1878–1918*. New Brunswick, NJ: Transaction Publishers, 2010.

Ercan, Yavuz, 'Non-Muslim Communities under the Ottoman Empire (Millet System)', in Halil Inalcik (ed.), *The Great Ottoman–Turkish Civilization*, Ankara: Yeni Türkiye, 2000, pp. 381–91.

Ergene, Boğaç A., *Local Court, Provincial Society and Justice in the Ottoman Empire: Legal Practice and Dispute Resolution in Çankırı, 1652–1744*, Leiden: E. J. Brill, 2003.

Ergut, Ferdan, 'State and Social Control: Police in the Late Ottoman Empire and the Early Republican Turkey, 1839–1939', PhD dissertation, New School of Social Research, 1999.

——, 'Policing the Poor in the Late Ottoman Empire', *Middle Eastern Studies*, 38 (2002), 149–64.

——, 'The State and Civil Rights in the Late Ottoman Empire', *Journal of Mediterranean Studies*, 13 (2003), 53–74.

——, *Modern Devlet ve Polis: Osmanlı'dan Cumhuriyet'e Toplumsal Denetimin Diyalektiği*. Istanbul: İletişim Yayınları, 2004.

Espisito, John (ed.), *The Oxford Encyclopedia of the Modern Islamic World*, 4 vols. Oxford: Oxford University Press, 1995.

Fahmy, Khaled, *All the Pasha's Men: Mehmed Ali, His Army and the Making of Modern Egypt*, Cambridge: Cambridge University Press, 1997.

——, 'The Police and the People in Nineteenth-century Egypt', *Die Welt des Islams*, 39 (1999), 340–77.

——, 'Medical Conditions in Egyptian Prisons in the Nineteenth Century', in R. Ostle (ed.), *Marginal Voices in Literature and Society*. Strasbourg: European Science Foundation; Maison Mediterraneene des Sciences de l'Homme d'Aix-en-Provence, 2000, pp. 135–55.

F.D.E., *Système des Mesures, Poids et Monnaies de l'Empire Ottoman et des principaux États*, Constantinople: n.p., 1910.

Fernea, Elizabeth Warnock (ed.), *Women and the Family in the Middle East: New Voices of Change*, Austin, TX: University of Texas Press, 1985.

——, *Children in the Muslim Middle East*, Austin, TX: University of Texas Press, 1995.

——, *Remembering Childhood in the Middle East: Memoirs from a Century of Change*, Austin, TX: University of Texas Press, 2002.

Findely, Carter, *Bureaucratic Reform in the Ottoman Empire: The Sublime Porte 1789–1922*. Princeton: Princeton University Press, 1980.

Foucault, Michel, 'Essays on Governmentality', in Graham Burchell, *et al.* (eds), *The Foucault Effect: Studies in Governmentality: With Two Lectures by and an Interview with Michel Foucault*. Chicago: The University of Chicago Press, 1991, Chapter 4.

——, *Discipline and Punish: The Birth of the Prison*, trans. Alan Sheridan. New York: Pantheon Books, 1995.

Frierson, Elizabeth B., 'Women in Late Ottoman Intellectual History', in Elizabeth Özdalga (ed.), *Late Ottoman Society: The Intellectual Legacy*. London: Routledge, 2005, pp. 135–61.

Garland, David, *Punishment and Modern Society: A Study in Social Theory*. Chicago: The University of Chicago Press, 1990.

Gelvin, James, 'Post Hoc Ergo Proptor Hoc?: Reassessing the Lineages of Nationalism in Bilad Al-Sham', in Thomas Philipp and Christoph Schumann (eds), *From the Syrian Land to the States of Syria and Lebanon*. Beirut: Ergon Verlag Würtzburg in Kommission, 2004, pp. 127–44.

——, *The Modern Middle East, A History*, 2nd edn. Oxford: Oxford University Press, 2005.

——, 'The "Politics of Notables" Forty Years After', *Middle East Studies Association Bulletin*, 40(1) (June 2006), 19–30.

——, 'Modernity, Tradition, and the Battleground of Gender in Early Twentieth-Century Damascus', *Die Welt des Islams* (January 2012).

Gerber, Haim, *State, Society, and Law in Islam: Ottoman Law in Comparative Perspective*. Albany, NY: SUNY Press, 1994.

Gil'adi, Avner, *Children of Islam: Concepts of Childhood in Medieval Muslim Society*. New York: St. Martin's Press, 1992.

Gillis, John R, *Youth and History: Tradition and Change in European Age Relations*. New York: Academic Press, 1974.

Ginio, Eyal, 'The Administration of Criminal Justice in Ottoman Selanik

(Salonica) during the Eighteenth Century', *Turcica*, 30 (1998), 185–210.

——, 'Childhood, Mental Capacity, and Conversion to Islam', *Byzantine and Modern Greek Studies*, 25 (2001), 90–119.

Gluck, Carol, 'The End of Elsewhere: Writing Modernity Now', *AHR* 116(3) (June 2011), 676–87.

Goffman, Erving, *Asylums: Essays on the Social Situation of Mental Patients and Other Inmates*. Chicago: Aldine Pub. Co., 1962.

Gorman, Anthony, 'Regulation, Reform and Resistance in the Middle Eastern Prison', in Frank Dikötter and Ian Brown (eds), *Cultures of Confinement: A History of the Prison in Africa, Asia, and Latin America*. Ithaca, NY: Cornell University Press, 2007, pp. 95–146.

Göçek, Fatma Müge, *Rise of the Bourgeoisie, Demise of the Empire: Ottoman Westernization and Social Change*. Oxford: Oxford University Press, 1996.

Gökçen, Ahmet, 'Criminal Law', in John Espisito (ed), *The Oxford Encyclopedia of the Modern Islamic World*, vol. I. Oxford: Oxford University Press, 1995, pp. 329–33.

Gönen, Yasemin, 'Osmanlı İmparatorluğunda Hapishaneleri İyileştirme Girişimi, 1917 Yılı', in Emine Gürsoy (ed.), *Hapishane Kitabı*. Istanbul: Kitabevi, 2005, pp. 173–83.

Guha, Ranajit and Gayatri Chakravorty Spivak (eds), *Selected Subaltern Studies*. New York: Oxford University Press, 1988.

Gürsoy, Emine (ed.), *Hapishane Kitabı*. Istanbul: Kitabevi, 2005.

Hacking, Ian, *Historical Ontology*. Cambridge: Cambridge University Press, 2002.

Hallaq, Wael, *An Introduction to Islamic Law*. Cambridge: Cambridge University Press, 2009a.

——, *Shari'a: Theory, Practice, and Transformations*. Cambridge: Cambridge University Press, 2009b.

Hanioğlu, Şükrü, *The Young Turks in Opposition*. New York: Oxford University Press, 1995.

——, *Preparation for a Revolution: The Young Turks, 1902–1908*. New York: Oxford University Press, 2001.

Hardy, M. J. L., *Blood Feuds and the Payment of Blood Money in the Middle East*. Leiden: E. J. Brill, 1963.

Hatem, Mervat F., 'Economic and Political Liberation in Egypt and the Demise of State Feminism', *IJMES*, 24(2) (May 1992), 231–51.

Heyd, Uriel *Foundations of Turkish Nationalism: The Life and Teachings of Ziya Gökalp*. London: Harvill Press, 1950.

——, *Studies in Old Ottoman Criminal Law*. Oxford: The Clarendon Press, 1973.

Hill, Christopher, *The World Turned Upside Down: Radical Ideas during the English Revolution*. New York: Viking Press, 1972.

Howard, John, *The State of Prisons in England and Wales, with an Account of Some Foreign Prisons*. Warrington, Cheshire, UK, 1777.

Bibliography

——, *An Account of the Principle Lazarettos in Europe and Additional Remarks on the Present State of Prisons in England and Ireland*, Warrington, UK, Cheshire, 1787.

Hurewitz, J. C., *The Middle East and North Africa in World Politics: A Documentary Record, Vol. 1: European Expansion, 1535–1914*. New Haven: Yale University Press, 1975.

Ignatieff, Michael, *A Just Measure of Pain: The Penitentiary and the Industrial Revolution, 1750–1850*. New York: Pantheon Books, 1978.

Imber, Colin, *The Ottoman Empire, 1300–1600*. London: Palgrave Macmillan, 2002.

——, *Ebu's-Su'ud: The Islamic Legal Tradition*. Stanford: Stanford University Press, 2007.

Inalcik, Halil, *The Ottoman Empire: The Classical Age 1300–1600.* London: Phoenix, 1973.

Jenkins, Roy, *Churchill: A Biography*. New York: Farrar, Straus and Giroux, 2001.

Kabacalı, Alpay, *Türkiye'de Gençlik Hareketleri*. Istanbul: Altın Kitaplar, 1992.

Kalkan, İbrahim Halim, 'Medicine and Politics in the Late Ottoman Empire: 1876–1909', MA thesis, Boğazici Üniversitesi, 2004.

Kandiyoti, Deniz, 'End of Empire: Islam, Nationalism, and Women in Turkey', in Deniz Kandiyoti (ed.), *Women, Islam, and the State*. Philadelphia: Temple University Press, 1991, pp. 22–47.

Kansu, Aykut, *The Revolution of 1908 in Turkey*. Leiden: E. J. Brill, 1997.

——, *Politics in Post-revolutionary Turkey, 1908–1913*. Leiden: E. J. Brill, 2000.

Kaplan, Martha, 'Panopticon in Poona: An Essay on Foucault and Colonialism', *Cultural Anthropology*, 10(1), 85–98.

Karpat, Kemal, *An Inquiry into the Social Foundations of Nationalism in the Late Ottoman State: From Social Estates to Classes, from Millets to Nations*. Princeton: Center of International Studies, Princeton University, 1973.

——, *Ottoman Population, 1830–1914*. Madison, WI: University of Wisconsin Press, 1985.

——, *The Politicization of Islam: Reconstituting Identity, State, Faith, and Community in the Late Ottoman State*. New York: Oxford University Press, 2001.

——, *Studies on Ottoman Social and Political History: Selected Articles and Essays*. Leiden: E. J. Brill, 2002.

Kayalı, Hasan, 'Elections and the Electoral Process in the Ottoman Empire, 1876–1919', *IJMES* 27(3) (1995), 265–86.

——, *Arabs and Young Turks: Ottomanism, Arabism, and Islamism in the Ottoman Empire, 1908–1918*. Los Angeles: University of California Press, 1997.

Koç, Yunus, and Fatih Yeşil, *Nizâm-i Cedîd Kanunları, 1791–1800*. Ankara: Türk Tarih Kurumu, 2012.

Kornrumpf, Hans-Jürgen, 'Islahhaneler', in Jean-Louis Bacque-Grammont and

Paul Dumont (eds), *Économie et Sociétés Dans L'Empire Ottoman, Fin du XVIII-Début du XX siècle*. Paris: Editions Du Centre National de la Recherche Scientifique, 1983, pp. 149–56.

Kranzler, Katherine Linnea, 'Health Services in the Late Ottoman Empire: 1827–1914', MA thesis, Boğazici Üniversitesi, 1991.

Kuru, Alev, *Sinop Hapishane*. Ankara, 2004.

Kushner, David, *The Rise of Turkish Nationalism, 1876–1908*. London: Frank Cass, 1977.

Lane-Poole, Stanley, *The Life of Lord Stratford de Redcliffe*. London: Longmans, Green and Co., 1890.

Le Bon, Gustav, *The Psychology of the Crowd*. Dunwoody, GA: N. S. Berg, 1968 [1895].

Lefebvre, Henri, *The Production of Space*, trans. Donald Nicholson-Smith. Oxford: Oxford University Press, 1991.

Lerner, Gerda, *The Creation of Patriarchy*. New York: Oxford University Press, 1986.

Lewis, Bernard, *The Emergence of Modern Turkey*. Oxford: Oxford University Press, 1961.

Levine, Mark, *Overthrowing Geography: Jaffa, Tel Aviv, and the Struggle for Palestine, 1880–1948*. Berkeley: California University Press, 2005.

Lévy, Noémi, and Alexandre Toumarkine (eds), *Osmanlı'da Asayiş, Suç ve Ceza, 18.–20. Yüzyıllar*. Istanbul: Tarih Vakfı Yurt Yayınları, 2007.

Lévy, Noémi, Nadir Özbek, *et al.* (eds), *Jandarma ve Polis: Fransız ve Osmanlı Tarihçiliğine Çapraz Bakışlar*. Istanbul: Tarih Vakfı Yurt Yayınları, 2009.

Lévy-Aksu, Noémi, *Ordre et désordres dans l'Istanbul ottomane*. Paris: Karthala, 2013.

Lockman, Zachary, *Contending Visions of the Middle East: The History and Politics of Orientalism*, 2nd edn. New York: Cambridge University Press, 2010.

McCarthy, Justin, *Muslims and Minorities: The Population of Ottoman Anatolia and the End of the Empire*. New York: New York University Press, 1983.

——, *Population of Palestine: Population, History, and Statistics of the Late Ottoman Period and the Mandate*. New York: Columbia University Press, 1990.

——, *Death and Exile: The Ethnic Cleansing of Ottoman Muslims, 1821–1922*. Princeton: Darwin Press, 1995.

——, *The Ottoman Peoples and the End of Empire*. New York: Oxford University Press, 2001.

——, *Population History of the Middle East and the Balkans*. Istanbul: İsis Press, 2002.

Maksudyan, Nazan, 'Orphans, Cities, and the State: Vocational Orphanages (*ıslahhanes*) and Reform in the Late Ottoman Urban Space', *IJMES* 43 (2011), 493–511.

Mardin, Şerif, *The Genesis of Young Ottoman Thought: A Study in the*

Bibliography

Modernization of Turkish Political Ideas. Princeton: Princeton University Press, 1962.

Messick, Brinkley, *The Calligraphic State: Textual Domination and History in a Muslim Society*. Berkeley: California University Press, 1993.

Miller, Ruth, *Legislating Authority: Sin and Crime in the Ottoman Empire and Turkey*. New York: Routledge, 2005.

Mitchell, Timothy, 'The Limits of the State: Beyond Statist Approaches and their Critics', *American Political Science Review*, 85(1) (March 1991), 77–96.

Mohsen, Safia K., 'New Images, Old Reflections: Working Middle-Class Women in Egypt', in Elizabeth Warnock Fernea (ed.), *Women and the Family in the Middle East: New Voices of Change*. Austin, TX: University of Texas Press, 1985, pp. 56–71.

Montesquieu, Baron de, *The Spirit of the Laws*. Berkeley: California University Press, 1977 [1748].

Morris, Norval, and David Rothman (eds), *The Oxford History of the Prison: The Practice of Punishment in Western Society*. Oxford: Oxford University Press, 1998.

O'Brien, Patricia, 'Crime and Punishment as Historical Problem', *Journal of Social History*, 11(4) (Summer 1978), 508–20.

_____, *The Promise of Punishment: Prisons in Nineteenth-Century France*. Princeton: Princeton University Press, 1982.

Owen, Roger, The Middle East in the World Economy 1800–1914. London: Methuen, 1981.

Özbek, Nadir, 'Osmanlı İmparatorluğu'nda İç Güvenlik, Siyaset ve Devlet, 1876–1909', *Türklük Araştırmaları Dergisi*, 16 (Güz 2004), 59–95.

_____, 'Policing the Countryside: Gendarmes of the Late 19th-century Ottoman Empire (1876–1908)', *IJMES* 40 (2008), 47–67.

Özen, İmdat, 'II. Meşrutiyet'e Kadar Islahhaneler ve Darülaceze', MA thesis (Ankara Üniversitesi, 2001).

Pamuk, Şevket, *The Ottoman Empire and European Capitalism, 1820–1913*. Cambridge: Cambridge University Press, 1987.

Paz, Omri, 'Crime, Criminals, and the Ottoman State: Anatolia between the Late 1830s and the Late 1860s', PhD dissertation, Tel Aviv University, 2010.

Peters, Rudolph, 'The Codification of Criminal Law in 19th Century Egypt; Tradition or Modernization', in Jamil M. Abun-Nasr, Ulrich Spellenberg, *et al.* (eds), *Law, Society, and National Identity in Africa*. Hamburg: Helmut Buske Verlag, 1990, pp. 211–25.

_____, 'The Islamization of Criminal Law: A Comparative Analysis', *Die Welt Des Islams* 34 (1994), 246–60.

_____, 'Islamic and Secular Law in Nineteenth-century Egypt: The Role and Function of the Qadi', *Islamic Law and Society*, 4(1) (1997), 70–90.

_____, 'Controlled Suffering: Mortality and Living Conditions in 19th-century Egyptian Prisons', *IJMES*, 36 (2001), 387–407.

_____, 'Prisons and Marginalisation in Nineteenth-century Egypt', in Eugene

Rogan (ed.), *Outside in: On the Margins of the Modern Middle East*. London: I. B. Tauris (2002a), pp. 31–52.

_____, 'Egypt and the Age of the Triumphant Prison: Legal Punishment in Nineteenth-century Egypt', *Annales Islamologiques*, 32 (2002b), 253–85.

_____, *Crime and Punishment in Islamic Law: Theory and Practice from the Sixteenth to the Twenty-first Century*. Cambridge: Cambridge University Press, 2005.

Pierce, Leslie, *Morality Tales: Law and Gender in the Ottoman Court of Aintab*. Berkeley: California University Press, 2003.

Platt, A. M., *The Child Savers: The Invention of Delinquency*. Chicago: The University of Chicago Press, 1977.

Porter, Theodore, *The Rise of Statistical Thinking 1820–1900*. Princeton: Princeton University Press, 1986.

Powers, David, 'Kadijustiz or Qadi-Justice? A Paternity Dispute from Fourteenth-century Morocco', *Islamic Law and Society*, 1(3) (1994), 332–66.

Pratt, John, *Punishment and Civilization: Penal Tolerance and Intolerance in Modern Society*. London: Sage Publications, 2002.

Quataert, Donald, 'The 1908 Young Turk Revolution: Old and New Approaches', *Middle East Studies Association Bulletin*, 13(1) (July 1979a), 22–9.

_____, 'The Economic Climate of the "Young Turk Revolution of 1908"', *Journal of Modern History*, 51 (1979b), D1,147–61.

_____, *Social Disintegration and Popular Resistance in the Ottoman Empire, 1881–1908: Reactions to European Economic Penetration*. New York: New York University Press, 1983.

_____, *The Ottoman Empire, 1700–1922*, 2nd edn. New York: Cambridge University Press, 2005.

Quataert, Donald, and David Gutman, 'Coal Mines, the Palace, and Struggles over Power, Capital, and Justice in the Late Ottoman Empire', *IJMES*, 44(2) (May 2012), 215–35.

Ramsaur, Ernest Edmondson, *The Young Turks: Prelude to the Revolution of 1908*. New York: Russell & Russell, 1957.

Redfield, Peter, 'Foucault in the Tropics: Displacing the Panopticon', in Jonathan Xavier India (ed.), *Anthropologies of Modernity: Foucault, Governmentality, and Life Politics*. Oxford: Oxford University Press, 2005, pp. 50–79.

Redhouse, Sir James, *A Turkish and English Lexicon, New Edition*. Beirut: Librairie du Liban, 1996.

——, *Redhouse Sözlüğü: Türkçe/Osmanlıca-İngilizce*, 18th edn. Istanbul: Sev Matbaacılık, 2000 [1968].

Rengger, N. J., *Political Theory, Modernity, and Postmodernity: Beyond Enlightenment and Critique*. Oxford: Blackwell, 1995.

Rogan, Eugene, *Frontiers of State in the Late Ottoman Empire*. Cambridge: Cambridge University Press, 1999.

Bibliography

Rothman, David, *The Discovery of the Asylum: Social Order and Disorder in the New Republic*. New York: Aldine de Gruyter, 2002 [1971].

Rubin, Avi, 'Legal Borrowing and its Impact on Ottoman Legal Culture in the Late Nineteenth Century', *Continuity and Change*, 22(2) (2007), 279–303.

——, 'Ottoman Judicial Change in the Age of Modernity: A Reappraisal', *History Compass*, 6 (2008), 1–22.

——, *Ottoman Nizamiye Courts: Law and Modernity*. New York: Palgrave Macmillan, 2011.

Rugh, Andrea, *The Family in Contemporary Egypt*. Syracuse: Syracuse University Press, 1984.

Rusche, George, and Otto Kirchheimer, *Punishment and Social Structure*. New York: Columbia University Press, 1939.

Said, Edward, *Orientalism*. New York: Vintage Books, 1979.

Salvatore, Ricardo Donato, and Carlos Aguirre (eds), *The Birth of the Penitentiary in Latin America: Essays on Criminology, Prison Reform, and Social Control, 1830–1940*. Austin, TX: University of Texas Press: Institute of Latin American Studies, 1996.

Saner, Yasemin, 'Osmanlı'nın Yüzlerce Yıl Süren Cezalandırma ve Korkutma Refleksi: Prangaya Vurma', in Noémi Lévy and Alexandre Toumarkine (eds), *Osmanlı'da Asayiş, Suç ve Ceza: 18.–20. Yüzyıllar*. Istanbul: Tarih Vakfı Yurt Yayınları, 2007, pp. 163–89.

Schull, Kent F., 'Tutuklu Sayımı: Jön Türklerin Sistematik Bir Şekilde Hapishane İstatistikleri Toplama Çalışmaları ve Bunların 1911–1918 Hapishane Reformu Üzerine Etkileri', in Noémi Lévy and Alexandre Toumarkine (eds), *Osmanlı'da Asayiş, Suç ve Ceza: 18.–20. Yüzyıllar*. Istanbul: Tarih Vakfı Yurt Yayınları, 2007a, pp. 212–38.

——, 'Hapishaneler ve Cezalandırmaya İlişkin Yaklaşımlara Eleştirel Bir Bakış', in Noémi Lévy and Alexandre Toumarkine (eds), *Osmanlı'da Asayiş, Suç ve Ceza: 18.–20. Yüzyıllar*. Istanbul: Tarih Vakfı Yurt Yayınları, 2007b, pp. 46–54.

——, 'Penal Institutions, Nation-state Construction, and Modernity in the Late Ottoman Empire, 1908–1919', PhD dissertation, University of California, Los Angeles, 2007c.

——, 'Identity in the Ottoman Prison Surveys of 1912 and 1914', *IJMES*, 41(3) (2009), 365–7.

——, 'Conceptualizing Difference during the Second Constitutional Period: New Sources, Old Challenges', in Jorgen Nielson (ed.), *Religion, Ethnicity and Contested Nationhood in the Former Ottoman Space*, Leiden: Brill, 2012, pp. 63–87.

Semerdjian, Elyse, *'Off the Straight Path': Illicit Sex, Law, and Community in Ottoman Aleppo*. Syracuse: Syracuse University Press, 2008.

Shaw, Stanford, 'The Ottoman Census System and Population, 1831–1914', *IJMES* 9(3), (October 1978), 325–38.

——, 'Ottoman Expenditures and Budgets during the Late Nineteenth and Early Twentieth Centuries', *IJMES* 9(3), (October 1978), pp. 373–8.

Shissler, A. Holly, *Between Two Empires: Ahmet Ağaoğlu and the New Turkey*, London: I. B. Tauris, 2003.

Singha, Radhika, *A Despotism of Law: Crime and Justice in Early Colonial India*. New York: Oxford University Press, 1998.

Stone, Lawrence, *The Family, Sex and Marriage in England, 1500–1800*. New York: Harper & Row, 1979.

Sutton, John, *Stubborn Children: Controlling Delinquency in the USA, 1640–1981*. Berkeley: California Unversity Press, 1988.

Swanson, Glen W., 'The Ottoman Police', *Journal of Contemporary History*, 7(1&2) (1972), 243–60.

Şen, Hasan, 'Transformation of Punishment Politics and Birth of the Prison in the Ottoman Empire (1845–1910)', MA thesis, Boğazici Üniversitesi, 2005.

Şen, Ömer, *Osmanlı'da Mahkum Olmak*. Istanbul: Kapı Yayınları, 2007.

Şimşar, Nahide, 'Karesi Hapishanesi', in Emine Gürsoy-Naskali and Halil Oytun Altun (eds), *Zindanlar ve Mahkumlar*. Istanbul: Babil Yayınları, 2006, pp. 65–70.

Tekeli, Ilhan, 'The Public Works Program and the Development of Technology in the Ottoman Empire in the Second Half of the Nineteenth Century', *Turcica*, 28 (1996), 195–234.

Tilly, Charles (ed.), *The Formation of National States in Western Europe*. Princeton: Princeton University Press, 1975.

——, *The Contentious French*. Cambridge, MA: Belknap Press, 1986.

Toledano, Ehud, 'Mehmet Ali Paşa or Muhammad Ali Basha? An Historiographical Appraisal in the Wake of a Recent Book', *Middle Eastern Studies*, 21 (1985), 141–59.

Toprak, Zafer, 'İttihat ve Terraki'nin Paramiliter Gençlik Örgütleri', *Boğaziçi Üniversitesi Dergesi Beşeri Bilimler*, VII (1979), 95–113.

——, *'Milli İktisat' 1908–1918*. Ankara: Yurt Yayınları, 1982.

——, 'II. Meşrutiyet Döneminde Paramiliter Gençlik Örgütleri', in *Tanzimat'tan Cumhuriyet'e Türkiye Ansiklopedisi*, vol. 2, Istanbul: İletişim Yayınları, 1985, pp. 531–6.

——, 'Modernization and Commercialization in the Tanzimat Period: 1838–1875', *New Perspectives on Turkey*, 7 (1992), 57–70.

——, *Milli İktisat, milli burjuvazi*. Istanbul: Tarih Vakfı Yurt Yayınları, 1995.

——, 'From Liberalism to Solidarism: The Ottoman Economic Mind in the Age of the Nation State (1820–1920)', in Raoul Motika, *et al.* (eds), *Studies in Ottoman Social and Economic Life*. Heidelberg: Heidelberger Orientverl, 1999, pp. 171–90.

——, *İttihad-Terraki ve Cihan Harbi: Savaş Ekonomisi ve Türkiye'de Devletçilik, 1914–1918*. Istanbul: Homer Kitabevi, 2003.

Trumpener, Ulrich, 'Germany and the End of the Ottoman Empire', in Marian

Bibliography

Kent (ed.), *The Great Powers and the End of the Ottoman Empire*. London: George Allen and UNWIN, 1984, pp. 111–39.

——, *Germany and the Ottoman Empire, 1914–1918*, 2nd edn. New York: Caravan Books, 1989.

Turfan, M. Naim, *The Rise of the Young Turks: Politics, the Military and Ottoman Collapse*. London: I. B. Tauris, 2000.

Türker, Ebru Aykut, 'Alternative Claims on Justice and Law: Rural Arson and Poison Murder in the 19th Century Ottoman Empire', PhD thesis. Boğazici Üniversitesi, 2011.

Uslu, Muharrem, 'Erzincan'da Suç, Suçlu ve Hapishane (XIX. Yüzyılın Sonu-XX. Yüzyılın Başı)', MA thesis, Erzincan University, 2010.

Ülker, Erol, 'Centextualising "Turkification": Nation-building in the Late Ottoman Empire, 1908–18', *Nations and Nationalism*, 11(4) (2005), 613–36.

Üstel, Füsun, *İmparatorluktan Ulus Devlete Türk Milliyetçiliği: Türk Ocakları, 1912–1931*. Istanbul: İletişim Yayınları, 1997.

Weber, Eugen, *Peasants into Frenchmen: The Modernization of Rural France, 1870–1914*. Stanford: Stanford University Press, 1976.

Weber, Max, *Economy and Society*, vol. II. Berkeley: California University Press, 1978.

Werrett, Simon, 'Potemkin and the Panopticon: Samuel Bentham and the Architecture of Absolutism in Eighteenth Century Russia,' *Journal of Bentham Studies*, 2 (1999), 1–25.

Wolff, Larry, *Inventing Eastern Europe: The Map of Civilization on the Mind of the Enlightenment*. Stanford: Stanford University Press, 1994.

Yakut, Kemal, 'The Exertions for the Depoliticisation of the Military in the Second Constitutionalist Era (1908–1912)', in Halil Inalcik (ed.), *The Great Ottoman-Turkish Civilization*. Ankara: Yeni Türkiye, 2000, pp. 691–704.

Yıldırım, Nuran, 'Tanzimat'tan Cumhuriyet'e Koruyucu Sağlık Uygulamaları', in *Tanzimat'tan Cumhuriyet'e Türkiye Ansiklopedisi*, vol. 5. Istanbul: İlestişim Yayınları, 1985, pp. 1,318–38.

Yıldız, Gültekin, 'Osmanlı Devleti'nde Hapishane Islahatı (1838–1908)', MA thesis (Marmara Üniversitesi, 2002).

——, *Mapusane: Osmanlı Hapishanelerinin Kuruluş Serüveni, 1839–1908*. Istanbul: Kitabevi, 2012.

Yıldıztaş, Mümin, 'Mütareke Döneminde Suç Unsurları ve İstanbul Hapishanleri', MA thesis, (İstanbul Üniversitesi, 1997).

Yosmaoğlu, İpek K., 'Counting Bodies, Shaping Souls: The 1903 Census and National Identity in Ottoman Macedonia', *IJMES*, 38 (2006), 55–77.

Zarinebaf, Fariba, *Crime and Punishment in Istanbul, 1700–1800*. Berkeley: California University Press, 2010.

Zinoman, Peter, *The Colonial Bastille: A History of Imprisonment in Vietnam, 1862–1940*. Los Angeles: California University Press, 2001.

Zürcher, Erik J, 'The Vocabulary of Muslim Nationalism', *International Journal of Sociology Of Science*, 137 (1999), pp. 81–92.

——, 'Young Turks, Ottoman Muslims and Turkish Nationalists: Identity Politics 1908–1938', in Kemal Karpat (ed.), *Ottoman Past and Today's Turkey*. Leiden: E. J. Brill, 2000, pp. 150–79.

——, *Turkey: A Modern History*. London: I. B. Tauris, 2001.

——, 'Islam in the Service of the National and Pre-national State: The instrumentalisation of Religion for Political Goals by Turkish Regimes between 1880–1980', *Turkology Update Leiden Project: TULP Working Papers* (October 2005), 1–15.

Index

Index

221

military mobilisation (*seferberlik*), 153–4,
177–8, 195–6
millet see identity
Millet System, 95
Milne, General, 192–3
Minister of War (*Serasker*), 22
Ministry (Ottoman)
Finance, 52, 56
Interior, 23, 49, 51–2, 54–5, 57–9, 98,
105, 125, 130, 147–8, 150, 155–6,
159, 162n
Justice, 24, 46–7, 115, 120, 125, 145–6,
155–6, 158–9, 172
Police, 51
War, 86, 177–8
misconduct *see* corruption
Modern World System, 27–8, 198–9
modernity, 4–6, 11, 17–18, 19, 22, 25,
43–4, 60–1, 132–4, 143–4, 153,
168–70, 196–7
money changers *see* bankers
Montesquieu, Baron de, 6–7
Mosul, 73, 75, 77–9, 81–2, 97, 102, 103,
104, 107n, 110n, 136n, 148, 162n,
184, 189n, 190n
mufti see jurisconsult
Muslim, 2, 19, 36, 48, 69–70, 93, 101,
109n, 128, 168, 177, 191
bourgeoisie, 91, 132, 140n
constituency, 95–6
prisoners, 73, 90, 94, 96–7, 99, 100,
104–5, 109n, 123–4, 128, 135, 166–7
refugees, 50, 170
Müfettiş Pasha, 47, 63n
Mürzsteg Programme, 91–3, 135n

nanny state *see* state patriarchy
nation-in-arms, 177–8
nation-state construction (modern state
construction), 3, 6, 49–50, 53, 68, 93,
195–9
national economy (*milli iktisat*) *see*
Committee of Union and Progress,
economic policy
nationalism, 5, 96, 188n, 199
CUP, 101, 108n, 187–8n
Ottoman (*Osmanlılık*), 101, 108n
Turkish, 101, 108n
neo-Marxism and neo-Marxist, 6–7, 8, 91
Nigeria, 36
Niş, 179–80
Nizam-i Cedid Kanunları, 22
nizamiye courts *see* courts, criminal

nominalism *see* Ian Hacking
non-Muslim, 48–9, 95–6, 109n

O'Brien, Patricia, 9–10, 16n, 163n
Office of Population Registers (*Ceride-i
Nüfus Nezareti*), 69
Orientalist, 1–3, 43, 195
orphan, 169–70
orphanage *see Darülaceze*
Osmanlı Güç Dernekleri (Ottoman
Strength Association), 177–8
Ottoman Constitution of 1876, 24, 28, 50,
70, 84, 179
Ottoman Parliament (Grand Assembly),
29, 31–2, 50, 52–4, 88, 89–90, 173,
175–6, 178–9, 184
Ottomanism (*Osmanlılık*) *see* nationalism

Palmer, Lieutenant, 191–2
pardon, 88–9, 107n, 126–7, 182–6,
190n
Parfitt, Harold, 177
Paris Peace Conference, 2, 191
penal institutions, 3–4, 5–10, 15n, 17,
51–61, 62n, 102, 169, 197–9
penitentiary (*hapishane-yi umumi*), 9–10,
26–7, 43, 45–7, 56–7, 62n, 116–18,
120–5, 128–32, 133, 144, 149,
153–61, 182, 184, 194
physician (doctor), 47, 67, 74, 83, 121–2,
138n, 145, 148, 181–2
Plain of Sharon, 166
police (policing and *zaptiye*), 3, 5, 10, 12,
18–20, 22–4, 29–30, 35, 46, 49–51,
53, 68, 85, 87–8, 101, 111, 125, 144,
146, 171–4, 176, 192–3, 195, 199
Pollitz, Paul, 56–60, 65n, 132, 139n, 141n,
162n, 164n, 182–5, 189n, 190n, 195
salary, 57
poor house *see Darülaceze*
Positivism and Positivist *see* Comtian
press censorship, 50
prison (*hapishane*)
administration (*hapishane idaresi*), 13,
24–5, 44–5, 49, 52–5, 64n, 67–8,
71–2, 83–7, 89, 93, 95–8, 106n, 109n,
112–17, 120–34, 135n, 136n, 137n,
138n, 144–5, 147–8, 150–5, 159–61,
162n, 164n, 180–5
architecture (blueprints, designs, plans),
4, 48, 51–2, 53, 55–6, 113–14, 121,
138n, 142
cadre *see* prison employee

Index

Index